A Prince of Cornwall

A Story of Glastonbury and the West in the Days
of Ina of Wessex

Charles W. Whistler

Alpha Editions

This edition published in 2024

ISBN 9789362091581

Design and Setting By

Alpha Editions

www.alphaedis.com

Email - info@alphaedis.com

Contents

PREFACE.

A few words of preface may save footnotes to a story which deals with the half-forgotten days when the power of a British prince had yet to be reckoned with by the Wessex kings as they slowly and steadily pushed their frontier westward.

The authority for the historical basis of the story is the Anglo-Saxon Chronicle, which gives A.D. 710 as the year of the defeat of Gerent, king of the West Welsh, by Ina of Wessex and his kinsman Nunna. This date is therefore approximately that of the events of the tale.

With regard to the topography of the Wessex frontier involved, although it practically explains itself in the course of the story, it may be as well to remind a reader that West Wales was the last British kingdom south of the Severn Sea, the name being, of course, given by Wessex men to distinguish it from the Welsh principalities in what we now call Wales, to their north. In the days of Ina it comprised Cornwall and the present Devon and also the half of Somerset westward of the north and south line of the river Parrett and Quantock Hills. Practically this old British "Dyvnaint" represented the ancient Roman province of Damnonia, shrinking as it was under successive advances of the Saxons from the boundary which it once had along the Mendips and Selwood Forest. Ina's victory over Gerent set the Dyvnaint frontier yet westward, to the line of the present county of Somerset, which represents the limit of his conquest, the new addition to the territory of the clan of the Sumorsaetas long being named as "Devon in Wessex" by the chroniclers rather than as Somerset.

The terms "Devon" or "Dyvnaint," as they are respectively used by Saxon or Briton in the course of the story, will therefore be understood to imply the ancient territory before its limitation by the boundaries of the modern counties, which practically took their rise from the wars of Ina.

With regard to names, I have not thought it worth while to use the archaic, if more correct, forms for those of well-known places. It seems unnecessary to write, for instance, "Glaestingabyrig" for Glastonbury, or "Penbroch" for Pembroke. I have treated proper names in the same way, keeping, for example, the more familiar latinised "Ina" rather than the Saxon "Ine," as being more nearly the correct pronunciation than might otherwise be used without the hint given by a footnote.

The exact spot where Wessex and West Wales met in the battle between Ina and Gerent is not certain, though it is known to have been on the line of the hills to the west of the Parrett, and possibly, according to an identification deduced from the Welsh "Llywarch Hen," in the neighbourhood of Langport. Local tradition and legend place a battle also at the ancient Roman fortress of Norton Fitzwarren, which Ina certainly superseded by his own stronghold at Taunton after the victory. As Nunna is named as leader of the Saxons, together with the king himself, it seems most likely that there were two columns acting against the Welsh advance on the north and south of the Tone River, and that therefore there were battles at each place. On the Blackdown Hills beyond Langport a barrow was known until quite lately as "Noon's barrow," and it would mark at least the line of flight of the Welsh; and if not the burial place of the Saxon leader, who is supposed to have fallen, must have been raised by him over his comrades.

The line taken by the story will not be far wrong, therefore, as in any case the Blackdown and Quantock strongholds must have been taken by the Saxons to guard against flank attacks, from whichever side of the Tone the British advance was made.

The course of the story hangs to some extent on the influence of the old feud between the British and Saxon Churches, which dated from the days of Augustine and his attempt to compel the adoption of Western customs by the followers of the Church which had its rise from the East. There is no doubt that the death of the wise and peacemaking Aldhelm of Sherborne let the smouldering enmity loose afresh, with the result of setting Gerent in motion against his powerful neighbour. Ina's victory was decisive, Gerent being the last king of the West Welsh named in the chronicles, and we hear of little further trouble from the West until A.D. 835, when the Cornish joined with a new-come fleet of Danes in an unsuccessful raid on Wessex.

Ina's new policy with the conquered Welsh is historic and well known. Even in the will of King Alfred, two hundred years later, some of the best towns in west Somerset and Dorset are spoken of as "Among the Welsh kin," and there is yet full evidence, in both dialect and physique, of strongly marked British descent among the population west of the Parrett.

There is growing evidence that very early settlements of Northmen, either Norse or Danish, or both, contemporary with the well-known occupation of towns, and even districts, on the opposite shores of South Wales, existed on the northern coast of Somerset and Devon. Both races are named by the Welsh and Irish chroniclers in their accounts of the expulsion of these settlers from Wales in A.D. 795, and the name of the old west country port of Watchet being claimed as of Norse origin, I have not hesitated to place the Norsemen there.

Owen and Oswald, Howel and Thorgils, and those others of their friends and foes beyond the few whose names have already been mentioned as given in the chronicles, are of course only historic in so far as they may find their counterparts in the men of the older records of our forefathers. If I have too early or late introduced Govan the hermit, whose rock-hewn cell yet remains near the old Danish landing place on the wild Pembrokeshire coast between Tenby and the mouth of Milford Haven, perhaps I may be forgiven. I have not been able to verify his date, but a saint is of all time, and if Govan himself had passed thence, one would surely have taken his place to welcome a wanderer in the way and in the name of the man who made the refuge.

CHAS. W. WHISTLER.

STOCKLAND, 1904.

CHAPTER I
HOW OWEN OF CORNWALL WANDERED
TO SUSSEX, AND WHY HE BIDED THERE.

The title which stands at the head of this story is not my own. It belongs to one whose name must come very often into that which I have to tell, for it is through him that I am what I may be, and it is because of him that there is anything worth telling of my doings at all. Hereafter it will be seen, as I think, that I could do no less than set his name in the first place in some way, if indeed the story must be mostly concerning myself. Maybe it will seem strange that I, a South Saxon of the line of Ella, had aught at all to do with a West Welshman--a Cornishman, that is--of the race and line of Arthur, in the days when the yet unforgotten hatred between our peoples was at its highest; and so it was in truth, at first. Not so much so was it after the beginning, however. It would be stranger yet if I were not at the very outset to own all that is due from me to him. Lonely was I when he first came to me, and lonely together, in a way, have he and I been for long years that for me, at least, have had no unhappiness in them, for we have been all to each other.

I have said that I was lonely when he first came to me, and I must tell how that was. I suppose that the most lonesome place in the world is the wide sea, and after that a bare hilltop; but next to these in loneliness I would set the glades of a beech forest in midwinter silence, when the snow lies deep on the ground under boughs that are too stiff to rustle in the wind, and the birds are dumb, and the ice has stilled the brooks. Set a lost child amid the bare grey tree trunks of such a winter forest, in the dead silence of a great frost, with no track near him but that which his own random feet have made across the snow, and I think that there can be nought lonelier than he to be thought of: and in the depth of the forest there is peril to the lonely.

I had no fear of the forest till that day when I was lost therein, for the nearer glades round our village had been my playground ever since I could remember, and before I knew that fear therein might be. That was not so long a time, however, save that the years of a child are long years; for at this time, when I first learned the full wildness of the woods of the great Andredsweald and knew what loneliness was, I was only ten years old. Since I could run alone my old nurse had tried to fray me from wandering out of sight of those who tended me, with tales of wolf and bear and pixy, lest I should stray and be lost, but I had not heeded her much. Maybe I had proved so many of her tales to be but pretence that, as I began to think for myself, I deemed them all to be so.

But now I was lost in the forest, and what had been a playground was become a vast and desolate land for me, and all the things that I had ever heard of what dangers lurked within it, came back to my mind. I remembered that the grey wolf's skin on which I slept had come hence, and I minded the calf that the pack had slain close to the village a year ago, and I thought of the girl who went mazed and useless about the place, having lost her wits through being pixy led, as they said, long ago. The warnings seemed to me to be true enough, now that all the old landmarks were lost to me, and all the tracks were buried under the crisp snow. I did not know when I had left the road from the village to the hilltop, or in which direction it lay.

It was very silent in the aisles of the great beech trunks, for the herds were in shelter. There was no sound of the swineherds' horn, though the evening was coming on, and but for the frost it was time for their charges to be taken homeward, and the woodmen's axes were idle. Even the scream of some hawk high overhead had been welcome to me, and the harsh cry of a jay that I scared was like the voice of a friend.

It was the fault of none but myself that I was lost. I had planned to go hunting alone in the woods while the old nurse, whose care I was far beyond, slept after her midday meal before the fire. So, over my warm woollen clothing I had donned the deerskin short cloak that was made like my father's own hunting gear, and I had taken my bow and arrows, and the little seax {¹} that a thane's son may always wear, and had crept away from the warm hall without a soul seeing me. I had thought myself lucky in this, but by this time I began to change my mind in all truth. Well it was for me that there was no wind, so that I was spared the worst of the cold.

I went up the hill to the north of the village by the track which the timber sleds make, climbing until I was on the crest, and there I began to wander as the tracks of rabbit and squirrel led me on. Sometimes I was set aside from the path by deep drifts that had gathered in its hollows with the wind of yesterday, and so I left it altogether in time. Overhead the sky was bright and clear as the low sun of the month after Yule, the wolf month, can make it. I wandered on for an hour or two without meeting with anything at which to loose an arrow, and my ardour began to cool somewhat, so that I thought of turning homewards. But then, what was to me a wondrous quarry crossed my way as I stood for a moment on the edge of a wide aisle of beech trees looking down it, and wondering if I would not go even to its end and so return. Then at once the wild longing for the chase woke again in me, and I forgot cold and time and place and aught else in it.

Across the glade came slowly and lightly over the snow a great red hare, looking against the white background bigger than any I had ever set eyes on before. It paid no heed at all to me, even when I raised my bow to set an arrow on the string with fingers which trembled with eagerness and haste. Now and again it stopped and seemed to listen for somewhat, and then loped on again and stopped, seeming hardly to know which way it wished to go. Now it came toward me, and then across, and yet again went from me, and all as if I were not there.

It was thirty paces from me when I shot, and I was a fair marksman, for a boy, at fifty paces. However, the arrow skimmed just over its back, and it crouched for a second as it heard the whistle of the feathers, and then leapt aside and on again in the same way. But now it crossed the glade and passed behind some trees before I was ready with a second arrow, and I ran forward to recover the first, which was in the snow where it struck, hoping thence to see the hare again.

When I turned with the arrow in my hand I saw what made the hare pay no heed to me. There was a more terrible enemy than even man on its track. Sniffing at my footprints where they had just crossed those of the hare was a stoat, long and lithe and cruel. I knew it would not leave its quarry until it had it fast by the throat, and the hare knew it also by some instinct that is not to be fathomed, for I suppose that no hare, save by the merest chance, ever escaped that pursuer. The creature seemed puzzled by my footprint, and sat up, turning its sharp eyes right and left until it spied me; but when it did so it was not feared of me, but took up the trail of the hare again. And by that time I was ready, and my hand was steady, and the shaft sped and smote it fairly, and the hare's one chance had come to it. I sprang forward with the whoop of the Saxon hunter, and took up and admired my prey, not heeding its scent at all. It was in good condition, and I would get Stuf, the house-carle, who was a sworn ally of mine, to make me a pouch of it, I thought.

I mind that this was the third wild thing that I had slain. One of the others was a squirrel who stayed motionless on a bough to stare at me, in summer time, and the second was a rabbit which Stuf had shown me in its seat. This was quite a different business, and I was proud of my skill with some little reason. I should have some real wild hunting to talk of over the fire tonight.

Then I must follow up the hare, of course, and I thrust the long body of the stoat through my girdle, so that its head hung one way and its tail the other, and took up the trail of the hare where my prey had left it. Now, I cannot tell how the mazed creature learned that its worst foe was no longer after it, but so it must have been, else it had circled slowly in lessening rings until the stoat had it, and presently it would have begun to scream dolefully. But

I only saw it once again, and then it seemed to be listening at longer spaces. Yet it took me a long way before it suddenly fled altogether, as its footmarks told me. A forest-bred lad learns those signs soon enough, if he is about with the woodmen in snow time.

Then I turned to make my way home, following my own track for a little way. That was crooked, and I went to take a straighter path, and after that I was fairly lost.

Yet I held on, hoping every minute to come into some known glade or sight, some familiar landmark, before the sun set. But I found nought but new trees, and new views over unknown white country all round me as I turned my steps hither and thither as one mark after another drew me. Then the sun set and the short day was over, and the grey twilight of snow weather came after the passing of the warm red glow from the west, shadowless and still.

That was about the time when I was missed at home, for my father came back from Chichester town, and straightway asked for me. And when I came not for calling, nor yet for the short notes of the horn which my father had always used to bring me to him, one ran here and another there, seeking me in wonted places about the village, until one minded that he had seen a boy, who must have been myself, go up the hill track forestwards.

Then was fear enough for me, seeing that from our village more than one child has wandered forth thus and been seen no more, and I was the only son of the long-widowed thane, and the last of the ancient line that went back to Ella, and beyond him even to Woden. So in half an hour there was not a man left in the village, and all the woods and hillsides rang with their calls to me, while in the hall itself bided only the old nurse, who wept and wailed by the hearth, and my father, whose tall form came and went across the doorway, restless; for he waited here lest he should miss my coming homeward. Up the steep street of the village the wives stood in the doorways silent, and forgetting their ailments for once in listening for the cries that should tell that I was found. If they spoke at all, they said that I should not be seen again, for the cold had driven the wolves close to the villages.

But I was by this time far beyond the reach of friendly voices, on the edge of the great hill that falls sheer down through many a score feet of hanging woods and thicket to the Lavington valley far below, and there at last I knew for certain that I was lost utterly, for this place or its like I had never seen before. Then I stayed my feet, bewildered, for the sun was gone, and I had nothing to tell me in which direction I was heading, for at that time the stars told me nought, though there were enough out now to direct any man who was used to the night. When I stood still I found that I was growing deadly cold, and the weariness that I had so far staved off began to creep over me, so that I longed to sleep.

And I suppose that I should have done so, and thereby met my death shortly, but for a thing that roused me in an instant, and set the warm blood coursing through me again.

There came a rustling in the undergrowth of the hillside below me, and that was the most homely sound that I had heard since the wild geese flew over me seaward with swish and whistle of broad wings and call that I knew well. The silence of the great brown owls that circled swiftly over me now and then was uncanny.

The rustling drew nearer, and then out into the open place under the tall bare tree trunks where I stood trotted a grey beast that was surely a shepherd's dog, for he stayed and looked back and whined a little as if his master must be waited for. I thought that I could hear the cracking of more branches once farther down the hill.

Then I called to the dog, knowing that he and the shepherd would not be far apart, and at the call the dog turned quickly toward me and leaped back a yard, cowering a little with drooping tail. So I called him again, and more loudly.

"Hither, lad! Hither, good dog!"

But the beast backed yet more from me, and I saw the dull gleam of yellow teeth and heard him snarl as he did so, and then he growled fiercely, so that I thought him sorely ill-tempered. But I had no fear of dogs, and I called him again cheerily, and at that he sank on his haunches and set back his head and howled and yelled as I had never heard any dog give tongue before. And presently from a long way off I heard the like howls, as if all the dogs of some village answered him, and I thought their tongue was strange also.

Then came the shout of a man, even as I expected, and there was the noise of one who tears his way through briers and brambles in haste; but at that shout the dog turned and fled like a grey shadow into the farther thickets, and was gone.

"Who calls?" one said loudly, and from the hillside climbed hastily into the open a tall man, bearded and strong, and with a pleasant-looking, anxious face. He was dressed in leather like our shepherds, and like them carried but quarterstaff and seax for weapons. I suppose that I was in some shadow, for at first he did not see me.

"Surely I heard a child's voice," he said out loud--"or was it some pixy playing with the grey beast of the wood?"

"Here I am," I cried, running to him; "take me home, shepherd, for I think that I am lost."

He caught me up in haste, looking round him the while.

"Child," he said, "how came you here--and to what were you calling?"

"I was calling your dog," I answered, "but he is not friendly. Does he look for a beating? for he ran away yonder when he heard you coming."

"Ay, sorely beaten will that dog be if he comes near me just now," the man said grimly. "Never mind him, but tell me how you came here, and where you belong."

So I told him that I was Oswald, the son of Aldred, the thane of Eastdean, thinking, of course, that all men would know of us, and so I bade him take me home quickly.

"I have been hunting," I said, showing him my unsavoury prey, which by this time was frozen stiff in my belt. "Then I followed the hare this was after, and I cannot tell how far I have come."

All this while the man had me in his strong arms, and he had looked at the track of the dog in the snow, and now was walking swiftly from it, through the beech trees, looking up at their branches as if wondering at the way the great trunks shot up smooth and bare from the snow at their roots before they reached the first forking, fathoms skyward.

"I am a stranger, Oswald, the thane's son," he said. "I do not rightly know in which direction your home may lie."

I know now that he was himself as lost as I, but that he did not tell me, for my sake. It is an easy thing for a stranger to go astray in the Andredsweald. But I could not tell him more than that I knew that I had left the sea always behind me so long as I knew where it lay. So he turned southwards at once when he heard that, and went on swiftly. Then I heard the howl of his dog again, and I laughed, for the other howls that answered him were nearer.

"Listen, shepherd," I said. "Your dog is making his comrades howl for him, and the beating that is to come.

"Are you cold?"

For he had shivered suddenly, and his pace quickened. He had heard the howl of the single wolf that has found its quarry, and calls the answering pack to follow. But he did not tell me of my mistake.

"I am not cold overmuch," he answered. "Let us run and warm me."

Then he ran until we came to the top of a hill whence the last glimmer of the sea over Selsea was plain before him, and there I asked him to set me down lest I tired him.

"Nay, but you keep me warm," he said. "Tell me, are there oak trees as one goes seaward?"

"Ay, many and great ones in some places."

Then he ran down the hill, and the sway of his even stride lulled me so that I dozed a little. I roused when he stayed suddenly.

"Sit here, Oswald, for a moment, and fear nought while I rest me," he said in a strange voice.

We were halfway up a long slope and among fresh trees. Then he lifted me and set me on the curved arm of a great oak tree, some eight feet from the ground, asking me if I was safe there. And when I laughed and answered that I was, he set his back against the trunk, and drew his heavy seax, putting his staff alongside him, where he could reach it at once if it was needed. It was light enough, with the clear frosty starlight on the snow.

Then I heard the swift patter of feet over the crisp surface, and the grey beast came and halted suddenly not three yards from us, and on his haunches he sat up and howled, and I heard the answering yells in no long space of time coming whence we had come. His eyes glowed green with a strange light of their own as he stared at my friend, and for a moment I looked to see him come fawning to his master's feet.

Suddenly he gathered himself together, and sprung silently at the throat of the man who waited him, and there was a flash of the keen steel, and a sound as of the cleaving of soft wood, and the beast was in a twitching heap at the man's feet. I knew what it was at last, yet I could say nothing. The wolf was quite dead, with its head cleft.

Swiftly my friend hewed the great head from the trunk and tore one of the leather cross garterings from his leg, and so leapt at a branch which hung above him and pulled it down. Then he bound the head to its end with the thong and let it go, so that it dangled a fathom and a half above him, and then he lifted me from my place and ran as I had not thought any man could run, until he stayed at the brow of the hill for sheer want of breath.

Behind us at that moment rose the sound as of hungry dogs that fight over the food in their kennels, and my friend laughed under his breath strangely.

"That will be a wild dance beneath the tree anon," he said, as if to himself.

Then he said to me, "Are you frayed, bairn?" as he ran on again.

"No," I answered, "You can smite well, shepherd."

"Needs must, sometime," he said. "Now, little one, have you a mother waiting you at home?"

"No. Only father and old nurse."

"Nor brother or sister?"

"None at all," I said.

"An only child, and his father lonely," the man said. "Well, I will chance it while the trees last. The head will stay them awhile, maybe."

Now he went swiftly across the rolling woodlands, and again I slept in his arms, but uneasily and with a haunting fear in my dreaming that I should wake to see the wild eyes of the wolf glaring across the snow on us again. So it happens that all I know of the rest of that flight from Woden's pack has been told me by others, so that I can say little thereof.

The howls of the pack as they stayed to fall on the carcass of their fellow, after their wont, died away behind us, and before they were heard again my friend had come across a half-frozen brook, and for a furlong or more had crashed and waded through its ice and water that our trail might be lost in it. Then he lit on the path that a sounder of wild swine had made through the snow on either side of it as they crossed it, and that he followed, in hopes that the foe would leave us to chase the more accustomed quarry. From that he leapt aside presently with a wondrous leap and struck off away from it. He would leave nothing untried, though indeed by this time he had reason to think that the pack had lost us at the brook, for he heard no more of them.

So at last he came within sound of some far-off shouts of those who were seeking me, and he guessed well what those shouts meant, and turned in their direction. Had he not heard them I do not know what place of refuge, save the trees, he would have found that night, for he was then passing across the valley that winds down to our home.

So it happened that when at last he saw the red light from the door of our hall gleaming across the snow, for it had been left open that perchance I might see it, he was close to the place, and he came into the courtyard inside the stockading without meeting any one, for he came from the side on which the village is not.

There I woke as the house dogs barked, and at first it was with a cry of fear lest the wolves were on us again; but the fear passed as I saw my father come quickly into the light of the doorway, and heard his voice as he stilled the dogs and cried to ask if the boy was found.

"Ay, Thane, he is here, and safe," my friend answered, and he set me down in the midst of the court, while the dogs leapt and fawned round me.

Then I ran to the arms that were held out for me, forgetting for the moment the one who had brought me back to them, and left him standing there.

Then the man who had saved me turned after one long look at that meeting, and I think that he was going his way in silence, content with that he had done, but my father saw it and called to him:

"Friend, stay, for I have not thanked you, and I hold that there is reward due to you for what you have brought back to me."

"It was a chance meeting, Thane, and I am glad to have been of use. No need to speak of reward, for it is indeed enough to have seen the boy home safely."

"Why, then," said my father, "I cannot have a stranger pass my hall at this time in the evening, when it is too late to reach the town in safety. Here you must at least lodge for the night, or Eastdean will be shamed. Your voice tells me that you are a stranger--but maybe you have your men waiting for you at hand? There will be room for them also."

For there was that in the tones of the voice of this man which told my father that here he had no common wanderer.

"I am alone," my friend said. "But your men seek the little one even yet in the forest. Will you not call them in?"

My father looked at the man for a moment, and smiled.

"Ay, I forgot in my joy. They are well-nigh as anxious as I have been."

Then he took down the great horn that hung by the door, and wound the homing call that brings all within its hearing back to the hall, and its hoarse echoes went across the silent woods until it was answered by the other horns that passed on the message until the last sounds came but faintly to us. I heard men cheering also, for they knew by the token that all was well. My father had me in his arms all this time, standing in the door.

"There would have been sorrow enough had he been lost indeed," my father said. "He is the last of the old line, and the fathers of those men whom you hear have followed his fathers since the days of Ella. Come in, and they will thank you also. Where did you find him?"

Then as he turned and went into the hall the light flashed red on my jerkin suddenly, and he cried, "Here is blood on his clothing!--Is he hurt?"

"No," I said stoutly; "maybe it is the blood of the stoat I slew, or else it has come off the shepherd's sleeves. He hewed off the wolf's head and hung it on the tree."

Then my father understood what my peril had been--even that which he and all the village had feared for me, and his face paled, and he held out his hand to the man, drawing in his breath sharply.

"Woden!" he cried, "what is this, friend? Are you hurt, yourself? For the wolf must be slain ere his head can be hefted, as we say."

"No hurt to any but the wolf," the man said, smiling a little. "We did but meet with one who called the pack on us. So I even hung his head on a tree, that the pack when it came might stay to leap at it. They were all we had to fear, and maybe that saved us."

"I marvel that you are not even now in the tree, yourself--with the boy."

"Nay, but the frost is cruel, and he would have been sorely feared with the leaping and howls of the beasts. There were always trees at hand as we fled, if needs were to take to them. It was in my mind that it were best to try to get him home, or near it."

Then said my father, gripping the hand that met his: "There is more that I would say, but I cannot set thoughts into words well. Only, I know that I have a man before me. Tell me your name, that neither I nor the boy may ever forget it."

"Here, in the Saxon lands, men call me Owen the Briton," he answered simply.

"I thought your voice had somewhat of the Welsh tone," my father said. "And your English is of Mercia. I have heard that there are Britons in the fenland there."

"I am of West Wales, Thane, but I have bided long in Mercia."

Then came my old nurse, and there were words enough for the time. Her eyes were red with weeping, but it was all that my father could do to prevent her scolding me soundly then and there for the fright I had given her. But she set a great bowl of bread and milk before me, and the men began to come in at that time, and they stood in a ring round me and watched me eat it as if they had never seen me before, while my father spoke aside of the flight to Owen on the high place. But concerning his own story my father asked the stranger no more until he chose to open the matter himself.

After supper there was all the tale to be told, and when that was done the Welshman slept before the hall fire with the house-carles, but my father had me with him in the closed chamber beyond the high seat, for it seemed that he would not let me go beyond his sight again yet.

Now, that is how Owen came to me at first, and the first thing therefore that I owe to him is nothing less than life itself. And from that time we have been, as I have said, together in all things.

On the next morning my father made his guest take him back over the ground we had crossed together, for no fresh snow had fallen, and the footprints were plain to be followed almost from the gate of the hall stockade. So they came at last to the tree, and on it the head hung yet, but the body was clean gone. All round the tree the snow was reddened and trampled by the fierce beasts who leapt to reach the head, and the marks of their clawing was on the trunk, where they had tried to climb it. From the footmarks it seemed that there were eight or nine of them. Three great ones had left the head and followed us presently as far as the brook, half a mile away.

After that the two men went on to the place where Owen had found me, and there my father, judging from the dress and loneliness of the Briton that he might be able to help him somewhat, said:

"I do not know what your plans may be, but is there any reason why you should not bide here and help me tend the life you have kept for me?"

Then answered Owen: "You know nought of me, Thane. For all you ken, I may be but an outlaw who is fleeing from justice."

"Do I know nought about you? I think that last night and what I have seen today have told me much, and I have been held as a good judge of a man. If so be that you were an outlaw, which I do not think, what you have done is enough to inlaw you again with any honest man--even had you taken a life, for you have saved one. Did I know you were an outlaw I would see to your pardon. But maybe you are on a journey that may not be hindered?"

Now Owen was silent for a little, and there came a shadow over his face as he answered, slowly and with his eyes on the far sea:

"No man's man am I, and I am but drifting Westward again at random. Yet I can say in all truth, that I am no wanderer for ill reason in any wise. I will tell you, Thane, here and alone, that there are foes in my home for whose passing, in one way or another, I must needs wait. Even now I was on my way to Bosham, where they tell me are Western monks with whom I might bide for a time, if not altogether. I was lost in the forest last night."

Now my father saw that some heavy sorrow of no common sort lay beneath the quiet words of the man before him, and he forbore to ask him more. Also, he deemed that in the Welsh land he would surely rank as a thane, for his ways and words bespoke more than his dress would tell. Therefore he said:

"Wait here with us for a while at least. There will be no more welcome guest."

"Let me be of some use, rather," Owen answered. "If I bide with you, Thane, and I thank you for the offer, let it be as I have bided elsewhere from time to time--as one of the household, not as an idle guest, if it were but to help the woodmen in the forest."

"Why, that will be well. I need a forester, and it is plain that you are a master of woodcraft. Let it be so. Yet I must tell you one thing fairly, and that is, that I am what you would call a heathen. I know that you are a good Christian man, for I saw you sign your holy sign before you ate last night and this morning. Yet I do not hate Christians."

"I had heard that all Sussex was turned to the faith," Owen said.

"If one says that all the men have gone to market, one knows that here and there one is excepted for good reason. It is not for a thane of the line of Woden to give up the faith of his fathers idly. I do not know what may be in the days to come, but here in the Andredsweald some dozen of us will not leave the old gods. It was the bidding of Ethelwalch the king that we should do so, but that is not a matter wherein a king may meddle, as it seems to us."

"I do not know why I should not bide with you, Thane, if so be that there is no hindrance to my faith."

"That there will be none. Why, the most of my folk are Christian enough. And if a man of the Britons did not honour his old faith it would be as strange as if I honoured not that of my fathers. I have no quarrel with the faith of any man, either king or thrall."

"Then I will be your forester, Thane, for such time as I may, and I thank you."

"Nay, but the thanks are all on my side," answered my father. "Now I shall know that the boy will have one with whom he may live all day in the woods if he will, and I shall be content."

So Owen bided with us, half as honoured guest and half as forester, and as time went on he was well loved by all who knew him, for he was ever the same to each man about the place. As for me, it was the best day that could have dawned when he found me in the woods as a lost child. And that my father said also.

CHAPTER II
HOW ALDRED THE THANE KEPT HIS FAITH, AND OWEN FLED WITH OSWALD.

Our Sussex was the last land in all England that was heathen. I suppose that the last heathen thanes in Sussex were those whose manors lay in the Andredsweald, as did ours. Most of these thanes had held aloof from the faith because at the first coming of good Bishop Wilfrith, some twelve years ago, those who had hearkened to him were mostly thralls and freemen of the lower ranks, and they would not follow their lead. Yet of these there were some, like my father, who had no hatred, to say the least, of the Christian and his creed, and did but need the words of one who could speak rightly to them to turn altogether from the Asir.

Maybe the only man who was at this time really fierce against the faith was Erpwald, the thane of Wisborough, some half-score miles from us northwards across the forest. He had been the priest of Woden in the old days, and indeed held himself so even now, though secretly, for fear of Ina the Wessex king, who ruled our land well and strongly. This Erpwald was no very good neighbour of ours, as it happened, for he and my father had some old feud concerning forest rights and the like which he had taken to heart more than there was any occasion for, seeing that it was but such a matter as most thanes have, unless they are unusually lucky, in a place where boundaries are none. It is likely enough that but for the easy ways of my father, who gave in to him so far as he could, this feud would have been of trouble some time ago, for as the power of Erpwald, as priest, waned he seemed to look more for power in other ways. Yet in the end both the matter of the faith and the matter of the feud seemed to work together in some way that brought trouble enough on our house, which must be told; for it set Owen and me out into the world together for a time, and because of it there befell many happenings thereafter which have not all been sad in their ending.

Owen had been with us for a year and a half when what I am going to tell came to pass, and in that time my father had come to look on him rather as a brother than as a guest, and the thought that he might leave him at any time was one which he did not like to keep in his mind.

That being so, it was not at all surprising that in this summer my father had at last borne witness that he wished to become a Christian altogether, and so it had come to pass that he and Owen and I used to ride to Bosham, the little seacoast village beyond Chichester town, to speak with Dicul, the good old Irish priest, who yet bided there rather than in the new monastery which Wilfrith built at Selsea, until we were taught all that was needful, and the time came when we should be baptized.

That my father would have done here at Eastdean, that all his people, who were Christians before him, should see and rejoice. Yet it was not an easy matter for him as it had been for them, for now he would stand alone among his fellows, the heathen thanes; and most of all Erpwald the priest would be wroth with him for leaving that which he had held so long. He must meet these men often enough, and he knew that they would have biting words to hurl at him, but that thought did not stay him for a moment. It was more than likely that one or two more would follow him when once the old circle was broken.

So on a certain day Dicul rode over from Bosham on his mule, and early on the next morning he set up a little wooden cross by the spring above the hall, and there my father and I and Stuf, the head man of the house-carles, who had bided in the old faith for love of my father, were baptized, Owen and one of the village freemen standing sponsors for us, and that was a wondrous day to us all, as I think. For when all was done my father gave their freedom to all our thralls, for the sake of the freedom that had been given him, and he promised that here, where he and they had been freed, a church should be built of good forest oak, after the woodcutting of the winter to come.

Then Dicul went his way homewards, with one of our men to lead his mule and carry some few presents for his people to Bosham, and after he was gone we had a quiet feasting in our hall until the light was gone. And even as our feasting ended there came in a swineherd from the forest with word that from the northward there came a strong band of armed men through the forest, and he held it right that my father should be warned thereof, for he feared they were some banded outlaws, seeing that there was peace in the land. That was no unlikely thing at all, for our forests shelter many, and game being plentiful they live there well enough, if not altogether at ease. As a rule they gave little trouble to us, and at times in the winter we would even have men who were said to be outlaws from far off working in the woods for us.

Yet now and then some leader would rise among them and gather them into bands which waxed bold to harry cattle and even houses, so that there might be truth in what the swineherd told. Nevertheless my father thought of little danger but to the herds, and so had them driven into the sheds from the home fields, and set the men their watches as he had more than once done before in like alarms.

Presently I was awakened, for I had gone to rest before the message came, by the hoarse call of a horn and the savage barking of the dogs. I heard the hall doors shut and open once or twice as men passed in and out, and in the hall was the rattle of weapons as the men took them from their places on the walls, but I heard no voices raised more than usual. Then I got out of my bed and tried to open the sliding doors that would let me out on the high place from my father's chamber, where I always slept now, but I could not move them. So I went back to my place and listened.

What was happening I must tell, therefore, as Owen has told me, for I saw nothing to speak of.

As the horn was blown, one of the men who had been on guard came into the hall hastily and spoke to my father.

"The house is beset, Lord. Stuf blew the horn and bade me tell you. There are men all round the stockade."

"Outlaws?"

The man shook his head.

"We think not, Lord. But it is dark, and we cannot fairly see them. We heard them call one 'Thane.' Nor are there any outland voices among them, as there would be were they outlaws."

Then my father armed himself in haste and went out. The night was very dark, and it was raining a little. Stuf had shut the stockade gates, which were strong enough, and had reared a ladder against the timbers that he might look over.

Close to the ladder stood Owen, armed also, for he had been out to see that all was quiet and that the men were on guard.

"There are men everywhere," he said. "I would we had some light."

"Heave a torch on the straw stack," my father answered; "there will be enough then."

The stack was outside the stockade, and some twenty yards from its corner. One of the men ran to the hall and brought a torch from its socket on the wall, and handed it to Stuf, who threw it fairly on the stack top, from the ladder. It blazed up fiercely as it went through the air, and from the men who beset us there rose a howl as they saw it. Several ran and tried to reach it with their spears, but they were not in time. The first damp straws of the thatch hissed for a moment, dried, and burst into flame, and then nought could stop the burning. The red flames gathered brightness every moment, lighting up two sides of the stockading, in the midst of which the hall stood. Then an arrow clicked on Stuf's helm, and he came down into shelter.

"This is a strange affair, Master," he said. "I have seen three men whom I know well among them."

"Who are they?"

"Wisborough men--freemen of Erpwald's."

My father and Owen looked at one another. Words my father knew he should have to put up with, after today, from Erpwald, but this seemed token of more than words only.

Then came the blast of a horn from outside, and a strange voice shouted that the thane must come and speak with those who called him. So my father went to the gate and answered from within it:

"Here am I. What is all the trouble?"

"Open the gate, and you shall know."

"Not so, Thane," cried one of our men, who was peering through the timbers of the stockade. "Now that I can see, I have counted full fifty men, and they are waiting as if to rush in."

Then said my father:

"Maybe we will open the gate when we are sure you are friends. One may be forgiven for doubting that when you come thus at midnight to a peaceful house."

"We are friends or not, as you choose, Aldred," the voice answered. "I am Erpwald, Woden's priest, and I am here to stay wrong to the Asir of which I have heard."

"I will not pretend not to know what you mean, Erpwald," answered my father. "But this, as it seems to me, is a matter that concerns me most of all."

"If it concerns not Woden's priest, whom shall it concern?" answered Erpwald. "It is true, then, that you have left the Asir to follow the way of the thralls, led aside by that Welshman you have with you?"

"It is true enough that I am a Christian," said my father steadily. "As for leaving the Asir, that is not to be said of one whose line goes back to Woden, his forefather. But I cannot worship him any longer. Forefather of mine he may be, but not a god."

"Ho! that is all I needed to hear. Now, I will not mince matters with you, Aldred. Either you give up this foolishness, or I am here to make you do so."

Now, my father looked round at the men and saw that all the house-carles and one or two from the village were in the courtyard, fifteen of them altogether, besides himself and Owen. They were all Christian men, and they stood in a sort of line behind him across the closed gate with their faces set, listening.

"Don't suppose that there is any help coming to you from the village," said the hard voice from outside. "There is a guard over every house."

"Erpwald," said my father, "it is a new thing that any man should be forced to quit his faith here in Sussex. Nor is it the way of a thane to fall on a house at night in outlaw fashion. Ina the king will have somewhat to say of this."

"If there is one left to tell him, that is," came back the reply. "There will not be shortly, unless I have your word that tomorrow you come to me at Wisborough and make such atonement to the Asir as you may, quitting your new craze."

Then said Stuf, the leader of the house-carles, growling:

"That is out of the question, and he knows it. He means to fall on us, else had he spoken to you elsewhere first, Thane. It seems to me that here we shall die."

He looked round on his fellows, and they nodded, and one set his helm more firmly on his head, and another tightened his belt, and one or two signed the cross on their broad chests, but not one paled, though they knew there was small hope for them if Erpwald chose to storm the house. The court was light as day with the flames of the stack by this time.

"What think you of this, Owen," my father said.

"That it is likely that we must seal our faith with our blood, brother," he answered. "Yet I think that there is more in this than heathenism, in some way."

"There is an old feud of no account," said my father, "but I would not think hardly of Erpwald. After all, he was Woden's priest, and is wroth, as I myself might have been. It is good to die thus, and but for the boy I would be glad."

"I do not think that he will be harmed," said Owen, "even if the worst comes to the worst."

"Well, if I fall, try to get him hence. After that maybe Erpwald will be satisfied. I set him in your charge, brother, for once you have saved him already. Fail me not."

Owen held out his hand and took his.

"I will not fail you," he said--"if I live after you."

Now from outside the voices began to be impatient, and Erpwald had been crying to my father to be speedy, unheeded. But in the midst of the growing shouts of the heathen my father turned to the men and asked them if they were content to die with him for the faith. And with one accord they said that they would.

Then with a thundering crash a great timber beam was hurled against the gate, shaking its very posts with the force of the six men who wielded it at a run, and in the silence that fell as they drew back Erpwald cried:

"For the last time, Aldred, will you yield?"

But he had no answer, and after a short space the timber crashed against the gate again and again. And across it waited our few, silent and ready for its falling.

I heard all this in the closed chamber, and the red light of the fire shone across the slit whence the light and fresh air came into it, but it was too high for me to look out of. I got up and dressed myself then, for no reason but that I must be doing something. I waxed excited with the noise and flickering light, and no one came near me. My old nurse was the only woman in the house, for the married house-carles lived in the village, and I daresay she slept through it all in her own loft. There was no thunderstorm that could ever wake her.

At this time my father sent a few of the men to the back of the house, that they might try at least to keep off the foe from climbing the stockade and so falling on them in the rear. But the timbers were high, and the ditch outside them full of water, and as it happened there was no attack thence.

Erpwald watched the back indeed, but all his force was bent on the gate.

It was not long before that fell, crashing inwards, and across it strode the heathen priest into the gap. He was fully armed, and wore the great golden ring of the temple--all that was left him of his old surroundings since Ethelwalch the king, who sent Wilfrith to us, had destroyed the building that stood with the image of Woden in it hard by his house. Men used to take oath on that ring, as do we on the Book of the Gospels, and they held it holier than the oaken image of the god itself. I do not think that any man had seen it since that time until this night.

Now Erpwald stood for a moment in the gate, with his men hard behind him, expecting a rush at him, as it would seem. But our folk stood firm in the line across the courtyard, shoulder to shoulder, with my father and Owen before them. So they looked at one another.

Then Erpwald slipped the golden ring from his arm and held it up. There may have been some thought in his mind that my father was hesitating yet.

"By the holy ring I adjure you, Aldred, for the last time, to return to the Asir," he said loudly.

My father shook his head only, but Stuf the house-carle, who had stood beside him at the font this morning, had another answer which was strange enough.

"This for the ring!" he said.

And with that he hurled a throwing spear at it as it shone in the firelight, with a true aim. The spear went through the ring itself without harming the hand of the holder, and coming a little slantwise, twitched it away from him and stuck in the timber of the stockade whence the gatepost had been riven. The ring hung spinning on the shaft safely enough, but to Erpwald it seemed that his treasure had gone altogether, and he yelled with rage and sprang forward. After him came his men, and in a moment the two parties were hand to hand.

Then was fighting such as the gleemen sing of, with the light of the red fire waxing and waning across the courtyard the while. The strange lights and shadows it cast were to the advantage of our men for a little while, but the numbers were too great against them for that to be of much avail. Soon they who had not fallen were borne back to the hall door, and there stood again, but my father was not with them.

He fell at the first, as Owen tells me. Another has told me that Owen stood across his body and would have fallen with him, but that Stuf drew him away, calling on him to mind his promise concerning me, and so he went back, still fighting, until he stood in the door of the hall.

There Erpwald and his men stayed their hands, like a ring of dogs that bay a boar. There was a little porch, so that they could not get at him sideways, and needs must that they fell on him one at a time. It seemed that not one cared to be the first to go near the terrible Briton as he stood, in the plain arms and with the heavy sword my father had given him, waiting for them. Well do I know what he was like at that time, and I do not blame them. There is no man better able to wield weapons than he, and they had learnt it.

Then the light of the straw stack went out suddenly, as a stack fire will, and the darkness seemed great. Yet from the well-lit hall a path of light came past Owen and fell on his foes, so that he could well see any man who was bold enough to come, and they held back the more.

There were but six men of ours in the house behind Owen.

Then came Erpwald, leaning, sorely wounded, on one of his men, and Owen spoke to him.

"You have wrought enough harm, Erpwald, for this once. Let the rest of the household go in peace."

"Harm?" groaned the heathen. "Whose fault is it? How could I think that the fool would have resisted?"

"As there are fifty men in the yard at this moment, it seems that you were sure of it," answered Owen in a still voice. "If you knew it not before, now at least you know that a Christian thinks his faith worth dying for."

Now, whether it was his wound, or whether he saw that he had gone too far, Erpwald bethought himself, and seemed minded to make terms.

"I wish to slay no more," he said. "Yield yourselves quietly, and no harm shall come to you."

"Let them not go, Thane," said one of his men, "else will they be off to Ina, and there will be trouble. You mind what you promised us."

Now, Owen heard this, and the words told him that he was right in thinking that there was more than heathenry in the affair. It seemed to him that the first thing was to save me, and that if he could do that in any way nought else mattered much. It was plain that no man was to be left to bring Ina on the priest for his ill deeds.

"If that is all the trouble now," he said, therefore, "as we are in your power you can make us promise what you like. Give us terms at least; if not, come and end us and the matter at once."

One of the men flew at him on that, and bided where he fell, across the doorway of the porch; none stirred to follow him.

"Swear that you will not go to Ina for a month's time with any tales, and you and all shall go free," Erpwald said.

The man who had spoken before put in at once:

"What of the blood feud, Erpwald?--There is Aldred's son yet."

At that the priest lost temper with his follower, and turned on him savagely:

"Is it for men to war with children? What care I for a blood feud? Can I not fend for myself? Hold your peace."

Then he said to Owen:

"They say that you are the child's foster-father now. If I give him to you, will you swear that you or he shall cross my path no more? You need not trouble to go to Ina, for he will not hearken to a Briton in any case."

Owen reddened under the last, but for my sake he did not answer, save to the first part of the saying.

"I will swear to take the child hence and let this matter be for us as if it had not been," he said, seeing that it was the best he could win for me.

What other thoughts were in his mind will be seen hereafter, but I will say now that it was not all so hopeless as it seemed to Erpwald.

"What of the other men," asked one or two of Erpwald's following.

"They shall bide here, where we can keep an eye on them," the priest answered. "They will not hurt us, nor we them, save only if they try to make trouble."

Then some of our house-carles said in a low tone to Owen: "Better to die with the master. Let us out and fall on them."

But he said: "This is for the boy's sake. Let me be, my brothers; I have the thane's word to carry out."

Then they knew that he was right, but they bade him make Erpwald swear to keep faith with them all.

So he spoke again with the priest, asking for honest pledges in return for his own oath. Whereon from across the courtyard, where a few wounded men lay--a voice weak with pain cried, with a strange laugh:

"Get him the holy ring, that he may be well bound. It hangs yonder where I put it, in the gateside timbers."

Erpwald glowered into the darkness, but he could see nothing of the man who had spoken. But one of his men had seen the spear cast, and knew what was meant, though the fight had set it out of his mind. So he ran, and found the shaft easily in the darkness, and took the ring from it, bringing it back to Erpwald.

"It is luck," he said. "Spear and ring alike have marked the place for Woden."

"Hold your peace, fool," snarled Erpwald, with a sharp look at Owen.

And at that Stuf laughed again, unheeded.

Then Owen swore as he had promised, on the cross hilt of his sword, and Erpwald swore faith on the ring, and so the swords were sheathed at last; and when they had disarmed all our men but Owen, Erpwald's men took torches from the hall and went to tend the wounded, who lay scattered everywhere inside the gate, and most thickly where my father fell.

Owen went to that place, with a little hope yet that his friend might live, but it was not so. Therefore he knelt beside him for a little while, none hindering him, and so bade him farewell. Then he went to Stuf, who was sorely hurt, but not in such wise that he might not recover.

"What will you do with the child?" the man asked.

"Have no fear for him. I shall take him westward, where my own people are. He shall be my son, and I think that all will be well with him hereafter."

"I wit that you are not what you have seemed, Master," Stuf said. "It will be well if you say so."

Then Owen bade him farewell also, and went to find me and get me hence before the ale and mead of the house was broached by the spoilers. And, as I have said, I was already dressed, and I ran to his arms and asked what all the trouble was, and where my father had gone, and the like. I think that last question was the hardest that Owen ever had put to him, and he did not try to answer it then. He told me that he and I must go to Chichester at once, at my father's bidding; and I, being used to obey without question, was pleased with the thought of the unaccustomed night journey. And then Owen bethought him, and left me for a moment, going to the chest where my father had his store of money. It was mine now, and he took it for me.

It seemed strange to him that there was no ransacking of the house, as one might have expected. Had the foe fired it he would not have been surprised at all, but all was quiet in the hall, and the voices of the men came mostly from the storehouses, whence he could hear them rolling the casks into the courtyard; so he told me to bide quietly here in the chamber for a few minutes, and went out on the high place swiftly, closing the door after him, that I might see nothing in the hall.

There he found Erpwald himself close at hand, sitting in my father's own chair while the wound that Owen himself had given him was being dressed. At the side of the great room sat the rest of our men, downcast and wondering, and half a dozen of the foe stood on guard at the door. It was plain that nought in the house was to be meddled with.

Erpwald turned as he heard the sliding door open.

"Get you gone as soon as you may," he said sullenly.

"There is one thing that I must ask you, Erpwald," Owen said. "It is what one may ask of one brave man concerning another. Let Aldred's people bury him in all honour, as they will."

"There you ask too much, Welshman. But I will bury him myself in all honour in the way that I think best. He shall have the burial of a son of Woden for all his foolishness."

At least, there would be no dishonour to his friend in that, and Owen thought it best to say no more, but he had one more boon, as it were, to ask.

"Let me take a horse from the stable for the child," he said. "We may have far to go."

He thought that he would have been met with rage at this, but it was worth asking. However, Erpwald answered somewhat wearily, and not looking at him:

"Take them all, if you will. I am no common reiver, and they are not mine. The farther you go the better. But let me tell you, that it will be safer for you not to make for Winchester and the king. I shall have you watched."

"A plain warning not to be disregarded," answered Owen. "We shall not need it."

Erpwald said no more, and Owen came back to me, closing the door after him again. There was another door, seldom used, from this chamber to the back of the house where the servants had their quarters, and through that he took me, wrapped in such warm furs as he could find. Then he went to the stables, and in the dark, for he would not attract the notice of Erpwald's men, who were round the ale in the courtyard, he saddled my forest pony, and another good horse which he was wont to ride with my father at times. He did not take the thane's own horse, as it would be known, and he would risk no questions as to how he came by it.

Then we rode away by the back gate, and when the darkness closed on us as we passed along the well-known road towards Chichester the voices of the foe who revelled in our courtyard came loudly to us. And I did but think it part of the rejoicing of that day as I listened.

Through the warm summer rain we came before daylight had fully broken to Bosham, not passing through Chichester, for the gates would be closed. And just before the sun rose, Dicul the priest came from his house to the little church and saw us sitting in the porch, waiting him, while the horses cropped the grass on the little green outside the churchyard, hobbled in forest fashion.

He bade us back to his house, and there I fell asleep straightway, with the tiredness that comes suddenly to a child. And Owen and he talked, and I know that he told him all that had happened and what his own plans for me were, under the seal of secrecy. And then he begged the good priest to tell me of my loss.

So it came to pass that presently Dicul took me on his knee and told me wonderful stories of the martyrs of old time, and of his own land in times that are not so far off; and when it seemed to me that indeed there is nought more wonderful and blessed than to give life for the faith, he told me how my father had fallen at the hands of heathen men, and was indeed a martyr himself. I do not know that he could have done it more wisely or sweetly, for half the sting was lost in the wonder of it all.

But he did not tell me who it was had slain my father, and that I did not know for many a long day.

After that we ate with him, and he gave us some little store for a journey, and so Owen and I rode on again, westward, homeless indeed, but in no evil case.

Now, as one may suppose, Owen's first thought was to get me beyond the reach of Erpwald, whose mood might change again, from that in which he let us go with what we would, to that in which he came on us. So all that day we went on steadily, sleeping the night in a little wayside inn, and pushing on again in the early morning, until Owen deemed it safe for us to draw rein somewhat, and for my sake to travel slowly.

At this time he had no clear plan in his head for the ending of our journey, nor was there need to make one at once. We had store of money to last us for many a long day, what with my father's and that which Owen had of his own, and we were well mounted, and what few things we needed to seem but travellers indeed Owen bought in some little town we passed through on the third day. After that we went easily, seeing things that had nought in them but wonder and delight for me.

Then at last we came in sight of the ancient town of Sarum on its hill, and there we drew up on the wayside grass to let a little train of churchmen pass us, and though I did not know it, that little halt ended our wandering. In the midst of the train rode a quiet looking priest, who sang softly to himself as his mule ambled easily along, and he turned to give us his blessing as Owen unhelmed when he passed abreast of us. Then his hand stayed as he raised it, and I saw his face lighten suddenly, and he pulled up the mule in haste, crying to Owen by name, and in the Welsh tongue. And I saw the face of my foster-father flush red, and he leapt from his horse and went to the side of the priest, setting his finger on his lip for a moment as he did so.

Then the priest signed that his people should go on, and at once they left him with us, and Owen bade me do reverence to Aldhelm, the abbot of Malmesbury, before whom we stood. And after that they talked long in Welsh, and that I could not follow, though indeed I knew a fair smattering of it by this time, seeing that Owen would have me learn from him, and we had used it a good deal in these few days as we rode.

It seemed to me that Aldhelm was overjoyed to see Owen, and I know now that those two were old friends of the closest at one time, when they met in Owen's own land.

So from that meeting it came to pass that we found a home with the good abbot at Malmesbury for a time, and there I learned much, as one may suppose, while Owen trained me in arms, and the monks taught me book learning, which I liked not at all, and only suffered for love of Owen, who wished me to know all I might.

Then one day, after two years in quiet here, came Ina the king with all his court to see the place and the new buildings that were rising under the hand of Aldhelm and Owen, who had skill in such matters, and then again was a change for us. It seems that Ethelburga the queen took a fancy to me, and asked that I might be with her as a page in the court, and that was so good a place for the son of any thane in the land that Owen could not refuse, though at first it seemed that we must be parted for a time.

But it was needful that the king should hear my story, that he might have some surety as to who I was, and if I were worthy by birth to be of his household, and Owen hardly knew how to tell him without breaking his oath to Erpwald. Yet it was true that the heathen thane had scoffed at him, rather than forbidden him to seek Ina, though indeed it was plain that he meant to bind us from making trouble for him in any way. But at last Owen said that if the king would forbear to take revenge for a wrong done to me, he might speak, and so after promise given he told all.

Very black grew the handsome face of the king as he heard.

"Am I often deceived thus?" he said. "I will even send some to ask of all the ins and outs of such another case hereafter. This Erpwald sent to me to say that Aldred and all his house had been slain by outlaws, and that he himself had driven them off and I believed him. After that I made over the Eastdean lands to him, and I take it that they were what he wanted. Well, he has not lived long to enjoy them, for he died not long ago, and now his brother holds the lands after him, and I know that he at least is a worthy man.

"Let it be. The child is my ward now, as an orphan, and I should have had to set his estate in the hands of some one to hold till he can take them. There will be no loss to him in the end."

Then he smiled and looked Owen in the face.

"I know you well, Owen, though it is plain that you would not have it so. Mind you the day when I met Gerent at the Parrett bridge? I do not often forget a face, and I saw you then, and asked who you were. Now there is good and, as I hope, lasting peace between our lands, thanks to the wisdom of our good Aldhelm here, and I will ask you somewhat, for I know that you also wrought for that peace while you might. Come to me, and be of the nobles who guard me and mine, and so wait in honour until the time comes when you may return to your place. Then you will be with the boy also."

So it came to pass that we took leave of that good friend the abbot, and went from Malmesbury in the train of Ina of Wessex. Thereafter for six years I served Ethelburga the queen, being trained in all wise as her own child, and after that I was one of the athelings of the court in one post or another, but always with the king when there was war on the long frontier of the Wessex land.

CHAPTER III
HOW KING INA'S FEAST WAS MARRED,
AND OF A VOW TAKEN BY OSWALD.

At this time, when I take up my story again, I was two and twenty, not very tall indeed, but square in the shoulder, and well able to hold my own, at the least, with the athelings who were my comrades, at the weapon play or any of our sports. It would have been my own fault if I were not so, for there was no better warrior in all Ina's following than Owen, and he taught me all I knew. And that knowledge I had tested on the field more than once, for Ina had no less trouble with his neighbours than any other king in England, whether in matters of raiding to be stopped or tribute to be enforced. Since I was too old to serve the queen as page any longer I had been of his bodyguard, and where he went was not always the safest place on a field for us who shielded him.

A court is always changing, as men come and go again to their own places after some little service there, but Owen and I were of those to whom the court was home altogether. Owen was the king's marshal now, and I was in command of the house-carles, and had been so for a year or more. It was no very heavy post, nor responsible after all, for Ina's guard was the love of his people, and beyond these warriors from the freemen who served as palace guard and watch, were the athelings of the household, from whose number I had been chosen for this post by right of longest service more than for any other reason, as I think. I knew all the ins and outs of every house where Ina went, and had nothing fresh to learn in the matter. Still, if the men under me were few, the post had its own privileges, and was always held to lead to somewhat higher, and I was more than content therewith, for it kept me near Owen and the king, whom I loved next to my foster father.

I do not think that by this time any one knew, save the king, that I was not Owen's own son. I was wont to call him father always, and I cannot be blamed, for he was foster father and godfather to me, and well did he take the father's place to the orphan whom he had saved. And I had forgotten Eastdean, save as one keeps a memory of the home where one was a child. I never thought of it as a place that should have been mine, for neither the king nor Owen ever spoke to me concerning it. Sometimes, in remembrances of my father, I would wonder into whose hands the manors had passed, but rather in hopes that some day those who owned them now would suffer me to see that the grave where he lay was honoured, rather than as a matter which at all concerned me in any closer way.

For, since I was but a child, the court had been my home, with Owen as my father, and Ina the king as the loved guardian for whom I would gladly give my life in need. All my training and thoughts were centred here, not as what one calls a courtier at all, but as one of the household who feared the king and queen no more than Owen himself, and yet reverenced all three as those to whom all homage was due since he could remember.

Thus things were with us at the end of the tenth year after we left Aldhelm at Malmesbury, and now the court was at Glastonbury in fair Somerset, keeping the Christmastide there in the place that is the holiest in all England by reason of the coming thither of Joseph of Arimathea, and the first preaching of the Gospel in our land by him. It was not by any means the first time I had been in the place, and here I had some good friends indeed; for Ina loved the vale of Avalon well, and often came hither with a few of us, or with the whole court, to the house which he had made that he might watch the building of the wondrous church which he was raising over the very spot where the little chapel of the saint had been in the old days.

Fair is the place indeed, for it lies deep among green hills, and from the westward slope where the church stands, at their foot stretch great meres to lesser hills toward the sunset beyond. Very pleasant are the trees and flowers of the rich meadows of the island valley, and the wind comes but gently here even at Yuletide, hardly ruffling the clear waters that have given the place its name, "Inys Vitryn," and "Avalon" men called the place before we Saxons came, by reason of those still meres and the wondrous orchards which fear no frost among the hills that shelter them. The summer seems to linger here after it has fled from the uplands.

There was a goodly company gathered in Ina's hall for the twelfth night feasting. Truly, the hall was not so great as that in the palace at Winchester, but it was all the brighter for that reason. It was hard to get that great space well lighted and warmed at times, when the wind blew cold under eaves and through narrow windows; but here all was well lit and comfortable to look on and to feel also, as one sat and feasted with the sweet sedges of the mere banks deep under foot on the floor and the great fire in the hall centre near enough to every one. I think that this hall in Glastonbury was as pleasant as any that I know in all Wessex.

There was a great door midway in the southern side of the hall, and as one entered, to right and left along that wall ran the tables for the house-carles and other men of the lower ranks, and for strangers who might come in to share the king's hospitality and had no right to a higher place. Then at either end of the hall were cross tables, where the thanes and their ladies had their places in due order, above the franklins whose cross tables were next to those of the house-carles. And then, right over against the south wall and across the fire on the hearth, was the longest table of all, and in the midst of that was the high place for the king and queen and a few others. That dais was the only place where the guests did not sit on both sides of the tables, for the king's board stood open to the midst of the hall on its three low steps that he might see and be seen by all his guests, and be fitly served from in front.

On the hearth a great yule log burnt brightly, and all round the wall were set torches in their sconces, so that the hall was very bright. On the walls were the costly hangings that we took everywhere with us, and above them shone the spare arms and helms and shields of the house-carles, mixed with heads of boar and stag and wolf from the Mendips and Quantocks where Ina hunted, each head with its story. Up and down in the spaces between the tables hurried the servants who tended the guests, so that the hall was full of life and brightness from end to end. There was peace in all Wessex at this time, and so here was a full gathering of guests to the little town.

Ina and Ethelburga the queen were on the high place, and to their left was Herewald, the Somerset ealdorman, who lived in Glastonbury, and was a good friend of mine, as will be seen, with his fair daughter Elfrida, and on the right of the king was Nunna, his cousin, and his wife. Owen was next to Herewald, at one end of the high place, and at the other end was Sigebald, the Dorset ealdorman, under whom I had fought not so long ago. There were many others of high rank in the west to the right and left of these again at the long tables.

Indeed, there was but one whom I missed in all the gathering. My old friend Aldhelm was gone. He died in the last year, after having been Bishop of Sherborne for a little while. I missed him sorely, as did every man who knew him.

I do not think that if one searched all England through there could have been found a more noble looking group than that at Ina's high table. It is well known that our king and queen were beyond all others for royalty of look and ways, and I will venture to say that neither of the ealdormen had their equals, save in Nunna, anywhere. But it is not my word only, for it was a common saying, that Owen seemed most royal next to the king himself. Grave he always was, but with a ready smile and pleasant, in the right place, and though he was now about five-and-forty he had changed little to my eyes from what he was twelve years ago, when he saved me from the wolves. He was one of those men who age but slowly.

One other on the high place I have not mentioned in this way. That was Elfrida, the Somerset ealdorman's daughter, of whom it was said that she was the fairest maiden in all Wessex. Certainly at this time I for one would have agreed in that saying. She was two years younger than I, if I dare say it, and it seemed to me that in the last three years she had suddenly grown from the child that I used to play with to a very stately lady, well fitted to take the place of her mother, who used to be kind to me when I first came here as the queen's somewhat mischievous page, and had but died a year or so ago. I think that this feast was the first Elfrida and her father had been present at since then, and at least, that was the reason I heard given for her presence on the high place.

Now I must say where my place was in the hall, for it may make more plain what happened hereafter. The young nobles of the court who had no relatives present sat at one of the cross tables at the king's right hand, and at the head of these tables was my seat by reason of my post as captain of the house-carles. So I sat with my back to the long chief table, with its occupants just behind me, and to my left was the open space in the centre of the hall, so that if I was needed, or had to go out for the change of guard or other house-carle business, all that I had to do, being at one end of the bench, was to get up and go my way without disturbing any one. At the same time I could see all the hall before me, and a half turn of the head would set my eyes on the king himself.

The door of the hall was closed when the king entered from his own chambers and took his place, so that the cold, and the draughts, which might eddy the smoke of fire and torches about the guests too much, was kept out. But it was closed against weather only, for any man might crave admittance to the king's hall at the great feast, whether as wayfarer or messenger or suppliant, so that he had good reason for asking hospitality. Several men had come in thus as the feast went on, but none heeded the little bustle their coming made, nor so much as turned to see where they were set at the lower tables, except myself and perhaps Owen. There was merriment enough in the hall, and room and plenty for all comers, even as Ina loved to have it.

Now there is no need to tell aught of that feast, until the meat was done and the tables were cleared for the most pleasant part of the evening, when the servants, whether men or women, sat down at their tables also, and the harp went round, with the cups, and men sang in turn or told tales, each as he was best able to amuse the rest. There was a little bustle while this clearance went on, and men changed their seats to be nearer friends and the like, for the careful state of the beginning of the feast was over in some degree; but at last all was ready, and the great door, which had been open for a few minutes as the servants took out into the courtyard the great cauldrons and spits, was closed, and then there fell a silence, for we waited for a custom of the king's.

Here at Ina's court we kept up the old custom of drinking the first cup with all solemnity, and making some vows thereover. This cup was, of course, to be drunk by the host, and after him by any whom he would name, or would take a vow on him. In the old heathen days this cup was called the "Bragi bowl," and the vows were made in the names of the Asir, and mostly ended in fighting before the year was over. We kept the old name yet, but now the vows were made in the name of all the Saints, and if Ina or any other made one it was sure to be of such sort that it would lead to some worthy deed before long, wrought in all Christian wise. Maybe the last of the old pattern of vow was made when Kentwine our king swore to clear the Welsh from the Parrett River to the sea, and did it.

So when the time came we sat waiting, each with his horn or cup before him, brimming with ale or cider or mead, as he chose, and men turned in their seats that they might see the pleasant little ceremony at the high place the better. As for me, I just turned in my bench end so that my feet were clear of the table, on which my arm and cup rested, and faced right down the hall, with, of course, no one at all between me and the steps of the high place. For now all had taken their seats except one cup bearer, who waited at the lowest step with the king's golden cup in one hand, and in the other a silver flagon of good Welsh wine to fill it withal. One would say that this was but a matter of chance, but as it happened presently it was well that I moved.

Now, in the hush was a little talk and laughter among those who were nearest the king, and then I saw the queen smile and speak to Elfrida, who blushed and looked well pleased, and then rose and came daintily round the end of the king's board. There a thane who sat at the table at the foot of the steps rose and handed her down them to where the servant waited. Ina had asked her to hand him the cup after the old fashion, she being the lady of the chief house in Glastonbury next his own. There she took the cup from the man's hand, and held it while he filled it heedfully. A little murmur that was all of praise went round the hall, and her colour rose again as she heard it, for it was not to be mistaken, and from the lower tables the voices were outspoken enough in all honesty.

Then she went up the steps holding the cup, and the king smiled on her as she came, and so she stood on the dais before the table and held out the wine, and begged the king to drink the "Bragi bowl" from her hands in her father's town.

The king bowed and smiled again, and rose up to take the cup from this fair bearer, and at that moment there was a sort of scuffle, unseemly enough, at the lower end of the hall near the door, and gruff voices seemed to be hushed as Ina glanced up with the cup yet untouched by his hand.

Then a man leapt from the hands of some who tried to hold him back, and he strode across the hall past the fire and to the very foot of the high place--as rough and unkempt a figure as ever begged for food at a king's table, unarmed, and a thrall to all seeming. And as he came he cried:

"Justice, Ina the king!--Justice!"

At that I and my men, who had sprung to our feet to hinder him, sat down again, for a suppliant none of us might hinder at any time. I did not remember seeing this man come in, but that was the business of the hall steward, unless there was trouble that needed the house-carles.

Ina frowned at this unmannerly coming at first, but his brow cleared as he heard the cry of the man. He signed to Elfrida to wait for a moment, and looked kindly at the thrall before him.

"Justice, Lord," the man said again.

"Justice you shall have, my poor churl," answered the king gently. "But this is not quite the time to go into the matter. Sit you down again, and presently you shall tell all to Owen the marshal, and thus it will come to me, and you shall see me again in the morning."

"Nay, but I will have justice here and now," the man said doggedly, and yet with some sort of appeal in his voice.

"Is it so pressing? Well, then, speak on. Maybe the vow that I shall make will be to see you righted."

And so the king sat down again, and the lady Elfrida waited, resting one hand on the table at the end of the dais farthest from me, and holding the golden cup yet in the other.

"What shall be done to the man who slays my brother?" the thrall cried.

And the king answered:

"If he has slain him by craft, he shall die; but if in fair fight and for what men deem reason, then he shall pay the full weregild that is due according to my dooms."

Then said the man, and his voice minded me of Owen's in some way:

"But and if he slew him openly in cold blood, for no wrong done to himself?"

"A strange doing," said the king--"but he should die therefor."

The king leant forward, with his elbow on the table to hear the better, and the man was close to the lowest step to be near him. It seemed that he was very wroth, for his right hand clutched the front of his rough jerkin fiercely, and his voice was harsh and shaking.

"It is your own word, Ina of Wessex, that the man who has slain my brother in this wise shall die. Lo, you! I am Morgan of Dyvnaint--and thus--"

There flashed from under the jerkin a long knife in the man's hand, and at the king he leapt up the low steps. But two of us had seen what was coming, and even as the brave maiden on his left dashed the full cup of wine in the man's face, blinding him, I was on him, so that the wine covered him and my tunic at once. I had him by the neck, and he gripped the table, and his knife flashed back at me wildly once, but I jerked him round and hurled him from the dais with a mighty crash, and so followed him and held him pinioned, while the cups and platters of the overturned table rolled and clattered round us.

Then rose uproar enough, and the hall was full of flashing swords. I mind that I heard the leathern peace thongs of one snap as the thane who tried to draw it tugged at the hilt, forgetting them. Soon I was in the midst of a half ring of men as I held the man close to the great fire on the hearth with his face downward and his right arm doubled under him. He never stirred, and I thought he waited for me to loose my hold on him.

Then came the steady voice of Ina:

"Let none go forth from the hall. To your seats, my friends, for there can be no more danger; and let the house-carles see to the man."

Two of my men took charge of my captive, even as he lay, and I stood up. Owen was close to me.

"The man is dead," he said in a strange voice.

"I doubt it," I answered, looking at him quickly, for the voice startled me. Then I saw that my foster father's face was white and drawn as with some trouble, and he was gazing in a still way at the man whom the warriors yet held on the floor.

"His foot has been in the fire since you hove him there, yet he has not stirred," he said.

Then I minded that I had indeed smelt the sharp smell of burning leather, and had not heeded it. So I told the two men to draw the thrall away and turn him over. As they did so we knew that he was indeed dead, for the long knife was deep in his side, driven home as he fell on it. And I saw that in the hilt of it was a wonderful purple jewel set in gold. It was not the weapon of a thrall.

That Ina saw also, and he came down from the high place, and stood and looked in the face of this one who would have slain him, fixedly for a minute.

Then he said, speaking to Owen in a low voice:

"Justice has been done, as it seems to me. Justice from a higher hand than mine, moreover."

Then he went back to his place, and standing there said in the dead hush that was on us all:

"It would seem that this man thought that he had somewhat against me, indeed, but I do not know him, or who his brother may have been. Nor have I slain any man save in open field of battle at any time, as all men know, save and except that I may be said to have done so by the arm of the law. Yet even so, our Wessex dooms are not such as take life but for the most plain cause, and that seldom as may be. Is there any one here who has knowledge of this man who calls himself Morgan of Dyvnaint? It seems to me that I have heard the name before."

Now Owen had gone back to his place, and while one or two thanes came forward and looked in the face of the man, whom they had not yet seen plainly, he spoke to the king, and Ina seemed to wonder at what he heard.

Then Herewald the ealdorman said:

"That is the name of one of the two Devon princes of the West Welsh, cousins of Gerent the king. We have trouble with their men, who raid our homesteads now and then."

At that a big man with a yellow moustache and long curling hair rose from among the franklins and said loudly, in a voice which was neither like that of a Briton nor a Saxon at all:

"Let me get a nearer look at him, and I will soon tell you if he is what he claimed to be."

And with no more ceremony he came to where I and the two house-carles yet stood, and looked and laughed a little to himself as he did so.

"He is Morgan the prince, right enough," he said. "And I can tell you all the trouble. Your sheriff hung his brother, Dewi, three months since for cattle lifting and herdsman slaying on this side Parrett River, somewhere by Puriton, where no Welshman should be. I helped hunt the knaves at the time. The sheriff took him for a common outlaw like his comrades, and it was in my mind that there would be trouble. So I told the sheriff, and he said that if the king himself got mixed up with outlaws and cattle thieves he must even take his chance with the rest. And thereon I said--"

"Thanks, friend," said Ina. "The rest shall be for tomorrow. Bide here tonight, that you may tell all at the morning."

The man made a courtly bow enough, and went back to his seat, and then Ina bade Owen see to his lodgment, and after that the thralls carried out the body. I went quietly and walked along the lower tables, bidding my men see if more Welshmen were present, but finding none, and then I found the hall steward wringing his hands, with an ashy face, at the far end of the hall.

"Master Oswald," he said, almost weeping, "how that man came in here I do not know. I saw him not until he rose up. None seem to have seen him enter, but men have so shifted their places that it seemed not strange to any near him that they had not seen him before."

"Had you seen him you could not have turned him away," I said. "He came as a suppliant, and the king's word is strict concerning such at these times. Good Saxon enough he spoke, too, in the way of many of our half Welsh border thralls. I do not think that you will be blamed. Most likely he slipped in as the tables were cleared just now. There was coming and going enough, and we have many strangers here.

"Who is the yellow-haired man?"

"A chapman from the town. Some shipmaster whom the ealdorman knows."

Now, after I was back in my place and the bustle was ended, there fell an uneasy silence, for men knew not if the feast was to go on. Many of the ladies had gone, with the queen, and Elfrida was there no longer. But Ina stood up with a fresh cup in his hand, and he smiled and said, while the eyes of all were on him:

"Friends, we have seen a strange thing, but you have also seen the deeds of a brave maiden and a ready warrior to whom I am beholden for my life, as is plain enough. Yet we will not let the wild ways of our western neighbours mar the keeping of our holy tide. Maybe there is more to be learnt of the matter, but if so that can rest. Think now only of these two brave ones, I pray you, for I have yet the Bragi bowl to drink, and it is not hard to say whom I should pledge therein."

Then he looked round for Elfrida, not having noticed that she had gone with the queen.

"Why," he said, "it was in my mind to pledge the lady first, but I fear she has been fain to leave us. So I do not think that I can do better than pledge both my helpers together, and then Oswald can answer for the lady and himself at once."

He rose and held the cup high, and I rose also, not quite sure if I were myself or some one else, with all the hall looking at me.

"Drinc hael to the lady Elfrida, bravest and fairest in all the land of Somerset!" he cried. "Drinc hael, Oswald the king's thane--thane by right of ready and brave service just rendered!"

Then he drank with his eyes on me, and there went up a sort of cheer at his words, for men love to see any service rewarded on the spot if it may be so. Now I was at a loss what to say, and the lady should have been here to bring the cup to me in all formality. Maybe I should have stood there silent and somewhat foolish, but that the ealdorman, her father, helped me out.

"Come and do homage for the new rank, lad," he said in a low voice.

He was at the lower table near me now, for the high table had been broken and the king stood alone on the dais.

So I went to the steps, and bent one knee at their top, and kissed the hand of the king, and then held out the hilt of my sword, that he might seem to take it and give it me again. But he bade me rise, and so he took off his own sword, which was a wondrous one, and the token of the submission of some chief on the Welsh border beyond Avon, and he girt it on me with his own hands.

"You nigh gave your life for me, my thane," he said. "That man's knife was perilously near you."

He touched my tunic with his hand, and I looked. Across it where my heart beat was a long slit that I had not found out yet, where the knife flew at me. That stroke must have been the man's bane, because to reach me thus he had thrown his arm across his chest, and so had fallen on his weapon.

Then I was going, I think, though indeed I hardly know what I did at that moment, but the king stayed me, laughing.

"Do not think that I am going to let you off the cup, though. Now you shall pledge me, and if you have any vow to make which is fitting for a thane, make it and let us all hear it. But you have also the lady to think of in your words."

Then there was a little rustle at the door which was on the high place, and the queen returned with some of her ladies, hearing that all was seemly again, and she stood smiling at these last words. But Elfrida was not with her, and I was glad, else I had been more mazed yet. So I plucked up heart and took the cup from the hand of the king, trying to collect my thoughts into some sort of fitting words.

"Drinc hael Cyning," I said, while my voice shook. "Here do I vow before all the Saints and before this company--that I will do my best to prove myself worthy of this honour that has been set on me!"

"Why, Oswald," said the queen, "that is no sort of vow such as you should make, for we know that already, and you have proved it now if never before. And you have forgotten Elfrida."

Now, I thought to myself that the last thing that I was ever likely to do was to forget that maiden, and with that a thought came into my head, and as the queen was smiling at me, and every one was waiting, I grew desperate, and must needs out with it.

"Now, I cannot do better than this," I said, finding my courage all of a sudden. "Here do I add to my vow that so long as my life shall last I will not again forget the Lady Elfrida. Nor will I be content until I am held worthy by her to--to guard her all the rest of my days."

With that I drained the cup, and while the thanes laughed and cheered all round me, and Ina smiled as if well pleased enough, the queen set her hand on my arm, smiling also, and said:

"That was well said, my thane, but for one turn of the words. Why did you not tell us plainly that you mean to win her? We all know what you mean."

Then I went to my place, and I glanced at Herewald, to see how he would take all this. Somewhat seemed to have amused him mightily, and his eyes brimmed with a jest as he looked at me. Presently, when men forgot me in listening to the vow Ina made, that he would add somewhat to the new Church in thankfulness for this escape, the ealdorman came near me and whispered:

"You are a cautious youth, Oswald, for I never heard a man turn a hint from a lady better in my life. Nevertheless, if you are not careful, Ethelburga will wed you to Elfrida for all your craft."

He laughed again, and said no more. But I was looking at Owen, who seemed to have some thoughts of his own that were troubling him sorely. He smiled and nodded, indeed, when he caught my eye, but then he grew grave again directly, and afterwards his horn stood before him on the table untasted, and his look seemed far away, though round him men sang and all was merry.

However, as one may suppose, the merriment was not what it should have been, and none wondered much when Ina rose and left the table with a few pleasant parting words. He was never one to bide long at a feast, and he knew, maybe, that the house-carles and younger men would be more at ease when his presence was no longer felt by them. With him went Owen and the ealdorman, and Nunna, at some sign of his, and after they went I had to stand no little banter concerning my vow, as may be supposed.

I was not sorry when a page came and bade me join the king in his own chamber, though it was all good-natured and in no sort of unkindness. I will not say that I did not enjoy it either. So I went as I was bidden, and found that some sort of council was being held, and that those four were looking grave over it. I supposed they had some errand for me at first, but in no long time I knew that what was on hand was nought more or less than the beginning of parting between Owen and me.

I will make little of all that was said, though it was a long matter, and heavy in the telling, and maybe tangled here and there to me as I listened. I think that Ina understood that trouble fell on me as I heard all, for he looked kindly on me from his great chair, while Nunna sat on the table and was silent, stroking his beard, as if thinking. But Owen drew me to the settle by him, and bade me hearken while the king told me the tale I had to learn.

Then I heard how Owen, my foster father, was indeed a prince of the old Cornish line that came from Arthur, and how his cousins, Morgan and Dewi, had plotted to oust him from his place at the right hand of Gerent the king, and had succeeded only too well, so that he had had to fly. It matters not what their lies concerning him had been, nor do I think that Owen knew all that had been said against him, but Gerent had banished him, and so he had wandered to Mercia, and thence after a year or two to Sussex, having heard of the Irish monks of the old Western Church at Bosham. So he had met with me, and thus he and I had come to Ina's court together.

And as I heard all, I knew that it had been for my sake that he was content to serve as a simple forester at Eastdean, for Ina told me that across the Severn among the other princes of the old Welsh lands he would have been more than welcome. I could say nothing, but I set my hand on his and left it there, and he smiled at me, and grasped it.

"And now," said Ina, "your hand has in some sort avenged the old wrong, for you have brought about the end of Morgan, who was Owen's foe. But this is a matter we need to hear more concerning. Do you bring us that stranger that he may tell us what he knows."

I went to the hall again, and found him easily enough, for all men were looking at him. He was in the midst of the hall, juggling in marvellous wise with a heavy woodman's axe, which he played with as if it were a straw for lightness. Even as I entered from the door on the high place he was whirling it for a mighty stroke which seemed meant to cleave a horn cup which he had set on a stool before him, and I wondered. But he stayed the stroke as suddenly as if his great arms had been turned to steel, so that the axe edge rested on the rim of the vessel without so much as notching it, and at that all the onlookers cheered him.

"Now it may be known," said he, smiling broadly, "why men call me Thorgils the axeman."

Then he threw the unhandy weapon into the air whirling, and caught it as it came to hand again, so that it balanced on his palm, and so he held it as I went to him, and told him the king would speak with him.

Whereon he threw the axe at the doorpost, so that it stuck there, and laughed at the new shout of applause, and so turned down his sleeves and bade me lead him where I would.

He made a stiff, outlandish salute as he stood before Ina, and the king returned it.

"I have sent for you now, friend, rather than wait for morning," he said, "for it seems to me that we have business that must be seen to with the first light. Will you tell us what you know of this man who has been slain? I think you are no Welshman of Cornwall."

"I am Thorgils the Norseman of Watchet, king," he answered. "Thorgils the axeman, men call me, by reason of some skill with that weapon which your folk seem to hold in no repute, which is a pity. Shipmaster am I by trade, and I am here to seek for cargo, that I may make one more voyage this winter with the more profit, having to cross to Dyfed, beyond the narrow sea, though it is late in the year."

"I thought you might be a Dane from Tenby."

"The Welsh folk know the difference between us by this time," Thorgils said, with a little laugh. "They call them 'black heathen' and us 'white heathen,' though I don't know that they love us better than they do them. By grace of Gerent the king, to be politic, or by grace of axe play, to speak the truth, we have a little port of our own here on this side the water, at the end of the Quantocks, where we seek to bide peaceably with all men as traders."

"Ay! I have heard of your town," said Ina. "Now, can tell us how Morgan and his brother came to be in company with outlaws?"

"He fell out with Gerent over us, to begin with. I went with our chiefs to Exeter when we first came seeking a home, to promise tribute if we were left in peace in the place we had chosen. Gerent was willing enough, but Morgan, who claims some sort of right over the Devon end of the kingdom, was against our biding at all, and there were words. However,

Gerent and we had our way, and so we thought to hear no more of the matter. But the next thing was that Morgan gathered a force and tried to turn us out on his own account, and had the worst of the affair. That angered Gerent, for he lost some good men outside our stockades. And then other things cropped up between them. I have heard that the old king found out old lies told by Morgan concerning Owen the prince, whom men hope to see again, but I know little of that. Anyway, Morgan and his brother fled, and this is the end thereof. We heard too that he plotted to take the throne, and it is likely."

"Thanks, friend," Ina said. "That is a plain tale, and all we need to know. But what say men of Owen, whom you spoke of? Is it known that he lives?"

"Oh ay. They say that you know more of him than any one. Men have seen him here at Glastonbury. Moreover, Gerent came to Norton, just across the Quantocks, yesterday, and it is thought that he wants to send a message to you asking after him. There will be joy in West Wales if he goes back to the right hand of the king, for one would think that he was a fairy prince by the way he is spoken of."

Thereat Ina smiled at Owen, and Thorgils saw it, and knew what was meant in a moment. He turned to Owen with a quick look, and said frankly:

"True enough, Prince, but I did not know that I spoke of a listener. On my word, if you do go back, you will have hard work to live up to what is expected of you. Maybe what is more to the point is this, that Morgan has more friends than enough, and it is likely that they will stick at little to avenge him.

"Howbeit," he added with a quaint smile, "it shall not be said that Thorgils missed a chance. Prince, if you do go back to Gerent you will be his right hand, as they say. Therefore I will ask you at once to have us Norsemen in favour, so far as we need any. Somewhat is due to the bearer of tidings, by all custom."

Ina laughed, and even Owen smiled at the ready Norseman, but Herewald the ealdorman and I wondered at him, for he spoke as to equals, with no sort of fear of the king on him, which was not altogether the way of men who stood before Ina.

Then said Owen quietly:

"Friend, I think there is a favour I may ask you, rather. I have bided away from my uncle, King Gerent, because I would not return to him unasked, being somewhat proud, maybe. But now it seems to King Ina and myself that needs must I go to him to take the news of this death of Morgan myself. It is a matter that might easily turn to a cause of war between Wessex and West Wales, for if the man tried to slay our king in his own court, it may also be told that here was slain a prince of Dyvnaint. There is full need that the truth should reach the king before rumour makes the matter over great. You have seen all, and are known to the Welsh court as a friend. Come with me, therefore, tomorrow and tell the tale."

"That I will, Prince," Thorgils said. "You will be welcome; but as I warn you, there will be need for care."

"You know somewhat of the ways of the Welsh court," said Ina.

"Needs must, Lord King. I am a shipmaster, and every trader I carry across the sea, sometimes to South Wales, and sometimes to Bristol, and betimes so far as to Ireland, tells me all he has learned. It were churlish not to listen, and then we need warning against such attacks as that of Morgan. Moreover, one likes somewhat to talk of."

"That is plain enough," said Nunna, laughing.

"Maybe I do talk too much," answered the Norseman. "It is a failing in my family. But my sister is worse than I."

Then the king laughed again, and so dismissed the shipman, and presently Owen bade me make all preparation for riding to Norton on the morrow early. Ina would have us take a strong guard, and I should bring them back, either with or without Owen, as things went.

But little sleep had I that night, for I knew too well that from henceforth my life and that of my foster father must lie apart, and how far sundered we might be I could not tell. There was no love of the Saxon in West Wales, nor of the Welshman in Wessex.

CHAPTER IV
HOW THE LADY ELFRIDA SPOKE WITH OSWALD, AND OF THE MEETING WITH GERENT.

Gerent, the king of the West Welsh, as we called him, ruled over all the land of Devon and Cornwall, from the fens of the Tone and Parrett Rivers to the Land's End. Only those wide fens, across which he could not go, had kept our great King Kenwalch from pushing Wessex yet westward, and along their line had been our frontier since his days until, not long before Ina came to the throne, Kentwine crossed them to the north and cleared the marauding Welsh of the Quantock hills and forests from the river to the sea, setting honest Saxon franklins here and there in the new-won land, to keep it for him. It was out of those deep wooded hills that Morgan had come on the raid that ended so badly for his brother and himself, for the wasted country was yet a sort of no-man's land, where outlaws found easy harbourage, coming mostly from the Welsh side. It would not need much to set the tide of war moving westward again, now that our men knew the fenland as well as ever the British learned the secrets of the paths.

Now that the time seemed to have come for him to leave Ina, Owen feared most of all that the long peace would end, for that would mean the rending of old friendships and certain parting from me. How much longer the peace would last was very doubtful, and men said that it was only the wisdom of Aldhelm that had kept it so well, and now he was dead. It was not so long since that a west Welshman would not so much as eat with a Saxon, so great was the hatred they had for us, though that had worn off more or less. Maybe it would have passed altogether but that there were the differences between the ways of the two Churches which were always cropping up and making things bitter again, and those were the troubles that Aldhelm, whom Gerent honoured, had most tried to smooth away with some sort of success. Yet it was well known that many of the Welsh priests and people were sorely against peace with the men who followed the way of Austin of Canterbury.

As for me, I almost wondered that Ina seemed so ready to part with Owen, but presently I saw that if Gerent owned him again, my foster father would be a link between the two kingdoms, which would make for peace in every way. But for all that, in my own heart was a sort of half hope that in spite of what the Norseman had heard, Owen would not be welcomed back to the west, else I should lose him altogether. There was no intercourse between our courts, now that Aldhelm was gone.

But in the morning, when I came to say some of this to Owen, he smiled at me, and said:

"Wait, Oswald. Time enough for trouble when it comes. Maybe you and I will be back here this evening, and if not, I hope that my staying with my uncle will mean peace between our lands. Let it be so till we have seen what may be our fortune at Norton."

So I tried to let the trouble pass, and indeed at the morning meal I had my new rank to think of, for my comrades would not forget it, nor would they let me do so. The first man to greet me as thane was Thorgils the Norseman, too, and he went with me to see to choosing men and horses for our journey, and I was glad of his gossip, for it kept me from thinking overmuch of the heavier things that had kept me waking.

He would guide us across the hills to Norton, where Gerent was; for though we knew somewhat of the Quantocks, beyond them we did not go. The palace where the king lay was an ancient Roman stronghold, and had belonged to Morgan, who was dead; and though Thorgils had heard that Gerent was there to seek Owen, it was more likely that he had come to see that the outlawed brothers did not gather any force against him in their own place. It was many a year since he had been so near our border.

Presently Thorgils would go down the town to the inn where he had bestowed his horse, and I went with him, having an hour left before we started, rather than face any more banter concerning my thanedom. It was almost in my mind to go to the ealdorman's house to ask after Elfrida, but I forbore, being shy, I suppose, and so left the Norseman to join us presently, and went back to the king's hall by a short cut from the village, whereby I had a meeting which was unlooked for altogether.

That way was a sort of stolen short cut across the king's orchard, which some of us used at times in coming from village to hall, for it lay between the two on the south side of the hall where the ground sloped sunwards. And as I leapt over the fence I was aware of a lady who was gathering some of the ruddy crab apples from the ground under their bare tree, for the hot ale of the wassail bowl, doubtless, for we leave them out to mellow with the frost thus. She did not heed me as I came over the soft snow, and when she did at last look up I saw that she was Elfrida. Just for a moment I wished that I had gone round by the road, but there was no escape for me now, for she had seen me. So I unbonneted and went to meet her.

There was a little flush on her face when she saw me, but it was not altogether one of pleasure, for when I wished her good morrow, all that I had in return was a cold little bow and the few words that needs must be spoken in answer. Whereat I felt somewhat foolish; but it did not seem to me that I had done aught to deserve quite so much coldness, not being a stranger by any means. So I would even try to find the way to a better understanding, and I thought that maybe the sight of me had brought back some of the terror of last night.

"Now, I hope that the rough doings of the feast have not been troublous to you, Lady Elfrida," I said, trying with as good a grace as I could not to see her cold looks.

I saw that she did indeed shrink a little from them as I spoke, even in the passing thought.

But she answered:

"Such things are best forgotten as soon as may be. I do not wish to hear more of them."

"Nevertheless," I answered, "there are some who will not forget them, and I fear that you must needs be ready to hear of your part in them pretty often."

"Ay," she said somewhat bitterly, "I suppose that I am the talk of the whole place now."

"If so, there would be many who would be glad to be spoken of as you must needs be. There is nought but praise for you."

Then she turned on me, and the trouble was plain enough in a moment.

"But for yourself, Thane, there would have been nought that I could not have put up with. But little thought for me was there when you made me the jest of your idle comrades over that foolish cup of the king's."

That was a new way of looking at the matter, in all truth. I supposed that a vow of fealty to any lady would have been taken by her as somewhat on which to pride herself maybe, from whomsoever it came. Which seemed to be foolishness in this fresh light. Still, it came to me that her anger was not altogether fair, for I was the one who had to stand the jesting, and not one of my honest comrades so much as mentioned her name lightly in any wise.

"That was no jest of mine, Elfrida," I said gravely enough. "If there is any jest at all that will come from my oath, it will be that I have been foolish enough to vow fealty to one who despises me. The last thing that I would do is anything that might hurt you. And my vow stands fast, whether you scorn me or not, for if it was made in a moment, it is not as if I had not had long years to think on in which we have been good friends enough."

"Ay," she said, turning from me and reaching some apples that yet hung on a sheltered bough, "I have heard the terms of that vow from my father, more than once. You can keep it without trouble."

"Have I your leave to try to keep it?"

"You have had full leave to be a good friend of ours all these years, as you say, and I do not see that the vow binds you to more. No one thinks that you are likely to forget last night, or any one who took part in that cruel business. And if a friend will not help to guard a lady--well, he would be just nidring, no more or less."

Then she took up her basket, which was pretty full and no burden for a lady, for she had picked fast and heedlessly as she spoke to me, and so turned away.

"Nay, but surely you know that there was more than that meant," I said lamely.

"No need to have haled my name into the matter at all," she said.

And then, seeing that my eyes went to the basket, she smiled a little, and held it to me with both hands.

"Well, if you meant some new sort of service, you can begin by carrying this for me. I am going to the queen's bower."

I took it without a word, and we went silently together to the door that led to the queen's end of the hall. There she stayed for a moment with her hand on the latch.

But she had only a question to ask me:

"Do you go with your father to the Welsh king's court, as it is said that he will go shortly?"

"We start together in an hour's time or thereabout," I answered, wondering.

"Well then, take this to mind you of your vow," she said, and threw a little bronze brooch, gilt and set with bright enamel, into the basket, and so fled into the house, leaving me on the doorstep with the apples.

I set them down there, and had a mind to leave the brooch also. However, on second thoughts I took it, and went my way in a puzzled state of mind. It certainly seemed that Elfrida was desperately angry with me for reasons which were not easy to fathom, and yet she had given me this--that is, if to have a thing thrown at one is to have it given. But I was not going to quarrel with the manner of a gift from Elfrida, and so I went on with it in my hand, and as I turned the corner into a fresh path I also ran into the abbot of the new minster, who was on his way to speak with Owen before he set out. He had been a great friend of Bishop Aldhelm's, and I had known him well since the old days of Malmesbury.

"So Oswald," he cried, "I have been looking for you, that I might wish you all good in your thaneship. Why, some of us are proud of you. And I, having known you since you were a child, feel as if I had some sort of a share in your honours. But what is amiss? One would look to see you the gayest of the gay, and it seems as if the world had gone awry with you."

Now, the abbot was just the friend to whom I could tell my present trouble without fear of being mocked, for he was wont to stand to us boys of the court as the good friend who would help us out of a scrape if he could, and make us feel ashamed thereof in private afterward, in all kindliness. So I told him what was on my mind, for he was at the feast last night.

"It is all that vow of mine," I said. "I have just met Elfrida, and she is angry with me for naming her at all."

"Unfair," said the abbot. "You could not have helped it, seeing that you were bidden to do so."

I had forgotten that, and it was possible that Elfrida did not know it. So I said that I did not look for quite the scorn I had met with, at all events. Whereon the abbot stayed in his walk and asked more, trying to look grave as he heard me, and soon he had all the story.

"So you carried the basket like any thrall, and had my Yuletide gift to her in payment," he said, with his eyes twinkling; "I will ask if she has lost it presently, and you will be avenged."

He laughed again, and then said more gravely, but with a smile not far off:

"Go to, Oswald, don't ask me to make the ways of a damsel plain to you, for that was more than Solomon himself could compass. But I think I know what is wrong. Her father has been making a jest to her of the way you worded your vow, laughing mightily after his manner, and she is revenging herself on you. Never mind. Wait till you come back from this journey, and then see how things are with her. Now let us talk of your errand, for it is important."

Then we went slowly together, and he told me how that he had foreseen for a long time that Owen would return to his uncle and take his right place again. Also he told me that Morgan had a strong party on his side, and that we might have trouble with them if Owen was taken into favour again.

"As I hope he may be," he added with a sigh; "for I have seen the war cloud drifting nearer every year under the guidance of Morgan and his fellows."

Then we turned into the courtyard, and he went to speak to Owen in the hall, turning with a last smile to bid me hide the brooch, lest Elfrida should hear some jesting about that next. So I pinned it under my cloak, and then went and donned my arms, and saw to all things for the journey, both for Owen and myself; and so at last the hour came when I led the men round to the great door of the hall, and sent one to say that all was ready.

Now the king came forth, and with him was Owen. Ina wore his everyday dress, but my foster father was fully armed, and as those two stood there I thought that I had never seen a more kingly looking pair, silent and thoughtful both, and with lines of care on their foreheads, and both in their prime of life.

Behind me I heard Thorgils say to Godred, the chief house-carle: "If there were choice, I would take the king that wears the war gear. That is the only dress that to my mind fits a man who shall lead warriors."

Now the king came and spoke with me, bidding me be on my guard against any attack while we were at Norton, telling me plainly also that he deemed that there was danger to both of us at the first, somewhat in the way in which the abbot had already spoken to me. I daresay the words were his, for he had been counselling Owen.

Then the queen came forth with her ladies, and there was an honour for us, for she herself brought the stirrup cup to Owen, bidding him farewell, at the same time that the king must needs send Elfrida with another cup to me, saying that it was my due for last night's omission. But there was no smile as she set it in my hand, and she waited with head turned away until I gave it back to her, as if she looked at Owen rather than any one else. Then it was only a short word of farewell that she said to me, and yet it did seem that her eyes were less grave than she would seem in face as she turned back to the other ladies on the hall steps.

Then Owen unhelmed and turned his horse to the gates, and after him we went clattering down the street. In a minute or two Thorgils came alongside me.

"So that was the lady of the vow, surely. Well, you may be excused for making it, though indeed it is rash to bind oneself--nay, but it seems that this is one of those matters whereon I must hold my tongue!"

For I had spurred my horse a little impatiently, and he understood well enough. I did not altogether care that this stranger should talk of my affairs--more particularly as they did not seem to be going at all rightly. So he said no more of them, but began to talk of himself gaily, while Owen rode alone at our head, as he would sometimes if his thoughts were busy.

Presently he reined up and came alongside us, taking his part in our talk in all cheerfulness. And from that time I had little thought but of the pleasantness of the ride in the sharp winter air and under the bright sun with him toward the new court which I had often longed to see, with its strange ways, in the ancient British-Roman palace that he had so often told me of.

So we rode along the ancient and grass-grown Roman road that lies on the Polden ridge, hardly travelled save by a few chapmen, since the old town they called Uxella was lost in the days of my forefathers. The road had no ending now, as one may say, for beyond the turning to the bridge across the Parrett for which we were making it passed to nought but fen and mere where once had been the city. All the wide waters on either side of the hills were hard frozen, and southward, across to where we could see the blue hill of ancient Camelot, the ice flashed black and steely under the red low sun of midwinter. Before us the Quantocks lay purple and deepest brown where the woods hid the snow that covered them. Over us, too, went the long strings of wild geese, clanging in their flight in search of open water--and it was the wolf month again, and even so had they fled on that day when Owen found me in the snow.

And therewith we fell into talk of Eastdean, and dimly enough I recalled it all. I knew that an Erpwald held the place even yet, but I cared not. It was but a pleasant memory by reason of the coming of Owen, and I had no thought even to see the place again. Only, as we talked it did seem to me that I would that I knew that the grave of my father was honoured.

Then we left the old road, and crossed the ancient Parrett bridge, where the Roman earthworks yet stood frowning as if they would stay us. They were last held against Kenwalch, and now we were in that no-man's land which he had won and wasted. Then we climbed the long slope of the Quantocks, whence we might look back over the land we had left, to see the Tor at Glastonbury shouldering higher and higher above the lower Poldens, until the height was reached and the swift descent toward Norton began. There we could see all the wild Exmoor hills before us, with the sea away to our right, and Thorgils shewed us where lay, under the very headlands of the hills we were crossing, the place where his folk had their haven. He said that he could see the very smoke from the hearths, but maybe that was only because he knew where it ought to be, and we laughed at him.

So we came to the outskirts of Norton, and all the way we had seen no man. The hills were deserted, save by wild things, and of them there was plenty. And now for the first time I saw men living in houses built of stone from ground to roof, and that was strange to me. We Saxons cannot abide aught but good timber. Here none of us had ever come, and still some of the houses built after the Roman fashion remained, surrounded, it is true, by mud hovels of yesterday, as one might say, but yet very wonderful to me. Many a time I had seen the ruined foundations of the like before, but one does not care to go near them. The wastes our forefathers made of the old towns they found here, and had no use for, lie deserted, for they are haunted by all things uncanny, as any one knows. Maybe that is because the old Roman gods have come back to their old places, now that the churches are no longer standing.

Through the village we went, and then came to the walls of the ancient stronghold, and they seemed as if they were but lately raised, so strong were they and high. The gates were in their places, and at them was a guard, and through them, for they stood open, I could see the white walls and flat roof of the house, or rather palace, which was either that of the Roman governor of the place, or else had been rebuilt or restored from time to time in exactly the same wise, so that it stood fair and lordly and fit for a king's dwelling even yet. Maybe the wattled hovels of the thralls that clustered round it inside the great earthworks were not what would have been suffered in the days of those terrible men who made the fortress, but I doubt not that they stood on the foundations of the quarters of the soldiers who had held it for Rome.

The guard turned out in orderly wise as we came to the gates, and they wore the Roman helm and corselet, and bore the heavy Roman spear and short heavy sword. But that war gear I had seen before on the other Welsh border, and I had a scar, moreover, that would tell that I had been within reach of one weapon or the other. I knew their tongue, too, almost as well as my own, for Owen had taught it me, saying that I might need it at some time. It had already been of use to the king in the frontier troubles, for I could interpret for him, but I think that Owen had in his mind the coming of some such day as this.

Now, Owen would have me speak to the guard and tell them our errand, and I rode forward and did so. The short day was almost over by this time; and the captain who came to meet me did not seem to notice my Saxon arms in the shadow of the high rampart. Hearing that we bore a message for the king, he sent a man to ask for directions, and meanwhile we waited. I asked him if there was any news, thinking it well to know for certain if aught had been heard yet of the end of Morgan. News of that sort flies fast.

"No news at all," he answered. "What did you expect?"

"I had heard of the death of a prince, and do not know the rights thereof."

"Why, where have you been? That is old news. It was only Dewi, and he is no loss. The Saxon sheriff hung him, even as the king said he would do to him an he caught him, so maybe it is the same in the end. I have not heard that any one is sorry to lose him."

He laughed, and if it was plain that Morgan's brother was not loved, it was also plain that nought was known of the end of the other prince yet. We were first with the tidings here, and that might be as well.

Now a message came to bid us enter, and the steward who brought it told us that we were to be lodged in some great guest chamber, and that we should speak with the king shortly.

The men bided outside the walls, the captain leading them to a long row of timber-built stables which stood close at hand by the gate. Presently, when the horses were bestowed, they would be brought to the guest hall; so Thorgils went with them, while the steward led Owen and myself through the gate and to the palace, which stood squarely in the midst of the fortress, with a space between it and the other buildings which filled the area.

By daylight I knew afterwards that it was uncared for, and somewhat dilapidated without, but in the falling dusk it looked all that it should. We entered through a wide door, and passed a guardroom where many men lounged, armed and unarmed, and then were in a courtyard formed by the four sides of the building, wonderfully paved, and with a frozen fountain in its midst. There were windows all round the walls which bounded this court, and the light shone red from them, very cheerfully, and already there was bustle of men who crossed and passed through the palace making ready for our reception. The steward led us to the northern wing of the house across this court, and so took us into an antechamber, as it seemed, warm and bright, with hanging lamps, and with painted walls and many-patterned tiled floor, but for all its warmth with no fire to be seen, which was strange enough to me.

And so soon as the bright light shone on Owen I saw the steward start and gaze at him fixedly, and then as Owen smiled a little at him he fell on his knees and cried softly some words of welcome, with tears starting in his eyes.

"Oh my Lord," he said, "is it indeed you? This is a good day.--A thousand welcomes!"

Owen raised him kindly, and set his finger on his lip.

"It is well that you have been the first to know me, friend," he said. "Now hold your peace for a little while till we see what says my uncle. I must have word with him at once, if it can be managed, before others know me. It will be best."

"He waits you, Lord. It was his word that he would see the Saxon alone."

Then he led us into another room like to that we left, but larger, and with rich carpets on the tiled floor, and there sat Gerent alone to wait us. I thought him a wonderful looking old man, and most kingly, as he rose and bowed in return when we greeted him. His hair was white, and his long beard even whiter, but his eyes were bright. Purple and gold he wore, and those robes and the golden circlet on his head shewed that he had put on the kingly dress to meet with the messenger of a king.

Almost had Owen sprung toward him, but he forbore, and when the king had taken his seat he went slowly to him, holding out a letter which Ina had written for him, saying nothing. And Gerent took it without a word or so much as a glance at the bearer from under his heavy brows, and opened it.

Owen stood back by me, and we watched the face of the king as he read. We saw his brows knit themselves fiercely at first, and then as he went on they cleared until he seemed as calm as when he first met us. But the flush that had come with the frown had not faded when at last he looked keenly at us.

"Come nearer," he said in a harsh voice, speaking in fair Saxon. "Know you what is written herein?"

"I know it," Owen said.

"Here Ina says that this is borne by one whom I know. Is it you or this young warrior?"

Then Owen went forward and fell on one knee before the king, and said in his own tongue--the tongue of Cornwall and of Devon:

"I am that one of whom Ina has spoken. Yet it is for Gerent to say whether he will own that he knows me even yet."

I saw the king start as the voice of Owen came to him in the familiar language, and he knitted his brows as one who tries to recall somewhat forgotten, and he looked searchingly in the face of the man who knelt before him, scanning every feature.

And at last he said in a hushed voice, not like the harsh tones of but now:

"Can it be Owen?--Owen, the son of my sister? They said that one like him served the Saxon, but I did not believe it. That is no service for one of our line."

"What shall an exile do but serve whom he may, if the service be an honoured one? Yet I will say that I wandered long, seeing and learning, before there came to me a reason that I should serve Ina. To you I might not return."

But the king was silent, and I thought that he was wroth, while Owen bided yet there on his knee before him, waiting his word. And when that came at last, it was not as I feared.

Slowly the king set forth his hand, and it shook as he did so. He laid it on Owen's head, while the letter that was on his knees fluttered unheeded to the floor as he bent forward and spoke softly:

"Owen, Owen," he said, "I have forgotten nought. Forgive the old blindness, and come and take your place again beside me."

And as Owen took the hand that would have raised him and kissed it, the old king added in the voice of one from whom tears are not so far:

"I have wearied for you, Owen, my nephew. Sorely did I wrong you in my haste in the old days, and bitterly have I been punished. I pray you forgive."

Then Owen rose, and it seemed to me that on the king the weight of years had fallen suddenly, so that he had grown weak and needful of the strong arm of the steadfast prince who stood before him, and I took the arm of the steward and pulled him unresisting through the doorway, so that what greeting those two might have for one another should be their own.

Then said the steward to me as we looked at one another:

"This is the best day for us all that has been since the prince who has come back left us. There will be joy through all Cornwall."

But I knew that what I dreaded had come to pass, and that from henceforth the way of the prince of Cornwall and of the house-carle captain of Ina's court must lie apart, and I had no answer for him.

CHAPTER V
HOW OSWALD FELL INTO BAD HANDS,
AND FARED EVILLY, ON THE QUANTOCKS.

It would be long for me to tell how presently Owen called me in to speak with the king, and how he owned me as his foster son in such wise that Gerent smiled on him, and spoke most kindly to me as though I had indeed been a kinsman of his own. And then, after we had spoken long together, Thorgils was sent for, and he told the tale of the end of Morgan plainly and in few words, yet in such skilful wise that as he spoke I could seem to see once more our hall and myself and Elfrida at the dais, even as though I were an onlooker.

"You are a skilful tale teller," the king said when he ended. "You are one of the Norsemen from Watchet, as I am told."

"I am Thorgils the shipmaster, who came to speak with you two years ago, when we first came here. Men say that I am no bad sagaman."

"This is a good day for me," Gerent said, "and I will reward you for your tale. Free shall the ship of Thorgils be from toil or harbourage in all ports of our land from henceforward. I will see that it is known."

"That is a good gift, Lord King," said the Norseman, and he thanked Gerent well and heartily, and so went his way back to the guest chambers with a glad heart.

Then Gerent said gravely:

"I suppose that there are men who would call all these things the work of chance or fate. But it is fitting that vengeance on him who wronged you should come from the hand of one whom you have cared for. That has not come by chance; but I think it will be well that it is not known here just at first whose was the hand that slew Morgan."

"For fear of his friends?" asked Owen thoughtfully.

"Ay, for that reason. Overbearing and proud was he, but for all that there are some who thought him the more princely because he was so. And there are few who know that he did indeed try to end my life, for I would not spread abroad the full shame of a prince of our line. Men have thought that I would surely take him into favour again, but that was not possible. Only, I would that he had met a better ending."

The old king sighed, and was silent. Presently Owen said that I must see to the men and horses, and I rose up to leave the chamber, and then the king said:

"We shall see you again at the feast I am making for you all. Then tomorrow you must take back as kingly a letter to Ina as he wrote to me, and so return to Owen for as long as your king will suffer you to bide with us."

So I went to the stables first of all, and there was Thorgils bidding a Welsh groom to get out his horse while he took off the arms that had been lent him from our armoury, for he was but half armed when he came.

"There is no need to do that," I said; "for if Ina arms a man, it is as a gift for service done, if he is not too proud to take it. But are you not biding for the feast?"

"First of all," he said, laughing, "none ever knew a Norseman too proud to accept good arms from a king. Thank Ina for me in all form. And as to my going, seeing that tide waits for no man, if I do not get home shortly I shall lose the tide I want for a bit of a winter voyage I have on hand; wherefore I must go. Farewell, and good luck to you. This business has turned out well, after all, and a great man you will be in this land before long. Don't forget us Norsemen when that comes about, and if ever you need a man at your back, send for me. You might have a worse fence than my axe, and I have a liking for you; farewell again."

I laughed and shook hands with him, and he swung himself into the saddle and rode away.

There was high feasting that night in the guest hall of Norton, as may be supposed. I sat on the left of the king, and Owen on his right, while all the great men who could be summoned in the time were present, and it was plain enough that the homecoming of their lost prince was welcome to every one in all the hall. Not one dark look was there as I scanned the bright company, and presently not one refused to join in the great shout of welcome that rose when Owen pledged them all.

It was a good welcome, and the face of the old king grew bright as he heard it.

Then the harpers sang; I did not think their ways here so pleasant as our own, where the harp goes round the hall, and every man takes his turn to sing, or if he has no turn for song, tells tale or asks riddle that shall please the guests. Certainly, these Welsh folk were readier to talk than we, and maybe the meats were more dainty and the wines finer than ours, and in truth the Welsh mead was good and the Welsh ale mighty, but men seemed to care little for the sport that should come after the meal was over. Yet these harpers sang well, and from them I learnt more about my foster father than he had ever cared to tell me, for they sang of old deeds of his. Doubtless they made the most of them, for it would seem from their songs that he had fought with Cornish giants as an everyday thing, and that he had been the bane of more than one dragon. But one knows how to sift the words of the gleeman's song, and they told me at least that Owen had been a great champion ere he left his home.

Still, I missed the bright fire on the hearth, and the ways of the court were too stately for me here. Men seemed not to like the cheerful noise of my honest house-carles, who jested and laughed as they would have done in the hall of Ina, who loved to see and hear that his men were merry. We should have thought that there was something wrong if there had not been plenty of noise at the end of the long tables below the salt.

Now, I will not say that there was not something very pleasant in sitting here at the side of the king as the most honoured guest next to my foster father, but there was a sadness at the back of it all in the knowledge that it was likely that from henceforth our ways must needs go apart more or less, and that I might see him only from time to time. For I was Ina's man, and a Saxon, and it could not be supposed that I should be welcome here. I knew that I must go back to my place, and he must bide in his that he had found again, and so there was the sorrow of parting to spoil what might else have made me a trifle over proud.

Gerent did not stay long at the feast, nor did the ladies who were present, and Owen and I stayed for but a little while after they had gone. Then we were taken in all state to the room where we should sleep, and so for the first time I was housed within stone walls. There were a sort of wide benches along the walls covered with skins and bright rugs for us to sleep on, but after I had helped Owen to his night gear I took the coverings that were meant for me and set them across the door on the floor and so slept. For I had a fear of treachery and the friends of Morgan.

It was in my mind to talk for a while before rest came, but Owen would not suffer me to do so, saying that it was best to sleep on all the many things that happened before we thought much of what was to be done next. So I wrapt myself in my rugs on the strangely warm floor and went to sleep at once, being, as may be supposed, fairly tired out with the long day and its doings. More than that little space of time it seemed since we left Glastonbury, and even my meeting with Elfrida was like a matter of long ago to me.

There was a bronze lamp burning with some scented oil, hanging from the ceiling, which seemed so low after our open roofs, and we had left it alight, as I thought it better to have even its glimmer than darkness, here in this strange house. And presently I woke with a feeling that this lamp had flared up in some way, shining across my eyes, so that I sat up with a great start, grasping my sword hastily. But the lamp burned quietly, and all that woke me was the light of a square patch of bright moonlight from a high window that was creeping across the broad chest of Owen as he slept, and had come within range of my eyelids, for my face was turned to him. The room was bright with it, and for a little I watched the quiet sleeper, and then I too slept, and woke not again until Owen roused me with the daylight from the same window falling on his face.

"That is where I should have slept," I said, "for it is my place to wake you, father."

He laughed, and said that it was his place in the old days, and there was a sigh at the back of the laugh as he thought of those times, and then we forgot the whole thing. Yet though it seems a little matter in the telling, in no long time I was to mind that waking in a strange way enough, and then I remembered.

We must part presently, as I found, at least for a little while. There was no question but that Owen would stay at the court here, and so Gerent had ready for me a letter which I should carry back to Ina at once. He spoke very kindly to me at that time, giving me a great golden bracelet from his own arm, that I might remember to come back to bide for a time with him ere long. And then we broke our fast, and my men were ready, and I parted from my foster father in the bright morning light that made the white walls of the old palace seem more wonderful to me than ever.

"Farewell, then, for a while," he said to me; "come back as soon as Ina will spare you. There will be peace between him and Gerent now, as I think."

Then came a man in haste from out of the gateway where we stood yet, and he bore a last gift from Gerent to me. It was a beautiful wide-winged falcon from the cliffs of Tintagel in the far west, hooded and with the golden jesses that a king's bird may wear on her talons.

"It is the word of the king," said the falconer, "that a thane should ride with hawk on wrist if he bears a peaceful message. Moreover, there will be full time on the homeward way for a flight or two. Well trained she is, Master, and there is no better passage hawk between here and Land's End."

That was a gift such as any man might be proud of, and I asked Owen to thank the king for me. And so we parted with little sorrow after all, for it was quite likely that I should be back here in a day or two for yet a little while longer with him.

So I and my men were blithe as we rode in the still frosty air across the Quantocks by the way we had come, and by and by, when we gained the wilder crests, I began to look about me for some chance of proving the good hawk that sat waiting my will on my wrist.

Soon I saw that the rattle and noise of men and horses spoiled a good chance or two for me, for the black game fled to cover, and once a roe sprang from its resting in the bushes by the side of the track and was gone before I could unhood the bird.

"Ho, Wulf!" I cried to one of the men who was wont to act as forester when Ina hunted, "let us ride aside for a space, and then we will see what sort of training a Welshman can give a hawk."

So we put spurs to our horses and went on until they were a mile behind us, and then we were on a ridge of hill whence a long wooded combe sank northward to the dense forest land at the foot of the hills, and there we rode slowly, questing for what might give us a fair flight. Bustard there were on these hills, and herons also, for below me I could see the bare branches of the tree tops on which the broad-winged birds light at nesting time, twigless and skeleton-like. For a while we saw nothing, however, and so rode wide of the track, across the heather, until we found the woodland before us, and had to make our way back to the road, which passed through it. But before we came in sight of the road, from almost under my feet, a hare bolted from a clump of long grass, and made for the coverts. I cast off the hawk and shouted, but we were too near the underwood, and it seemed that the hare would win to cover in time to save herself.

Yet in a moment the hare was back again out of the cover, and running along its edge in the open as though she had met with somewhat that she feared even more than the winged terror which she had so nearly baffled. And that was strange, for it is hard to get a hare to stir from her seat if there is a hawk overhead, so that sometimes men have even picked up the timid beast from her place.

"There is a fox in the underwood, and she has seen him," I cried, and then forgot all about the strangeness of the matter in watching the stoop of the ready hawk, who waited only for one more chance.

Not far did the hare win this time. The hawk swooped and took her close to the edge of the wood, and I rode quickly to take the bird again and give her her share of the quarry. And then, while my eyes were fixed on her, and I was just about to dismount, I was aware of something like a streak of light that flew from the underwood toward me, and suddenly my horse reared wildly, and fell back on me, pinning me to the ground.

At the same moment I heard Wulf roaring somewhat, and then he was between me and the cover, and I saw him, through the dazedness of my eyes with the fall, dismount and unsling his shield from his back, with his eyes ever on the wood. Then an arrow struck the ground close to me, and I heard another smite Wulf's shield with the clap that no warrior can mistake. At that his steed took fright and left us.

"Get my horn and wind it," I said, struggling to get free from the horse. It was no mean bowman who had sent that first arrow, for the poor beast never moved after it fell, and had spent its last strength in rearing.

"That is crushed flat, Master," Wulf said between his teeth, and he tried to lift the weight that was on me.

Then the arrows came thickly again, and he crouched over me with the shield, behind the horse. It was lucky that I was almost covered by it as I lay, for it was between me and the wood. I writhed and struggled and at last I was free again, and Wulf helped me to get my own shield from my back as I rose, and then we stood back to back and looked for our foes.

"Morgan's people, I suppose," I said. "We should not have left the men, for I knew that he was leagued with Quantock outlaws."

"A nidring set, too," said Wulf savagely. "Can't they show themselves?"

As if the men had heard him, they came from the cover even as he spoke. There were more than I could count after a few moments, for they poured out in twos and threes from all along the edge of the wood, and came cautiously toward us, in such wise as to surround us. Wild looking men they were, with never a helm or mail shirt among them, but they were all well armed enough with bow and spear and seax, and more than one had swords.

Then I looked round to see if I could see my men coming, and my heart sank. We were hidden from the road by the crest of the hill, and I knew that the flight of the hawk had led us some way from it. We could not be less than a full mile from them at the rate we had ridden, and I did not think it likely that they had hurried after us, for they would not spoil sport.

Now the men were round us in a ring that was closing quickly, and Wulf and I had our swords out and were back to back facing them. Not a word had been said on either side, and I was not going to begin to talk to outlaws. If they had anything to say they might say it. But they had not, and I knew that they would make a rush on us directly.

One who seemed to be the leader whistled sharply, and the rush came with a wild howl and flight of ill-aimed spears that were of no harm. The circle was too close for a fair throw at us, lest the weapon should go too far. I had time to catch one as it passed me, and send it back with the Wessex war shout, and there was one man less against us.

I think that I cut down one or two after that, and then I felt Wulf reel and prop himself against me. Then I had a score of men crowding on me, and they clogged my sword arm and gripped my shield and tore it aside, and then from behind or at the side one smote me on the head with a club or a stone hammer, and I went down. I heard one cry that I was not to be slain, as I fell.

Then Wulf stood over me for a little while and fought all that crowd, until he was on his knees at my side, and my senses were coming back to me. Then he fell over me, and the men threw themselves on me and pinioned me and thrust something into my mouth and then bound me.

I knew that Wulf was slain at that time, and that he had given his life for me. That was what he would have wished to do, but in my heart there grew a wild rage with these men and with myself for my carelessness that had led us into their hands.

Now they dragged me into the cover, and thither also they brought Wulf and the fallen men, and for a little while all sat silent, and soon I knew what they were waiting for. I heard the voices of my men and the very click and rattle of their arms as they trotted slowly through the wood along the road, and I tried to shout to them, but the gag would not let me. So their sounds died away beyond the hill, and after them crept some of the foe, to see that they did not halt or turn back, as one may suppose. I thought how that they had at least three miles to ride before they could come to any place whence they could see that I and Wulf were not before them, and then, when they missed us, how were they to begin to seek us?

I suppose that my wits were sharpened with my danger, for I saw one thing that might help them even while I was thinking this. My hawk had gorged herself with her prey when the fight had turned aside from her, and so she was sitting sleepily and contented on the high bough of one of the trees that stood at the wood's edge. And she still had her jesses on, so that my men would know her if they caught sight of her by any chance.

Now the men who had me, being sure that all fear was past, began to talk of what was to be done next, and they spoke in Welsh, plainly thinking that I could not understand them. There were three or four who seemed to take the lead under the one who had given the signal for attack, and the rest gathered round them.

At first they were for killing me offhand as it seemed, but the leader would not hear of that.

"Search him first, and let us see who he is," he said. "We may have caught the wrong man, after all."

So they came to me and searched my pouch and thrust their grimy hands into the front of my byrnie, and there they found the king's letter, which they seized with a shout of delight. Then they took my arms, wondering at the sword with its wondrous hilt. Only my ring mail byrnie they could not take from me, as they feared to untie my arms.

"Not much would I give for your life if this warrior got loose," said one of them to that one who had the letter. "See how he glares at you."

And true enough that was, moreover. I should surely have gone berserk, like the men Thorgils told me of as we rode yesterday, had I been able to get free for a moment.

They took my belongings to the leaders, and they asked for some one who could read the letter, and there was none, even as I had expected, so that I was glad.

"It does not matter much," the leader said; "doubtless it has a deal of talk in it which would mean nought to us. We will have it read the next time one of us goes to the church," and with that he grinned, and the others laughed as at a good jest. "Let me look at the sword he wore."

He looked and his eyes grew wide, and then he whistled a little to himself. The others asked him what was amiss.

"If we have got Owen's son, we have taken Ina's own sword as well," he said. "Many a time have I seen the king wear it before the law got the best of me. It is not to be mistaken. Now, if we are not careful we have a hornets' nest on us in good truth. Ina does not give swords like this to men he cares nought for, and there will be hue and cry enough after him, and that from Saxon and Welsh alike."

"Kill him and have done. That is what we meant to do when we laid up for him."

So said many growling voices, and I certainly thought that the end was very near.

"Ay, and have ourselves hung in a row that will reach from here to the bridge," the leader said coolly. "Mind you this, that with the Welsh up against us we cannot get to Exmoor, and with the Saxons out also we cannot win to the Mendips, as we have done before now."

"There is the fen."

"And all the fenmen Owen's own men. Little safety is there in that."

"But he slew Morgan, as they say."

"Worse luck for Morgan therefore. What is that to you and me, when one comes to think of it?"

Now I began to understand the matter more or less. It seemed to me that these were Morgan's outlaws, and that somehow they had heard all the story. No doubt that was easy enough, for it would be all over Norton before the night was very old after our coming. And these outlaws have friends everywhere. So they had laid up for me, and now the leader was frightened, as it would seem, or else he had some other plan in his head. It did not seem that he had wished me to be slain, from the first, if it could be helped. Maybe the others had forced him to waylay me. A leader of outlaws has little hold on his men.

"Let him swear to say nought of us, and let him go then," one of the other leaders said in a surly way.

Then the chief got up and laughed at them all.

"There are six of us slain and a dozen with wounds, and we will make him pay for that and for Morgan as well before we have done with him. Now we must not bide here, or we shall have his men back on us, seeking him. Let us get away, and I will think of somewhat as we go. There is profit to be made out of this business, if I am not mistaken."

Then they brought my man's horse, which they had caught, and set me on it, making my feet fast under the girth. The men who had fallen they hid in the bushes, and it troubled me more than aught to think that Wulf should lie among them. My horse they dragged into a hollow, and piled snow over him. Then they went swiftly down the hillside into the deep combe, leaving only the trampled and reddened snow to tell that there had been a fight.

I had a hope for a little while that the track they left would be enough for my men to follow if they hit on it, but there was little snow lying in the sheltered woodlands, and there the track was lost. And these men scattered presently in all directions, so that trace of them was none. Only the leader and some dozen men stayed with me.

So they took me for many a long mile, always going seaward, until we were in a deep valley that bent round among the hills until its head was lost in their folds, and there was some sort of a camp of these outlaws sheltered from any wind that ever blew, and with a clear brook close at hand. All round on the hillsides was the forest, but there was one landmark that I knew.

High over the valley's head rose a great hill, and on that was an ancient camp. It was what they call the "Dinas," the refuge camp of the Quantock side, which one can see from Glastonbury and all the Mendips.

Here they took me from the horse and bound my feet afresh, and took the gag from my mouth and set me against a tree, and so waited until the band had gathered once more, lighting a great fire meanwhile. Glad enough was I of its warmth, for it is cold work riding bound through the frost.

When that was done the leader bade some of those with him fetch the goods to this place, and catch some ponies ready against the journey. I could not tell what this might mean, but I thought that they had no intention of biding here, and I was sorry in a dull way. It had yet been a hope that they might be tracked by my men from the place of the fight.

After these men had gone hillward into the forest, others kept coming in from one way or another until almost all seemed to have returned.

One by one as these gathered, they came and looked at me, and laughed, making rough jests at me, which I heeded not at all, if they made my blood boil now and then. Once, indeed, their leader shouted roughly to them to forbear, when some evil words came with a hoarse gust of laughter to his ears, and they said under their breath, chuckling as at a new jest:

"Evan has a mind to tell Tregoz that he treated the Saxon well," and so left me. It seemed to me that I had heard that name at Norton.

When the best part of the band had gathered again they lit another fire fifty yards from me, and round it they talked and wrangled for a good half hour. It was plain that they were speaking about me and my fate, but I could hear little of what they said.

The leader took not much part in the talk at first, but let the rest have their say. And when they had talked themselves out, as it were, he told them his plans. I could not hear them, but the rest listened attentively enough, and at the end of his speech seemed to agree, for they laughed and shouted and made not much comment.

Then the leaders got up and came and looked at me.

"Tell him what we are going to do with him, Evan," one said to the chief.

So Evan spoke in the worst Saxon I had ever heard, and I thought that it fitted his face well.

"No good glaring in that wise," he said; "if you are quiet no harm will come to you. We are going to hold you as a hostage until your Saxon master or your British father pay ransom for you, and inlaw us again. That last is a notion of my own, for I am by way of being an honest man. The rest do not care for anything but the money we shall get for you from one side or the other, or maybe from both. By and by, when we have you in a safe place, you shall write a letter for us to use, and I will have you speak well of me in it, so that it shall be plain that you owe your life to me, and then I shall be safe. That is a matter between you and me, however. None of these knaves ken a word of Saxon."

I suppose that I showed pretty plainly what I thought of this sort of treachery to his comrades, for one of the others laughed at me, and said:

"Speak him fair, Evan, speak him fair, else we shall have trouble with him."

"I am just threatening him now," the villain said in Welsh--"after that is time to give him a chance to behave himself," and then he went on to me in Saxon: "Now, if you will give your word to keep quiet and go with me as a friend I will trust you, but if not--well, we must take you as we can. How do you prefer to go?"

He waited for an answer, but I gave him none. I would not even seem to treat with them.

"Don't say that I did not give you a chance," he said; "but if you will go as a captive, that is your own fault."

And as I said nothing he turned away, and said to the rest:

"We shall have to bind him. He will not go quietly."

"How shall we get him on board as a captive?" one asked.

"That would be foolishness," Evan said; "the next thing would be that every one would know who the captive that was taken out of Watchet was. I have a better plan than that. We will tie him up like a sorely wounded man, and so get him shipped carefully and quietly with no questions asked."

"Well, then, there is no time to lose. We must be at the harbour in four hours' time at the latest. Tide will serve shortly after that," one of the others said. "What about the sword?--shall we sell it to the Norsemen?"

"What! and so tell all the countryside what we have been doing?--it is too well known a weapon. No, put it into one of the bales of goods, and I can sell it safely to some prince on the other side. No man dare wear it on this, but they will not know it there, or will not care if they do. Now get a litter made, and bring me some bandages."

It seemed to me to be plain that they would try to get me across the channel into Wales, or maybe Ireland, and my heart sank. But after all, Owen would gladly pay ransom for me, and that was the one hope I had. And then I wondered what vessel they had ready, and all of a sudden I minded that Thorgils had spoken of a winter voyage that he was going to take on this tide, and my heart leapt. It was likely that these men were going to sail with him, so I might have a chance of swift rescue.

Now Evan went to work on me with the help of one of his men, who seemed to know something of leech craft.

"This," said Evan, "is a poor friend of mine who has met with a bad fall from his horse. His thigh is broken and his shoulder is out. Also his jaw is broken, because the horse kicked him as he lay. For the same reason he is stunned, and cannot move much. It is a bad case altogether," and he grinned with glee at his own pleasantry.

Then they fitted a long splint to my right leg from hip to ankle, so that I was helpless as a babe in its swaddlings, and made fast the other leg to that. They did not do more than loosen the cords that bound me just enough to suffer them to pass the bandages round until the splint was on, and the other men stood in a ring and gibed at me all the time. After that they bandaged my right arm across my chest as if for a slipped shoulder, but under the bandages were cords that pinioned my elbows to one another across my back, so that I could only move my left forearm. Evan said that he would tie that also if need was, but it might pass now. I could not reach my mouth with this free hand, if I did try to take out a gag.

Next they bandaged my head and chin carefully, so that only my eyes were to be seen. I suppose that I might be thankful that they left my mouth uncovered more or less. And Evan said that he would gag me by and by.

"No need to discomfort him more than this now," he added. "Maybe he will be ready to promise silence when he has gone some time in this rig."

By this time some had caught half a dozen hill ponies, and on them they loaded several bales of goods, which I thought looked like those of some robbed chapman, and I have reason to think that they were such. They opened one of these, and in it they stowed my sword and helm and the great gold ring that Gerent gave me. There was some argument about this, but the leader said that it was better to sell it for silver coin which they could use anywhere.

Now Evan and two others dressed themselves afresh, and washed in the brook. One would have taken them for decent traders when that was done, for they were soberly clad in good blue cloth jerkins, with clean white hose, and red garterings not too new. Good cloaks they had also, and short seaxes in their belts. Only Evan had a short Welsh sword, and the peace strings of that were tied round the hilt. I wondered where the bodies of the honest men they had taken these things from were hidden in the wild hills.

Half a dozen of the best clad of the other men took boar spears, and so they were ready for a start, for all the world like the chapmen they pretended to be. They put me into the litter they had ready then, and four of the men were told off to bear me, grumbling. It was only a length of sacking made fast to two stout poles, and when they had hoisted me to their shoulders a blanket was thrown over me, and a roll of cloth from one of the bales set under my head, so that I might seem to be in comfort at least.

Then the band set out, and we went across the hills seaward and to the west until we saw Watchet below us. There was a road somewhere close at hand, as I gathered, for we stopped, and some of the rabble crept onward to the crest of the hill and spied to see if it was clear. It was so, and here all the band left us, and only Evan and the other two seeming merchants went on with their followers, who bore me and led the laden ponies. The road had no travellers on it, as far as I could see, nor did we meet with a soul until we were close into the little town that the Norsemen had made for themselves at the mouth of a small river that runs between hills to the sea.

Maybe there were two score houses in the place, wooden like ours, but with strange carvings on the gable ends. And for fear, no doubt, of the British, they had set a strong stockade all round the place in a half circle from the stream to the harbour. There were several long sheds for their ships at the edge of the water, and a row of boats were lying on a sort of green round which the houses stood with their ends and backs and fronts giving on it, as each man had chosen to set his place.

CHAPTER VI
HOW OSWALD HAD AN UNEASY VOYAGE AND A PERILOUS LANDING AT ITS END.

I thought that Evan had forgotten to gag me, but before we went to the gate of the stockade he came and did it well. I could not see a soul near but my captors, and it would have been little or no good to shout. So I bore it as well as I might, being helpless. Then, within arrow shot of the gate, one of the men blew a harsh horn, and we waited for a moment until a man, armed with an axe and sword, lounged through the stockade and looked at us, and so made a gesture that bid us enter, and went his way within. I hope that I may never feel so helpless again as I did at the time when I passed this man, who stared at me in silence, unable to call to him for help.

Then we crossed the green without any one paying much heed to us, though I saw the women at the doors pitying me, and so we came to the wharf, alongside which a ship was lying. There were several men at work on her decks, and it was plain that she was to sail on this tide, for her red-and-brown striped sail was ready for hoisting, and there was nothing left alongside to be stowed. She was not yet afloat however, though the tide was fast rising.

Evan hailed one of the men, and he came ashore to him. The bearers set down my litter and waited.

"Where is the shipmaster?" Evan asked.

The man jerked his thumb over his shoulder, and lifted his voice and shouted "Ho Thorgils, here is the Welsh chapman."

I saw the head of my friend rise from under the gunwale amidships, and when he saw who was waiting he also came ashore. Evan met him at the gangway.

"I thought you were not coming, master chapman," he said. "A little later and you had lost your voyage. Tide waits for no man, and Thorgils sails with the tide he waits. Therefore Thorgils waits for no man."

Just for a moment a thought came to me that Thorgils was in league with the outlaws, and that was hard. But Evan's next words told me that in this I was wrong. It would seem that the taking of his ill-gotten goods across the channel had been planned by Evan before he fell in with me, and maybe that already made plan was the saving of my life, by putting the thought of an easy way to dispose of me to some profit into the outlaw's head.

"I had been here earlier," he said, "but for a mischance to my friend here. I want to take him with me, if you will suffer it."

He pointed to me as he spoke, and Thorgils turned and looked at me idly. I was some twenty yards from him as I lay, and I tried to cry out to him as his eyes fell on me, but I could only fetch a sort of groan, and I could not move at all.

"He seems pretty bad," said Thorgils, when he heard me. "What is amiss with him? I can have no fevers or aught of that sort aboard, with the young lady as passenger, moreover."

"There is nothing of that," Evan answered hastily. "It is but the doing of a fall from his horse. The beast rolled on him, and he has a broken thigh, slipped shoulder, and broken jaw, so that it will be long before he is fit for aught again, as I fear. Now he wants to get back to his wife and children at Lanphey, hard by Pembroke, and our leech said that he would take no harm from the voyage. It is calm enough, and not so cold but that we may hap him up against it. If I may take him, I will pay well for his passage."

Thorgils looked at me again for a moment.

"Well," he said, "if that is all, I do not mind. It would be better if the after cabin was empty, but of course the princess has that. There is room for him to be stowed comfortably enough under the fore deck with your bales, however, and it will be warm there. Ay, we will take the poor soul home, for his mind will be easier, and that will help his healing. It is ill to be laid up in a strange land. Get him on board as soon as you can, for there is but an hour to wait for tide. I will ask no pay for his passage, for he is but another bale of goods, as it were, swaddled up in that wise, and I told you that I would take all you liked to bring for what we agreed on."

Evan thanked him, and Thorgils laughed, turning away to go up the town, and saying that he would be back anon. I groaned again as he passed me, and he looked straight in my eyes, which were all that he could see of me.

"Better on board than in that litter, poor fellow," he said kindly; "it is a smooth sea, and we shall see Tenby in no long time if this breeze holds."

He passed on with a nod and smile, and I could almost have wept in my rage and despair. I could not have thought of anything more cruel than this, and there was a sour grin on Evan's face, as if he knew what was passing in my mind.

Now they lifted me once more and carried me to the ship, setting me down amidships while they got the bales of goods on board. She was a stout trading vessel, built for burden more than speed, but she seemed light in the water, as though she had little cargo for this voyage. She had raised decks fore and aft, and there were low doors in the bulkheads below them that seemed to lead to some sort of cabins. Under the forward of these decks the outlaws began to stow their bales, the man who had called Thorgils ashore directing them.

I lay just at the gangway, and a little on one side so as not to block it, and I watched all that went on, helplessly. There was no one near me, or I think that I should have made some desperate effort to call a Norseman to my help. Maybe Evan thought me safer here than nearer the place where all were busy, as yet, but presently I heard voices on the wharf as if some newcomers were drawing near, and Evan heard them also, and left his cargo to hasten to my side. I saw that he looked anxious, and a little hope of some fresh chance of escape stirred in me, though, as they had carried me on board feet foremost, I could not see who came.

When they were close at hand their voices told me that one at least was a lady, and that she and her companions were Welsh. I supposed that this was the princess of whom I had heard Thorgils speak just now. I should know in a moment, for the first footsteps were on the long gangplank and pattering across it, while Evan began to smile and bow profoundly.

Then there came past my litter, stepping daintily across the planks, a most fair and noble lady, tall and black haired and graceful, wrapped against the sea air in the rare beaver skins of the Teifi River, and wonderful stuffs that the traders from the east bring to Marazion, such as we Saxons seldom see but as priceless booty, paid for with lives of men in war with West Wales in days not long gone by.

She half turned as she saw me, and it gave me a little pang, as it were, to see her draw her dress aside that it might by no means touch me, no doubt with the same fear of fever that had been in the mind of my friend at the first. But then she stayed and looked at me and at Evan, who was yet cringing in some Welsh way of respect as she passed. Her companions stopped on the gangplank, and they were silent.

"Why is this sick man on the ship," she said to my captor, with some little touch of haughtiness. "And why is he swathed thus? What is wrong with him?"

Evan bowed again, and at once began his tale as he had told it to Thorgils. But he did not say that I came from near Pembroke at all. Now he named some other place whose name began with "Llan--" as my home.

"The good shipmaster has suffered me to take him home, Lady, subject to your consent," he ended. "I pray you let it be so."

Now the eyes of the princess had grown soft as she heard the tale, and when Evan ended it there was pity in her voice as she answered.

"Surely he may come, and if there is no fitting place for him he shall even have the cabin to himself. I can be well content in these warm things of mine on deck in this calm air, and he must have all shelter."

"Nay, Lady, but there is the fore cabin, where he will be well bestowed," Evan said hastily, beckoning at the same time to his comrades that they might take me from this too unsafe place at once.

He kept himself between me and her as much as he could all this time, and I made no sign. It seemed to me that I could not, even in my trouble, bring more pain to this soft-eyed princess by raising the groan which was all that I could compass. What good would it do? I could tell her nothing, and she could not dream of the true reason that made me try to cry out. Maybe she would listen through all the long hours to come to hear if the poor wretch she felt for was yet in that dire pain that made him moan so terribly.

"Is he well bandaged?" she said, then. "It is ill if broken bones are not closely set and splinted, and the ship will plunge and rock presently."

Evan assured her with many words that all was well done, and yet she lingered.

"I must see him well and softly bestowed in his place," she said, half laughing, and turning to some who stood yet beyond my range of sight. "Else I shall have no peace at all till we come to land again."

Evan turned to me at that saying, to hide his face. He was growing ashy pale, and the sweat was breaking out on his forehead. And that made me glad to see, for he was being punished. Even yet the princess might wish to see that my swathings were comfortable, and if I once had my mouth freed for a moment all was lost to him.

He signed to his comrades to lift me carefully, and then put a bold face on the matter, and thanked the princess for her kindness.

"Lady, I may be glad to beg a warm wrap or two from your store," he said. "If it pleases you, we will shew you where he is to lie."

So they went forward, I on my litter first, and the lady and her people following. Evan knew well enough that little fault could be found with the warm place that was ready for me among the bales under the deck, and he was eager to get me out of sight before Thorgils returned. They had made a place ready with some of the softer bales for me to lie on, and there they lifted me from the litter, very carefully indeed, that they might not have to rearrange any of my bonds. Then the princess looked in through the low doorway and seemed content.

"It is as well as one can expect on board a ship, I suppose," she said, with a little sigh. "But I will send him somewhat to cover him well."

And then she bade me farewell, bidding me be patient for the little while of the voyage, and also adding that presently, when she was at home, she would ask Govan the hermit to pray for me; and so went her way, with the two maidens who were with her, and followed by a couple of well-armed warriors, all of whom I could see now for the first time.

Then Evan drew his hand over his forehead and cursed. As for the other Welshmen, they looked at one another, saying nothing, but I could see that they also had been fairly terrified. One of the men of the princess came with a warm blanket to cover me, and he stayed to see it put over me. It was as well that he did so, for Evan had no time to see that my arm was yet loose, unless he had forgotten that it ever had been so. Then they all went out, shutting the door after them, and I was left to my thoughts, which were not happy.

I began to blame myself as a fool for not trying to let the princess see that all was not right. But still I could not lose hope, for Thorgils might yet wish to see me, or the princess might send her men to look in on me. There were more chances now than a little while ago, as I thought.

I began to think over all that was possible, presently, and I tried to get the gag from my mouth. I could not reach it with my free hand, however, my elbows being too tightly fastened back even after all the shaking of the journey. Then I thrust that free hand and forearm well among the bandages across my chest, so that either of my captors who thought of it might think that the other had bound it, for I dared not try to loosen myself more yet. There would be time for that when we were fairly at sea.

After that I lay still, and so spied the bale in which my sword had been put, and that gave me some sort of hope by its nearness to me, though indeed it did not seem likely that I should ever get it.

I heard Thorgils come on board before very long, and I could hear also the voice of the princess as she talked to him, though with the length of the vessel between us, and the wash of the ripples alongside in my ears, I did not make out if they spoke of me. Evan spoke with them also, and it is likely that they did so.

Presently I could tell by the sway of the ship that she was afloat, and the men began to bustle about the deck overhead, while Thorgils shouted some orders now and then. Soon the sides of the ship grated along the wharf as she was hauled out, and then the shore warps were hove on board with a thud above me. I felt the lift of a little wave and heard the rattle of the halliards as the sail was hoisted and the ship heeled a little, and then began the cheerful wash and bubble of the wave at her bows as she went to sea. The men hailed friends on shore with last jests and farewells, and then fell to clearing up the shore litter from the decks.

Then Evan came and looked at me. Through the door I could see the hills and the harbour beyond the high stern, and on that Thorgils was steering, with his eyes on the vane at the masthead. His men were coiling down ropes, and Evan's two men were sitting under the weather gunwale aft, talking with the guards of the princess. She was in the after cabin, I suppose, out of the way of the wind, with her maidens. I could not see her.

"Art all well, friend?" said Evan, loudly enough for the nearest Norseman to hear. "Well, that is good."

Then he sunk his voice to a whisper, and said: "That gag bides in your mouth, let me tell you. I will risk no more calling to the shipmaster."

He cast his eyes over me and grunted, and went out, leaving the low door open so that he could see me at any time. It was plain that he thought his men had fastened my arm.

Now I tried to get rid of the gag again, and I will say that the outlaw knew how to manage that business. It filled my mouth, and the bandage round the jaw held it firmly. In no way could I get it out, or so much as loosen it enough to speak. And then I was worn out, and the little heave of the ship lulled me, and I forgot my troubles in sleep that came suddenly.

I was waked by the clapping to of the cabin door and the thunder of the wind in the great square sail as the ship went on the other tack. We had a fair breeze from the southwest over our quarter as the tide set up channel, but now it had turned and Thorgils was wearing ship. The new list of the deck flung the door to, and none noticed it, for it was dark now except for the light of the rising moon, and I suppose that the other noises of the ship prevented Evan hearing that the door had closed.

I felt rested with the short sleep, and now seemed the time to try to get free if ever. I got my left hand out of the bandages where I had hidden it, and began to claw at my chin to try to free it from the swathings that kept my mouth closed, but I could hardly get at them, so tightly were my elbows lashed behind my back, and it became plain that I must get them loose first if I could. It was easy to get the bandages loose, but the knotted cord was a different matter, for the men who tied it knew something of the work, and the cord was not a new one and would not stretch.

Then I heard two of the Norseman talking close to the cabin bulkhead.

"This is as good a passage as we shall ever make in the old keel," one said; "but we shall not fetch Tenby on this tide. Will Thorgils put in elsewhere, I wonder?"

"We could make the old landing place in an hour," was the answer, "and we had better wait for tide there than box about in the open channel in this cold. There is snow coming, I think."

I heard the man flap his arms across his chest, and the other said:

"Where do these merchants want to get ashore? I expect that Thorgils will do as they think best. He is pretty good natured."

They went away, and it seemed that I might have an hour before me. I was sure that if he had a chance Evan would land as soon as he could, and at some other place than at the Danes' town if possible, so that he might get me away without questions that might be hard to answer.

So I strained at the cords which bound my elbows with all my might, but I only hurt myself as the lashings drew tighter. I twisted from side to side as I did this, and presently hit my elbow hard against some metal fitting of the ship that seemed very sharp. Just at first I did not heed this, but by and by, when I had fairly tired myself with struggling, I minded it again, and so turned on my side and set my free hand to work to find out what it was.

There was a stout post which came from beneath and through the rough flooring of the cabin on which I lay, and went upward to the deck. I daresay it was to make the cable fast to, but I could not see that, nor did it matter to me what it might be for. But what I had felt was a heavy angle iron that was bolted by one arm to the post and by the other to a thick beam that crossed the ship from side to side, so as to bind the two together. It had a sharp edge on the part which crossed the floor, and it seemed to me as if it had been set there on purpose, for if I could manage to reach it rightly I might chafe through the cords at my back. Of course, there was the chance of Evan coming in and seeing what I was at, but I could keep my covering on me, maybe, and if Thorgils came, so much the better. He would see that something was amiss.

It was no easy task to get myself in such wise that the cord was fairly on the edge of the iron, but I did it at last, and, moreover, I got the thick blanket that was over me to cover me afresh. Then I started to try to chafe the cord through, and of course I could only move a little at a time, and I could not be sure that I was always rubbing it on the same place. And the great post was sorely in my way, over my shoulder more or less, so that I must needs hurt myself now and then against it. But as this seemed my one chance I would not give up until I must.

Every now and then I stayed my sawing and had a great tug at the cords, in hopes that they would give way, but at last I knew I must saw them through almost to the last strand. It would have been easy if I could keep at work on the same spot, but that was impossible, for I could not see behind me, and the post kept shifting me as I struck it.

I wondered now that I had seen nothing of Evan for so long. Maybe if I had not been so busy the wonder would have passed, for I should have been seasick as he was. There was some sea over on this coast, and quite enough to upset a landsman. However, I was content that he did not come, without caring to know why.

Then I became aware that the movement of the ship had changed in some way. There was less of it, and the roll was longer. Soon I heard Thorgils calling to his men, and then the creak of the blocks and the thud of folds of canvas on deck told me that the sail was lowered. After that the long oars rattled as they were run out, and their even roll and click in the rowlocks seemed to say that they were making up to some anchorage or wharf. The end of the voyage was at hand, and I worked harder than ever at my bonds. I began to fear that the cords would never chafe through enough for me to snap them, and my heart fell terribly.

Now there was a shout from Thorgils, and his men stopped rowing. I heard another shout from on shore, as it seemed, and the sound of breakers on rocks was not so very distant as we slipped into smooth water. The men trampled across the deck over my head and cast the mooring ropes ashore, and then the ship scraped along a landing stage of some sort and came to rest. I worked wildly at the rope.

Judging from the voices I heard, there seemed to be a number of people on shore, and soon I heard steps coming along the deck towards the cabin door. Hastily I straightened myself, and got a fold of my blanket over my free forearm just as it opened, and Evan peered in. Past his shoulder I could see that it was bright moonlight, and I had a glimpse of tall snow-covered cliffs that towered over us.

"How goes it, friend?" he cried in a loud voice. "Hast slept well? We are in your own land, and will be ashore soon."

That was for others to hear. Then he stood aside to let a little more light into the cabin, and it seemed that he had no suspicions that all was not as he would have it. He came inside and felt me carelessly enough.

"Well," he said. "You are warm in here, and no mistake. If I mistake not, you have been trying to wriggle out of these bonds."

He set his hand under some of the lashings and pulled them without uncovering me much, though it would not have mattered if he had done so, as it was very dark in here.

As I knew only too well, they were fast as ever, and he said:

"Well, we can tie a knot fairly. Presently we will loosen you a bit--in the morning maybe."

He went and closed the door, and I fell to work again. He would leave me now for a while.

There was a long talk from ship to shore before the gangplank was run out, and presently Thorgils spoke to Evan, seemingly close to the cabin door:

"Here's a bit of luck for your princess," he said. "Her father is up in the camp yonder, with his guards behind him. Maybe there is trouble with the Tenby Danefolk, or going to be some. It is as well that we put in here. Now he bids us take the lady up to him and bide to feast with him, Will you come with me?"

"I stay by my goods," answered Evan, with a laugh. "If there is a levy in the camp there will be men who will need watching among them."

"Why, then, we six Norsemen can go, and leave you to tend the ship."

"That will be all right," said Evan, somewhat gladly, as I thought; "so long as we are here you need have no fear. Every one knows that a chapman will fight for his goods if need be. But a Welshman will not meddle with a Welshman's goods."

"So long as he is there to mind them," laughed Thorgils. "Then we can go. I do not know how soon we can be back, though."

"That is no matter. We are used to keeping watch."

"Ay. How is that hurt friend of yours after the voyage?"

"Well as one could expect," answered Evan, "He says he has slept almost all the way. He is comfortable where he is."

They went aft, and soon I heard the princess speaking with them. Then the well-known click and clash of armed men marching in order came to me, as the chief sent a guard for his daughter. It was terrible to hear the voices of honest men so close to me and to be helpless, and I worked at the rope feverishly.

I heard the princess and her party leave the ship, and almost as the last footstep left the deck one strand of the cord went. I worked harder yet, with a great hope on me.

"Presently the Norsemen will be full of Howel's mead," I heard Evan say to one of his men. "Then we will get ashore and leave swiftly. I think we need not stay to pay Thorgils for the voyage."

"Let us tell some of the shore men to bide here to help us," said the other-- "we have the Saxon to carry."

"That is a good thought."

They clattered over the plank ashore, and another strand of the rope went at that time. I thought it was but one of another turn of the line, however. Five minutes more of painful sawing and straining and I felt another strand give way. That made three, and now one of the two turns of line that held my arms could have but one strand left, and that ought to be no more than I could break by force. Then I wrestled with it with little care if my struggles as I bent and strove made noise that might call attention to me, for it was my last chance. The lines bruised and cut me sorely, even through my mail, but I heeded that no more than I did the hardness of the timbers against which I rolled; and at last it did snap, with a suddenness that let my elbow fly against the iron that had been my saving, almost forcing a cry from me.

I was yet bound to my splints, but with my arms free it was but the work of a few seconds to cast off the last of my bonds, and within five minutes after the strand had parted I was on my feet, and rubbing and stretching my bruised and cramped limbs into life again. Then I felt in the darkness for the bale that held my gear, and found it and tore it open.

How good it was to gird the sword on me again, and to feel the cold rim of the good helm round my hot forehead! I was myself again, and as I slipped Gerent's gold ring on my arm I thought that it was almost worth the bondage to know what pleasure can be in the winning of freedom. I forgot that I was troubled with thirst and hunger, having touched nothing since I broke my fast with Owen; though, indeed, there was little matter in that, for I had done well at that meal with the long ride before me, and one ought to be able to go for a day and a night without food if need be, as a warrior.

Still, I was not yet out of the trouble. Thorgils had gone to some place that I knew nothing of, and I had yet to learn if there was any hope from Evan's shore going, which might make things easier or might not. I could hear no one moving about the ship, so I pushed the door open for an inch or two, and looked out into the moonlight, with my drawn sword ready in my hand.

We were in a strange place. The ship's bows were landward, so that as I looked aft I could see that we lay just inside the mouth of a little cove, whose guarding cliffs towered on either side of the water for not less than ten-score feet above the fringe of breakers, falling sheer to the water with hardly so much as a jutting rock at their feet. There was no sign of house or man at the hilltop, so that it was plain that we were not at Tenby.

Then I was able to see that we were alongside a sort of landing place that was partly natural and partly hewn and smoothed from the living rock into a sort of wharf at the foot of the cliff. From this landing place a steep road, hewn with untold labour at some ancient day, slanted sharply upward and toward the head of the cove along the face of the rocks, which were somewhat less steep on this side than across the water. I could not see the top of this road, but no doubt it was that along which Thorgils and the princess had gone, and no doubt also Evan thought to carry me up it before long.

I had a hope that my friend would return too soon for that, but it was a slender one. It was plain that he had gone too far for me to call to him. Yet could I win clear of the ship I might find or fight my way up after him, and that seemed easy with only these three Welshmen against me, and they expecting no attack.

I looked for the two who were left if I slew Evan. One sat under the weather gunwale, wrapped in a great cloak, and seemed to be sleeping. The other was not far off on the landing place, watching Evan, who was speaking with a dozen men at the foot of the rock-hewn road. I suppose that the coming in of the ship had drawn idlers from the camp I had heard of to see her, for they all had arms of some sort.

This was bad, for it seemed certain that the whole crowd would join with Evan in falling on me if he called on them. If I came forth now I had full twenty yards to cover before I reached them from the ship's side after I had settled with the men on watch. In that space all would be ready for me, and they were too many for me to cut through to the roadway. I thought too that I heard the voices of more who came downward toward the ship, though I could not see them whence I was.

Then it came into my mind that if there was any place where I could hide myself on deck I would try to creep to it while none had their eyes on the ship. Then Evan, as he went to the cabin to seek me, would have to deal with me from the rear. But that I soon saw was hopeless. The deck was clear of lumber big enough to shelter me, and the moonlight was almost as bright as day on everything, and all the clearer for the snow that covered all the land. So I began to turn over many other plans in my mind, and at last it seemed that the only thing was to wait in the cabin for the best chance that offered. Most likely Evan would do even as he had said, and try and get away at once, with all he could lay hands on. If so, I thought it would be certain that in his hurry he would bring all these men on board in order to get his goods, and maybe those belonging to Thorgils also, out and away with all haste, and so I could cut through them with a rush that must take them unawares, and so win to the camp with none to hinder me. There might be sentries who would stay me, but I should be within calling distance of my friend. Moreover, a sentry would see that I was some sort of a leader of men, and might help me. So I began to wish for Evan to act, for my fingers itched to get one downward blow at him.

I had not long to wait. He finished his talk with the men, and they all came to the ship, even as I had hoped. But only half of them came on board, leaving the rest alongside on the rock so that they might help the goods over the side. That was not all that I could have wished, but I thought that I might get through them in the surprise that was waiting for them. So I drew my sword, and for want of shield wrapped the blanket from the floor round my left arm, and stood by for the rush.

Evan walked in a leisurely way toward the door, talking to one of the newcomers as he came. The rest straggled behind him.

"I wonder how my sick man fares now," he said, and set his hand to the latch.

Then he opened the door and I shouted and sprung forth, aiming a blow at him as I came. But I was not clear of the low deck, and my sword smote the beam overhead so that I missed him, and he threw himself on the deck out of reach of a second blow, howling. I was sorry, but I could not stop, for I had to win to the shore and to the road yet.

The other men shrank from me, and I went through them easily, and so reached the shoreward gunwale. There I was stayed, for Evan had never ceased to cry to his fellows to stop me, and there was a row of ready swords waiting for me. And there were more men coming down the path, Welshmen as I could see by their arms, and by their white tunics which glimmered in the moonlight. So that was closed to me, and it seemed that here I must fight my last fight.

Then as I could not go over the side I went to the high stern and leapt on it, half hoping that the men on shore might not be quick enough to stay me from a leap thence, but they were there alongside before me. Evan was up now, and cheering on the men on deck to attack me, but not seeming to care to lead them. They gathered together and came aft to me slowly, planning, as it would seem, how best to attack me, for the steering deck on which I was raised me four feet or so above them. The men on shore could not reach me at all unless I got too near the gunwale, when some of them who had spears might easily end me.

Something alongside the ship caught my eyes, and I glanced at it with a thought that here might be fresh foes. But it was only the little boat that belonged to the ship. The wind had caught her, and was drifting her at the length of her painter as if she wanted to cross the cove to its far side. Perhaps the men saw that my eyes were not on them for that moment, for they made a rush from the deck to climb the steering platform.

Then I had a good fight for a few minutes, until I swept them back to their place. Two had won to the deck beside me, and there they stayed. Now I had a hope that the men on shore would come round to the ship and leave the way clear for me, but Evan called to them to bide where they were. He had not faced me yet, and I bade him do so, telling him that this was his affair, and that it was nidring to risk other men's lives to save his own skin. But even that would not bring him on me.

Now the men whom I had seen coming down from the cliffs' top had hurried to see what all the shouting meant, and I saw that they were well-armed warriors and mostly spearsmen. Evan cried to them to come and help, and they ranged up alongside. He told them that I was a Norseman who had gone berserk, and must needs be slain.

"That is easily managed," said the leader. "Get to your bows, men."

I saw half a dozen unslinging them, and I knew that without shield I was done, and in that moment a thought came to me. I suppose that danger sharpens one's wits, for I saw that in the little boat was my last chance. I had not time to draw her to the side, and so I cut her painter, which was fast to a cleat close to me, and as I did so the first arrow missed my head.

Then I shouted and leapt from the high stern straight among the crowd at Evan, felling one of his outlaw comrades as I lit on the deck. But I could not reach him, and in a few seconds I should have been surrounded. So I cleared a way to the seaward side and went overboard, amid a howl from my foes. I thought that I should never stop sinking, for I had forgotten my mail; but I came to the surface close to the ship, and looked for the boat. She was drifting gently away from me, and I knew that I should have all that I could do to reach her before the bowmen got to work again from the ship's deck. Some one threw an axe at me as I swam, which was waste of a good weapon, and I hoped that it was not Thorgils' best. Strange what thoughts come to a man when in a strait.

The water struck icy cold to me, and I felt that I could not stand it long, but I gained on the boat with every stroke, though it was hard work swimming in my mail and with a sword in my hand. I got rid of the blanket that was hampering my left arm, and by that time I was far enough from the ship for my foes to be puzzled by it. The moonlight was bright on the water, but the little waves tossed it so that it must have been hard for them to know which was I and which the floating stuff. Certainly, the first arrows that were shot when the bowmen got a chance at me from the ship or over her were aimed at the blanket, for I heard them strike it. Then one leapt from wave to wave past me.

I won to the boat just in time, for I could not have held on much longer. The cold was numbing me, and if I stopped swimming I must have sunk with the weight of mail. None of our old summer tricks of floating and the like were of any use with that weight on me. The arrows were coming thickly by that time, and I was glad to get to the far side of the boat and rest my hand on the gunwale, while I managed to sheathe my sword. The men could not see plainly where I was, and the arrows pattered on the planks of the boat and hissed into the water still, on the chance of hitting me. So I thought it well to get out of range before I tried to get on board, and so held the gunwale with one hand and paddled on with the other, until the arrows began to fall short, and at last ceased. A Welshman's bow has no long range, so that I had not far to go thus. But all the while I feared most of all to hear the plash of oars that would tell me that they had put off another boat in chase of me.

A little later and I should have been helpless, as I found when I tried to get into the boat. The cold was terrible, and it had hold of my limbs in spite of the swimming. It was hard work climbing over the bows, as I must needs do unless I wanted to capsize the light craft as I had overset a fisher's canoe more than once, by boarding her over the side, as we sported in the Glastonbury meres in high summer; but I managed it, and was all the better for the struggle, which set the blood coursing in my veins again. Then I got out the oars and began to pull away from the ship, with no care for direction so long as I could get away from her.

The foe had no boat, for they were all clustered in the ship or close to her on the rock, and there was a deal of noise going on among them. When I was fairly out of their way, and I could no longer make out their forms, I began to plan where I had best go, and at first I thought of a little beach that I had seen on the far side of the cove, thinking that I could get up what seemed a gorge to the cliff's top, and so hide inland somewhere. But when I could see right into the gorge, I found that it was steep and higher than I thought. My foes would be able to meet me by the time I was at the top.

There was no other place that I could see, for none could climb from the foot of the cliffs elsewhere, since if he reached the rocks he would have to stay where he leapt to them. So as there was no help for it, I headed for the open sea. No doubt, I thought, I should find some landing place along the coast before I had gone far, and meanwhile I was getting a fair start of the enemy, who would have to follow the windings of the cliffs if they cared to come after me.

I pulled therefore for the eastern end of the cove, opposite to the place where the ship lay, and so rounded the point and was out in the open and tossing on the waves in a way that tried my rowing sorely, for I am but a fresh-water boatman. Lucky it was for me that there was little sea on, or I should have fared badly. Then I pulled eastward, and against the tide also, but that was a thing that I did not know.

The boat was wonderfully light and swift, and far less trouble to send along than any other I had seen. There are no better shipwrights than the Norsemen, and we Saxons have forgotten the craft.

The terrible numbness passed off as I worked, but now the wind grew cold, and the clouds were working up from the southwest quickly, with wind overhead that was not felt here yet. I knew that I must make some haven soon, or it was likely that I should be frozen on the sea, but the great cliffs were like walls, and at their feet was a fringe of angry foam everywhere. I could see no hope as yet. Far away to the east of me a great headland seemed to bar my way, but I did not think that I should ever reach it. And all the while I looked to see the black forms of men on the cliffs in the moonlight, but they did not come. That was good at least.

Then at last my heart leapt, for I saw, as a turn of the cliffs opened out to me, another white beach with a cleft of the rocks running up from it, and I thought it best to take the chance it gave me, for I feared the blinding snow that would be here soon, and I felt that the sea was rising. If my foes were after me they would have been seen before now, as they came to the edge of the cliffs to spy me out, and anyway I dreaded them less than the growing cold. Moreover, I thought that Evan would hardly get many men to follow him on a chase of what he had told them was a madman, and a dangerous one at that. He had his goods to see to also.

So I ran the boat into the black mouth of the gorge, and beached her well by good chance. I had little time to lose, but I tied her painter to a rock at the highest fringe of tide wrack, in hopes that she might be safe. It was so dark here that I did not think that Evan would see her from above. And then I began to climb up the rugged path that led out of the gorge to the hilltops.

There were bones everywhere in it. Bones and skulls of droves of cattle on all the strand above the tide mark for many score yards. Their ribs stuck out from the snow everywhere, and the sightless eye sockets grinned at me as I stumbled over them. But I had no time to wonder how they came there, for I must get to the summit before Evan and his men reached it by their way along the cliff. I ate handfuls of the snow and quenched my thirst that was growing on me again, and my strength began to come back to me as I hurried upward. I was a better man when at last I reached the top of the gorge than when I came ashore.

CHAPTER VII
HOW OSWALD CROSSED THE DYFED CLIFFS, AND MET WITH FRIENDS.

Now I halted before I lifted my head above the skyline, and listened with a fear on me lest I should hear the sound of running feet, and I was the more careful because I knew that the snow which lay white and deep on all the open land might deaden any sounds thereof. But I heard nothing save the wail of the wind overhead as it rose in gusts. I wondered if Thorgils would be able to bide in this little cove, or must needs put out to seek some other haven. There seemed to be a swell setting into it.

So I crept yet farther up the path, crouching behind a point of rock, and thence I saw a dark line on the snow that seemed to promise a road, and that must surely lead to some house or village. I went forward to it with all caution, and with my head over my shoulder, as they say, but I saw no man. This track led east and west, and was well trodden by cattle, but there were few footprints of men on it, so far as I could see. So I turned into it, going ever away from the ship, and hurrying. I had a thought that I heard shouts behind me, but there was more wind here on the heights than I had felt on the sea, or it was rising, and it sung strangely round the bare points of rock that jutted up everywhere. Maybe it was but that.

Inland I could see no sign of house or hut where I might find food at least, but the cloud wrack had drifted across the moon, and I could not see far now. It was a desolate coast, all unlike our own.

Then I came to a place where the track crossed stony ground and was lost in gathered snow. When I was across that I had lost the road altogether, and had only the line of the cliffs to guide me to what shelter I could not tell. And now a few flakes of snow fluttered round me, and I held on hopelessly, thinking that surely I should come to some place that would give me a lee of rock that I could creep under.

Then the snow swooped down on me heavily, with a whirl and rush of wind from the sea, and I tried to hurry yet more from the chill. Then I was sure that I heard voices calling after me, and I ran, not rightly knowing where to go, but judging that the coastline would lead me to some fishers' village in the end. There seemed no hope from the land I had seen.

Again the voices came--nay, but there was one voice only, and it called me by my name: "Oswald, Oswald!"

I stopped and listened, for I thought of Thorgils. But the voice was silent, and again I pressed on in the blinding snow, and at once it came, wailing:

"Oswald, Oswald!"

It was behind me now and close at hand, and I turned with my hand on my sword hilt. But there was nothing. Only the snow whirled round me, and the wind sung in the rocks. I called softly, but there was no answer, and I was called no more as I stood still.

"Oswald, Oswald!"

I had turned to go on my way when it came this time, and now I could have sworn that I knew the voice, though whose it was I could not say.

"Who calls me," I cried, facing round.

Then a chill that was not of cold wind and snow fell on me, for there was silence, and into my mind crept the knowledge of where I had last heard that voice. It was long years ago--at Eastdean in half-forgotten Sussex.

"Father!" I cried. "Father!"

There was no reply, and I stood there for what seemed a long time waiting one. I called again and again in vain.

"It is weakness," I said to myself at last, and turned.

At once the voice was wailing, with some wild terror as it seemed, at my very shoulder, with its cry of my name, and I must needs turn once more sharply:

"Oswald, Oswald!"

My foot struck a stone as I wheeled round, and it grated on others and seemed to stop. But as I listened for the voice I heard a crash, and yet another, and at last a far-off rumble that was below my very feet, and I sprang with a cry away from the sound, for I knew that I stood on the very brink of some gulf. And then the snow ceased for a moment and the moon shone out from the break in the clouds, and I saw that my last footprint whence the voice had made me turn was on the edge of an awesome rift that cleft the level surface on the downland, clean cut as by a sword stroke, right athwart my path. Even in clear daylight I had hardly seen that gulf until I was on its very brink, for I could almost have leapt it, and nought marked its edge. And in its depths I heard the crash and thunder of prisoned waves.

I do not know that I ever felt such terror as fell on me then. It was the terror that comes of thinking what might have been, after the danger is past, and that is the worst of all. I sank down on the snow with my knees trembling, and I clutched at the grass that I might not feel that I must even yet slip into that gulf that was so close, though there was no slope of the ground toward it. Sheer and sudden it gaped with sharp edges, as the mouth of some monster that waited for prey.

There on the snow I believe that I should have bided to sleep the sleep of the frozen, for I hardly dared to move. The snow whirled round me again, but I did not heed it, and with a great roar the wind rose and swept up the rift with a sound as of mighty harps, but it did not rouse me. Only my father's voice came to me again and called me, and I rose up shaking and followed it as it came from time to time, until I was once more on the track that I had lost.

There it left me, but the sadness that had been in its tones was gone when it last came. And surely that was the touch of no snowflake that lit on my hand for a moment and was gone.

Now I grew stronger, and the fear of the unseen was no longer on me, and I battled onward with wind and snow for a long way. Thanks to the wind, the track was kept clear of the snow, and I did not lose it again until it led me to help that was unlooked for.

There came the sound of a bell to me, strange sounding indeed, but a bell nevertheless, and I knew that somewhere close at hand was surely some home of monks who would take me in with all kindness. And presently the track led me nearer to the sound of the sea, and at last bent sharply to the right and began to go downhill, while the sound of the bell grew plainer above the roar of nearer breakers yet. I felt that I was passing down such a gorge as that up which I had come from the boat, but far narrower, for I had not gone far before I could touch the rocky walls with either hand. Then I came to steps, and they were steep, but below me still sounded the bell, and the hoarse breakers were very near at hand. I expected to see the lights of some little fishing village every moment, but the wind that rushed up the narrow space between the cliff walls and brought the salt spray with it almost blinded me.

Suddenly the stairway turned so sharply that I almost fell, and then I found my way downward barred by what seemed a great rough-faced rock that was right across the gorge, if one may call a mere cleft in the cliffs so, and barred my way, while the strange bell sounded from beyond it. But it was sheltered under this barrier, and I felt along it to find out where I had to climb over, thinking that the stairway must lead up its face. But there was no stair, and as I groped my hand came on cut stone, and when I felt it I knew that I had come to a doorway, for I found the woodwork, but in no way could I find how it opened.

I kicked on it, therefore, and shouted, but it seemed that none heard. The bell went on and then stopped, and I thought I heard footsteps on the far side of the barrier. They came nearer, and then were almost at the door, paused for a moment, and then the door was opened and the red light from a fire flashed out on me, showing the tall form of a man in monk's dress in its opening.

"Come in, my son," said a grave voice, speaking Welsh, that had no wonder in it, though one could hardly have expected to see an armed and gold-bedecked Saxon here in the storm.

I stumbled into what I had thought a rock, and found when my eyes grew used to the light that I was in a house built of great stones, uncemented but wonderfully fitted together, and warm and bright with the driftwood fire, though I heard the spray rattle on the roof of flat stones, and the wind howled strangely around the walls. Both ends of this house were of the living rock of the sides of the gorge, and at one end seemed to be a sort of cave with a narrow entrance.

The man who had bidden me in stood yet at the open door looking out on his staircase, but he did not bide there long. With a sigh he turned and closed the door and came in, hardly looking at me, but turning toward the cave I had just noticed. He was an old man, very old indeed, with a long white beard and pale face lined with countless wrinkles, and he stooped a little as he walked. But his face was calm and kind, though he did not smile at me, and I felt that here I was safe with one of no common sort.

"Come, my son," he said, "it is the hour of prime. Glad am I to have one with me after many days."

He waited for no answer, and I followed him for the few steps that led to the rock cavern; and there was a tiny oratory with its altar and cross, and wax lights already burning.

The old man knelt in his place and I knelt with him, and as he began the office straightway I knew how worn out I was, and of a sudden the lights danced before me and I reeled and fell with a clatter and clash of arms on the rocky floor. I seemed to know that the old man turned and looked and rose up from his knees hastily, and I tried to say that I was sorry that I had broken the peace of this holy place; but he answered in his soft voice:

"Why, poor lad, I should have seen that you were spent ere this. The fault is mine."

He raised me gently, and seemed to search me for some wound. And as he did so I came more to myself, and begged him to go on with his office.

"First comes care of the afflicted, my son, and after that may be prayer. In truth, to help the fainting is in itself a prayer, as I think. Come to the fireside and tell me what is amiss."

"Fasting and fighting and freezing, father," I said, trying to laugh.

"Are you wounded?" he asked quickly.

"No, not at all."

"That is well. It is a brave heart that will jest in such a case as yours, for you are ice from head to foot. Well, I had better hear your story, if you will tell it me, in the daylight. Now get those wet garments off you and put on this. I will get you food, and you shall sleep."

This was surely the last place where my foes would think of looking for me, and the snow would hide every trace of my path. So I made no delay, but took off my byrnie and garments. There was a pool on the floor where I stood, for it was true enough that I had been ice covered. Then I put on a rough warm brown frock with a cord round the waist, so that I looked like a lay brother at Glastonbury, and all the while I waxed more and more sleepy with the comfort of the place. But I wiped my arms carefully while the old priest was busy with a cauldron over the fire, and we were ready at the same time.

Then I had a meal of some sort of stew that seemed the best I ever tasted, and a long draught of good mead, while the host looked on in grave content. And then he spread a heap of dry seaweed in a corner near the fire, and blessed me and bid me sleep. Nor did I need a second bidding, and I do not think that I can have stirred from the time that I lay down to the moment when I woke with a feeling on me that it was late in the daylight.

So it was, and I looked round for my kind host, but he was not to be seen. Outside the wind was still strong, but not what it had been, for the gale was sinking suddenly as it rose, and into the one little window the sun shone brightly enough now and then as the clouds fled across it. There was a bright fire on the hearth, and over it hung a cauldron, whence steam rose merrily, and it was plain that my friend of last night was not far off, so I lay still and waited his return.

Then my eyes fell on my clothes and arms as they hung from pegs in the walls over against me, and it seemed as if the steel of mail and helm and sword had been newly burnished. Then I saw also that a rent in my tunic, made when my horse fell, had been carefully mended, and that no speck of the dust and mire I had gathered on my garments from collar to hose was left. All had been tended as carefully as if I had been at home, and I saw Elfrida's little brooch shining where I had pinned it.

That took me back to Glastonbury in a moment, but I had to count before I could be sure that it was but a matter of hours since I took that gift in the orchard, rather than of months. And I wondered if Owen knew yet that I was lost, or if my men sought me still. Then my mind went to Evan, the chapman outlaw, and I thought that by this time he would have given me up, and would be far away by now, beyond the reach of Thorgils and his wrath.

Now the seaward door opened, and a swirl of spray from the breakers on the rocks came in with my host, who set a great armful of drift wood on the floor, closed it, and so turned to me.

"Good morrow, my son," he said. "How fare you after rest?"

"Well as can be, father," I answered, sitting up. "Stiff I am, and maybe somewhat black and blue, but that is all. I have no hurt. But surely I have slept long?"

"A matter of ten hours, my son, and that without stirring. You needed it sorely, so I let you be. Now it is time for food, but first you shall have a bath, and that will do wonders with the soreness."

Thankful enough was I of the great tub of hot water he had ready for me, and after it and a good meal I was a new man. My host said nought till I had finished, and then it was I who broke the silence between us.

"Father," I said, "I have much to thank you for. What may I call you?"

"They name me Govan the Hermit, my son."

"I do not know how to say all I would, Father Govan," I went on, "but I was in a sore strait last night, and but for your bell I think I must have perished in the snow, or in some of the clefts of these cliffs."

"I rang the bell for you, my son, though I knew not why. It came on me that one was listening for some sign of help in the storm."

"How could you know?" I asked in wonder.

Govan shook his head.

"I cannot tell. Men who bide alone as I bide have strange bodings in their solitude. I have known the like come over me before, and it has ever been a true warning."

Now it was my turn to be silent, for all this was beyond me. I had heard of hermits before, but had never seen one. If all were like this old man, too much has not been said of their holiness and nearness to unseen things.

So for a little while we sat and looked into the fire, each on a three-legged stool, opposite one another. Then at last he asked, almost shyly, and as if he deemed himself overbold, how it was that I had come to be on the cliffs. That meant in the end that he heard all my story, of course, but my Welsh halted somewhat for want of use, and it was troublesome to tell it. However, he heard me with something more than patience, and when I ended he said:

"Now I know how it is that a Saxon speaks the tongue of Cornwall here in Dyfed. You have had a noble fostering, Thane, for even here we lamented for the loss of Owen the prince. We have seen him in Pembroke in past years. You will be most welcome there with this news, for Howel, our prince, loved him well. They are akin, moreover. It will be well that you should go to him for help."

He rose up and went to the seaward door again, and I followed him out. The sea was but just below us, for the tide was full, and the breakers were yet thundering at the foot of the cliffs on either hand. But I did not note that at first, for the thing which held my eyes at once was a ship which was wallowing and plunging past us eastward, under close reefed sail, and I knew her for the vessel in which I had crossed. Thorgils had left the cove, and was making for Tenby while he might. I should have to seek him there.

"How far is it to the Danes' town, Father Govan?" I asked. "Yonder goes my friend's ship."

"Half a day's ride, my son, and with peril for you all the way. Our poor folk would take you for a Dane in those arms, and you have no horse. Needs must that you seek Howel, and he will give you a guard willingly."

Then he turned toward a great rock that lay on the beach, as if it had fallen from the cliffs that towered above us.

"Here is the bell that you heard last night," he said.

He took a rounded stone that lay on the rock and struck it, and I knew that the clear bell note that it gave out was indeed that which had been my saving.

"Once I had a bell in the cote on the roof yonder," he said, "but the Danes caught sight of it when they first passed this way, and took it from me. Then as I sorrowed that the lonely shepherds and fishers might no more hear its call, I seemed to see a vision of an angel who bade me see what had been sent me instead. And when I went out as the vision bade me, I could see nought but this rock newly fallen, and was downcast. And so, from the cliff rolled a little stone and smote it, and it rang, and I knew the gift. To my hearing it has a sweeter voice than the bell made with hands."

Then he showed me his well, roofed in with flat stones because the birds would wash in it, and so close to the sea salt that it seemed altogether wonderful that the water was fresh and sweet. And then I saw that the cell did indeed stretch from side to side of the narrow cleft down which I had come, so that each end of the building was of living rock.

"I built it with my own hands, my son," he said. "I cannot tell how long ago that was, for time is nought to me, but it was many years. Once I wore arms and had another name, but that also I care not to recall."

Then there came footsteps from above us, and looking up I saw a man in a rough fisher's dress coming in haste down the long flight of rock-hewn steps that led from the cliff top down the cleft to the door that I had found last night, and soon we heard him calling to the hermit.

Govan left me, and went through the cell to speak with him, but was back very shortly.

"Howel the prince is coming hither," he said. "The man you saw has seen him on the way, and came to warn me to be at hand for him. It is well for you, my son, as I am sure."

So we went together into the house, and I thought to arm myself, but Govan smiled and asked me not to do so, saying that hither even Howel would come without his weapons, in all likelihood.

I understood him, and did but see that my sword was in reach before I sat down and waited for the coming of the Welsh prince, and I thought that all I need ask him was for help to reach Tenby, whither Thorgils must have gone. It was quite likely that Evan might have raised the country against me in hopes of taking me again. And maybe I would ask for justice on the said Evan. Also I wanted to hear what had happened after my going.

It was not long that I had to wait. There came the tramp of horses at the top of the gorge, and the sound of a voice or two, and then the tread of an armed man came slowly down the stair, and Govan went to meet him. I rose and waited for his entry.

Now there came in, following Govan, unhelmed as he had greeted the holy man, a handsome, middle-aged warrior, black haired and eyed and active looking. He wore the short heavy sword of the Roman pattern, gold hilted and scabbarded, at his side, and the helm he carried had a high plumed crest and hanging side pieces that seemed like those pictured on the walls of Gerent's palace. He had no body armour on, and his dress was plain enough, of white woollen stuff with broad crimson borders, but round his neck was a wonderful twisted collar of gold, and heavy golden bracelets rang as his arms moved. I saw that his first glance went to me, and that his face changed when he saw that I was not one of his own people, but a foreigner, as he would hold me. I saw too that he noted my arms as they hung on the wall behind me.

Govan saw it also, and made haste to tell him who I was.

"This is one who should be welcome to you, Prince, for the sake of old days, for he has come by mischance from Dyvnaint, being foster son of one of the princes of Gerent's court, though a Saxon by birth. Nevertheless he speaks our tongue well. He will tell you all that presently, and I think that he needs your help."

"I thought you one of our troublesome neighbours, the Danes," he said, with a smile now in place of the look of doubt. "But if you are from Dyvnaint there are many things that you can tell me. But I have come here to see that all is well with Father Govan, for there is talk of a mad Norseman who is roving the country, unless the cold has ended him in the night. It is good to see that nought is wrong here."

Now I stood apart, and Govan and his guest spoke together for a few moments before my turn to tell Howel of my plight should come, and almost the next thing that the prince said made me wonder that I had not thought who he was at once. Of course, he was the father of the kindly princess who had crossed the sea with Thorgils, and had so nearly been the means of my earlier rescue.

"Nona, my daughter, is here at the cliff top, Father Govan," Howel said. "She came home in the Norse ship last night, as we planned; but tide failed for Tenby, and it chanced that the ship had to put in at the old landing place. Now she wants to thank you for your prayers for her, and also to beg them for some sick man about whom she is troubling herself--some poor hurt knave of a trader who crossed in the ship with her."

"I will go out and speak with her," Govan said, smiling. "It is ever her way to think of the troubled."

"Tell her that I will not keep her long in the cold," Howel said. "Bid her keep her horse walking, lest he take chill, if I may ask as much, Father."

Govan threw his cowl over his head, and answered:

"I will tell her. Now, Prince, this friend of mine has come here in a strange way, and I think he needs help that you can give him."

He passed out of the cliffward door and went his way up the long stairway. Then Howel asked me how he could help me.

"Tell me about Dyvnaint also, for when I was a boy I was long at Gerent's court. Did not Govan say that you were fostered by one of the princes? It is likely that I knew your foster father well, if so; was he Morgan?"

"Not Morgan, but Owen," I answered, and at that Howel almost started to his feet.

"Owen!" he cried. "Does he yet live? Surely we all thought him dead, or else he had come hither to us when he was banished. I loved him well in the old days, and glad I am that you are not Morgan's charge. Tell me all about Owen. Is he home again?"

"Morgan is dead," I answered, feeling that here I had met with a friend in all certainty. "And because of that, Owen is in his place again, and I am here. It has all happened in this week, and to tell you of it is to tell you all my trouble."

Now he was all impatience to hear, and I told him all that needed to be told, until I came to the time when Owen was back at Norton with the old king. Then he asked me some questions about matters there, and in the midst of my answers sprang up.

"Why," he cried, "here I have forgotten the girl, and she ought to be hearing all this, instead of sitting in the cold on the cliff. She is Owen's goddaughter, moreover, and he was here only a little time before he was banished. She can remember him well."

"Stay, though," he said, sitting down again. "There is your own tale yet. Let us hear it. Maybe that is not altogether so pleasant."

My own thought was that I was glad I might tell it without the wondering eyes of the fair princess on me, being afraid in a sort of way of having her think of me as the helpless sick man she had pitied. So I hastened to tell all that story.

And when I came to the way in which Evan brought me, Howel's eyes flashed savagely, and a black scowl came over his handsome face, sudden as a thunderstorm in high summer.

"It will be a short shrift and a long rope for that Evan when I catch him," he said. "He comes here every year, and I suppose that the goods I have had from him at times have been plunder. I would that you had ended him last night. Now he has got away in peace, and is out of my reach, maybe, by this time. Well, how went it?"

Then I told him the end of the tale, wondering how it was that Thorgils had let him go. I asked the prince if he could explain that for me.

"Not altogether," he said. "Evan sent to me to ask me for men to guard the ship presently, after we began the feast, saying that he was going ashore with his goods, and was responsible to the shipmaster. I told Thorgils, and he said it was well. So I sent a guard, and presently Evan came and spoke with Thorgils for a little while, and drank a cup of wine, and so went his way. Next morning, before he sailed, Thorgils came and grumbled about the loss of his boat, saying that Evan had taken some sick friend of his ashore in her, and that she had not come back. I paid him for it too, because I like the man, and so does my daughter. He sailed, and then I heard of the fight for the first time."

Howel laughed a little to himself.

"Master Evan must have paid my rascals well to keep up the story of the sick man to Thorgils, for he said nothing to me of any fight. Maybe, however, he never spoke to any of them, and it is likely that they would not say much to him. And now, by the Round Table! if you are not the mad Norseman they prated of to me when I wanted to know who slew the two men, and if you are not the sick man that Nona is so anxious about! Here, she must come and see you!"

With that he got up and went to the door before I could stay him, and called gaily to the princess, whose horse I could hear stamping high above us.

"Ho, Nona, here is a friend of yours whom you will be glad to see. Ask Father Govan to let you come hither, and bid the men take your horse."

So I must make the best of it, and I will say that I felt foolish enough. It was in my mind, though, that I owed many thanks to the princess for all her kind thought for me as sick man. I had already said as much to Howel. So I began to try to frame some sort of speech for her. One never remembers how such speeches always fail at the pinch.

The light footsteps came down the steps in no long time, and then the princess entered, dressed much as yesterday, with a bright colour from the wind, and looking round to see the promised friend.

"I have kept you long, daughter," Howel said, taking her hand, "but I have been hearing good news. Here is Oswald of Wessex, a king's thane, but more than that to us, for he is the adopted son of your own godfather, Owen of Cornwall, and he brings the best of tidings of him."

Now the maiden's face flushed with pleasure, and she held out her hand to me in frank welcome. Yet I saw a little wondering look on her face as she let her eyes linger on mine for a moment, and that puzzled me.

"You are most welcome, Thane," she said. "It is a wonderful thing that here I should learn that my lost godfather yet lives. You will come to Pembroke with us, and tell me of him there?"

Then Howel laughed as if he had a jest that would not keep, and he cried: "Why, Nona, that is a mighty pretty speech, but surely one asks a sick man of his health first."

She blushed a little, and glanced again at me.

"Surely the thane is not hurt?" she said.

"Yesterday he was, and that sorely. What was it, Thane?--Slipped shoulder, broken thigh, and broken jaw? All of which a certain maiden pitied most heartily, even to lending a blanket to the poor man."

Then Nona blushed red, and I made haste to get rid of some of the thanks that were heartfelt enough if they came unreadily to my lips, and Howel laughed at both of us. I think that the princess found her way out of the little constraint first, for she began to smile merrily.

"There must be a story for me to hear about all this," she said. "But I was sure that I had seen your eyes before. I was wondering where it could have been."

"Well," said Howel, "I have sat with the thane for close on an hour, and now I do not know what colour his eyes are."

"They were all that I could see of him, father," laughed the princess, and then she put the matter aside. "Now we have been here long enough, and good Govan shivers on the hilltop. Surely the thane will ride home with us, and we can talk on the way."

Howel added at once that this was the best plan for me, and what he was about to ask me himself.

"I know you will want to get home again as soon as may be," he said. "No doubt Thorgils will take you at once. I will have word sent to him at Tenby to stay for you."

"Father, you have forgotten," the princess said, somewhat doubtfully, as I thought.

"Nay, but I have not," answered Howel grimly. "But honest Thorgils is a white heathen, and those Tenby men are black heathen. He does not come into our quarrels, and will heed me, if they will not."

I minded that I had heard of trouble between the Tenby Danes and this prince, and it seemed that he spoke of it again. However, that I might hear by and by. So I thanked him, and said that I could wish for nothing better than to be his guest until I could go on my way hence.

Now the princess went to the cliff top and called Govan, while I armed myself. The hermit came back, and I bade him farewell, with many thanks for his kindnesses during the hours I had been with him; and so I went from the little cell with the blessing of Govan the Hermit on me, and that was a bright ending to hours which had been dark enough. Govan the Saint, men call him, now that he has gone from among them, and rightly do they give him that name, as I think.

Howel dismounted one of his men, and set me on the horse in his place, and then we rode to the camp at the landing place by the track which had led me hither, passing the head of the rift from which I had escaped, so that I saw its terrors in full daylight. And they were even more awesome to me than as I hung on the brink with the depths unknown below me. Then Howel told me how once a hunter had come suddenly on that gulf with his horse at full gallop, and had been forced to leap or court death by checking the steed. He had cleared it in safety, but the terror of what he had done bided with him, so that he died in no long time; I could well believe it.

Then the princess told me many things of Govan, and among others that the poor folk held that when the Danes came and stole the bell from him he had been hidden from them in the rock wall of the chapel, which had gaped to take him in, closing on him and setting him free when danger was past. Certainly there was a cleft in the rock wall of the chapel wall that had markings as of the ribs of a man in its sides, and was just the height and width for one to stand in, but Govan said nought to me about it when he told of the taking of the bell. Danes also slew all these cattle whose bones I had passed among.

Then we came in sight of the camp, over which the red dragon banner of Wales floated, and Howel told me how it was that he had met us there with his guards.

"Men saw Thorgils' ship from the lookout, and so I came here, for they said that she could not make Tenby on this tide and must needs come in here. Nona has been for three months with her mother's folk in Cornwall--ay, she is half Cornish, and kin to Gerent and Owen. I was married over there, at Isca, and Owen was at the wedding as my best man, though he is ten years younger than I. That is how he came to be the girl's godfather, you see. Now I wanted her back, for it is lonely at Pembroke without her, and I am apt to wax testy with folk if she is not near to keep things straight. So I sent word by Thorgils six weeks ago that she was to come back, and he was to bring her. I have had the men watching for the ship ever since. Good it is to see her again, and she has brought good news also, with yourself. I have a mind to keep you with us awhile, and let the Norseman take back word of your safety."

But I said that, however pleasant this would be, it seemed plain that I must get back to Owen with all speed, to warn him of this trouble that was somewhat more than brewing. It could not be thought that I would send word and yet never move to his side to help.

"If I might say what comes into my mind," said the fair princess, "it seems almost better that none but Owen and yourself know that the plot is found out, while you guard against it. The traitors will be less careful if they deem that nought is known. Thorgils is somewhat talkative, you know."

"That is right," said Howel. "I have a good counsellor here, Thane, as you see. However, Thorgils will not sail today, for he has just put in, and I know that he was complaining of some sort of damage done, as the gale set a bit of a sea into the cove, and he had some ado to keep clear of the rocks for a time. We will even ride to Pembroke, and I will send for Thorgils that he may speak with you."

And then he added grimly:

"Moreover, I will send men on the track of Evan, the chapman, forthwith."

So we called out the guards from the camp, where there were lines of huts with a greater building in the midst as if it were often used thus, and so rode across the rolling land northwards till we came to Pembroke. And there Howel of Dyfed dwelt in state in such a palace as that of Gerent, for here again the hand of the Saxon had never come, and the buildings bore the stamp of Imperial Rome.

So once again I was lodged within stone walls, and with a roof above me that I could touch with my hand, and I need not say how I fared in all princely wise as the son of Owen. I suppose there could be no more frank and friendly host than Howel of Dyfed.

Tired I was that night also, and I slept well. But once I woke with a fear for Owen on me, for I had dreamed that I saw some man creeping and spying along the wide ramparts of Norton stronghold. And it seemed that the man had a bow in his hand.

CHAPTER VIII
HOW OSWALD LOST A HUNT, AND FOUND SOMEWHAT STRANGE IN CAERAU WOODS.

I thought Pembroke a very pleasant place when I came to see it in the fair winter's morning. The gale had passed, but it had brought a thaw with it, and there was a softness in the air again, and the light covering of snow had gone when I first looked abroad. There had been no such heavy fall here as we had in Wessex beyond the sea.

Maybe pleasant companionship had something to do with my thought of the place, for none can deny that a good deal does depend on who is with one. And, seeing that after the morning meal her father was busy with his counsellors for a time, Nona the princess would shew me all that was to be seen while we waited the coming of Thorgils.

Whoever chose the place for the building of this palace stronghold chose well, for it is set on a rocky tongue of land that divides the waters of an inland branch of the winding Milford Haven, so that nought but an easily defended ridge of hill gives access to the fortress. All the tongue itself has sheer rock faces to the water, and none might hope to scale them. They and the wall across the one way from the mainland, as one may call it, make Howel's home sure, and since the coming of the Danes into the land he had strengthened what had fallen somewhat into decay in the long years of peace that had passed.

We had never reached Dyfed, either from land or sea. So I saw hawks and hounds, stables and guardrooms and all else, and at last we walked on the terraced edge of the cliffs in the southern sun, and there a man came and said that Thorgils the Norseman had come.

"Oh," said Nona with a little laugh, "he knows not that you are here! Let us see his face when he meets you!"

"The prince is busy," said the servant. "Is it your will that the stranger should be brought here?"

"Yes, bring him. Tell him that I would speak with him, but say nought of any other."

The man bowed and went his way, and the princess turned to me with a new look of amusement on her face.

"Pull that cloak round you, Thane, and pay no heed to him when he comes; we may have sport."

They had given me a long Welsh cloak of crimson, fur bordered, and a cap to wear with it instead of my helm. And of course I had not on my mail, though Ina's sword was at my side, and Gerent's bracelet on my arm, setting off a strange medley of black-and-blue bruises and red chafed places from the cords, moreover. So I laughed, and did as she bade me, even as I saw Thorgils brought round the palace toward us from the courtyard where they had taken charge of his horse. There were two other men with him, tall, wiry looking warriors, and all three were well armed, but in a fashion which was neither Welsh nor Saxon, but more like the latter than the former.

"Danes from Tenby," said Nona; "I know them both, and like them. See what wondrous mail they have, and look at the sword hilt of the elder man. That is Eric, the chief, and I think he comes to speak with my father."

The two Danes hung back as they saw that Howel was not present, but Thorgils unhelmed and came forward quickly, with the courtly bow he knew how to make when he chose, as he saluted the princess. Then he turned slightly to me with his stiff salute, and as I nodded to him I saw him start and look keenly at me. Then he looked away again, and tried to seem unheeding, but it was of no use; his eyes came back to me.

"You seem to have met our friend before, Shipmaster," said Nona, whose eyes were dancing.

"I cannot have done so, Princess," he answered. "But on my word, I never saw so strange a likeness to one I do know."

"I trust that is a compliment to my friend," she said.

"Saving the presence of the one who is like the man I know, I may say for certain that it is nought else to him."

I turned away somewhat smartly, for I wanted to laugh, and this was getting personal. The princess was not unwilling, I think, that it should be more so.

"Now you have offended the present, and I shall have to say that the absent need not be so."

"Nor the present either, Princess. See here, Lord, the man you are so wondrous like in face did the bravest deed I have seen for many a day. Moreover, he saved the life of a king thereby. Shall I tell thereof?"

Now this was a new tale to Nona, for, as may be supposed, I had not said that it was myself who handled Morgan so roughly, as I told the tale of his end. It would have seemed like boasting myself somewhat, as I thought, so

I did but say that he was dragged away from the king in time. Nor had I spoken of Elfrida. The tale was told hurriedly, and when it was done there had been no thought but of Owen. It was greater news here that he lived than that Ina had narrowly escaped.

So she glanced round at me in some surprise, and then turned again to Thorgils.

"Some time you shall, for I love your songs. Not now, for we have not time."

"Thanks, Lady. It will be a good song, and is shaping well in my mind. There is a brave lady therein also."

"Well, you have not told us who the brave man is.

"Did I not know that Oswald, son of Owen the Cornish prince, was by this time in Glastonbury, I should have said he was here, so great is the likeness. It is a marvel.

"Now, Lord, you will forgive me, no doubt."

"Ay, freely," I said, turning round sharply. "That is, if your friend has a sword as good as this," and I shewed him the gemmed hilt of Ina's gift from beneath the folds of my great cloak.

He stared at it, and then at my face again, and I took off my cap to him with a bow.

"It is strange that a shipmaster knows not his own passenger," I said.

But he was dumb for a moment, and his mouth opened. Nona laughed at him and clapped her hands with glee, and I must laugh also.

"By Baldur," he gasped, "if it is not Oswald, in the flesh! What witchcraft brought you here? To my certain knowledge there is no ship but mine afloat now in the Severn Sea."

"Why, then, I crossed with you, friend," I said.

"That you did not--" he began, but stopped short.

"Thorgils, Thorgils--the sick man!" cried Nona.

"Oh!" said Thorgils, "can you have been Evan's charge?"

"Ay. Mind you that it was your own word that there might be danger from the friends of Morgan?"

Then I told him all, and he heard with growls and head shakings, which but for the presence of the lady might have been hard sayings concerning my captors.

But when I ended he said:

"If ever I catch the said Evan there will be a reckoning. All the worse it will be for him that for these five years past I have known him, and deemed him a decent and trustworthy man, for a Welsh trader. I have fetched him back and forth with his goods twice or thrice a year for all that time, and now I suppose he has made me a carrier of stolen wares! Plague on him. I mind me now that betimes I have thought he dealt in cast-off garments somewhat, but that was not my affair. Now one knows how that was."

"I liked the man well, also," said the princess, with a sigh. "He has come here every year, and betimes as he shewed me his goods--not those you spoke of, Thorgils--it has seemed to me that he was downcast, and as one who had sorrow in his heart. Maybe he had, for his ill doings. He deserves to be punished, but yet I would ask that--that if you lay hands on him you will be merciful."

"He shewed little mercy to Oswald the thane," growled Thorgils. "However, Princess, I think that you may be easy. He will not risk aught, and we shall see him no more. But the knave would beguile Loki. Never a word did I hear of any trouble, but he came and spoke to me as I sat with your men yonder, and paid me his passage money, and said he had asked for a guard for the ship as he wanted to be away with the sick man. Also he said he would borrow the boat for his easier passage ashore. I supposed she was smashed in the gale, as she came not back, and Howel paid me for her when I grumbled."

"I wonder he went near you," I said.

"Therein was craft. If he had not paid passage I would have let every shipmaster beware of him, and he would have fared ill. He thought you done for, no doubt, and so fell back on certainty, as one may say. It is a marvel you escaped the great rifts in yon cliffs in the storm. Now he will hear that you are none the worse, and he will be sorry he paid me."

Thorgils laughed grimly, but Nona sighed at the downfall of the man she had liked. As for myself, it mattered little what became of him, so far as I was concerned. Howel's men were hunting him as I knew, and I only hoped they might catch him, for then we might learn more of the plotting that was on hand from him. He would tell all to save his skin, no doubt.

But now I told Thorgils how I needed to be back in Norton with all speed, and it sent a sort of chill through me to see him shake his head.

"There is need, truly," he said, "and all that may be done I will do. But yestermorn we found that we had sprung a plank or two just above the waterline, as we were in a bad berth for shelter. I made shift to get the ship to Tenby, but on one tack she leaks like a basket, and she must be repaired. It will take all today, and maybe tomorrow; but it shall be done, if we have to work double tides, or to make a cobbler's job of it in haste. I must be off therefore to see to it. But I hope, if wind will serve us we may sail for home tomorrow night. Tide serves about midnight, and waits for no man. You had better be with us betimes."

He saw that I seemed downcast, and added thoughtfully enough: "It is in my mind that you need have little care yet. Gerent will not let Owen out of his sight for some time, as I think, and danger begins when he is abroad alone, and carelessly. Maybe not till he is at Exeter."

Then he beckoned to the two Danes who were waiting him, and made them known to me after they had saluted the princess. Eric the chief was a fine old warrior, iron grey and strong, and the other was his son, who bade fair to be like his father in time. He was a sturdy young man, and wore his arms well. They shook hands with me frankly, and from their words it was plain that Thorgils had told my story at Tenby already.

"This is the sick man I told you of," he said now. "He turns out to be a Thane of Glastonbury, and Evan had a hand in some plot of the friends of Morgan. Took him by craft and brought him here for ransom, doubtless. I had not thought that man such a knave, and shall distrust my judgment of men sorely in future."

Then Nona asked them what they would with the prince, and Eric told her.

"The deer are in the valleys, Lady, and we came to tell the prince that we have harboured the great stag of twelve points in the woods beyond Caerau. Will it please him to join our hunt?"

"Doubtless," she said. "Now there is no time to be lost, for the day is high already."

"None the worse, Princess," said Eric. "The last snow is passing hourly."

So we went round to the front of the palace toward the gates, and there waited half a dozen more men and horses by a gathering of men on foot with a pack of great hounds, the like of which I had never seen. They were the Danish hounds, which had come hither with their masters, and were big and strong enough for any quarry, even were it the bear that yet lurked in the Welsh mountain wilds.

Then Howel came, and would have me mounted well, and in less than half an hour we were riding eastward along the ancient way they call the Ridgeway, which crowns the long hill between the sea and the valleys where lie the windings of Milford Haven. And so we went till we could see Tenby itself far off on its rocky ness, and at that point left Thorgils to go his way, while we turned northward into the inland valleys, and sought the deep combe where they had harboured the stag.

The snow lay here and there yet, but it was almost gone, and the going was somewhat heavy, but overhead the sky was soft and grey, and the wind was pleasant if chill. North and west it was, and that would be fair for our crossing, if only it would hold, as Thorgils deemed that it surely would.

Now it was good to hear the horn and the cheer of the hunters as they drew the deep cover for the deer, and the half-dozen couple of hounds that were held back in leash while the rest were at their work strained and whimpered to be with them. And at last the great stag broke from the cover, in no haste, but in a sort of disdain of those who had disturbed him, and after him came a few scurrying hinds who huddled to him for safely. They trotted to another cover, and after them streamed the hounds, and then the great stag was driven alone from his hiding, and so the pack was laid on and we were away.

He headed for the far waters of the haven I had seen glittering from the hilltop, even as Howel told me was likely, and the pace was fast at the first. So I settled myself to the work and rode as one should ride on another man's horse, and a good one, moreover, carefully enough. But these hills were easier than ours, for heather was none, and the loose stones that trouble us on Mendips and Quantocks were not to be seen. It was fair grass land mostly. So I let my horse go, and in a little while had forgotten aught but the sheer joy of the pace, and the cry of the great hounds, and the full delight of such a run as one dreams of. Whereby I have little more to tell thereof.

For a country may seem to be open enough as one looks down on it from a height, but as one crosses it the difference in what has seemed easy riding is soon plain. Long swells of rolling ground rise as it were from nothing, and deep valleys that had been unseen cross the path, and the clustered trees are found to be deep woods as they are neared. Then the man who knows the country has the advantage, and it is as well to follow him. But I was well mounted, and the pace was good where the gale had thinned the snow, and it came about that before I had time to think what Howel and Eric and the Danes who were on horseback were doing I rode down one side of a little cover, past which the deer had gone with the hounds close on him, while the rest went on the other. I heard one shout, but it did not come into my mind that it was to me, for I thought that they needs must follow, and did not look round. Then I had to turn off yet more to the right as the best way seemed to take me, and meanwhile they were off to the left.

So when I was clear of the thicket and could see across the open again I had lost them. Unless I could hear the hounds I had nothing to guide me, and I drew rein and listened for them. As I heard nothing I rode on until I had a stretch of open country before me, but there I could see no more. Afterwards I learned that the deer had turned and made for the hill again, but it did not seem likely that he would do so with the waters of the haven so close at hand as I could see them. It was more likely that he would head straight for them, and so I spurred on once more in that direction. It was certainly the best thing that I could do, and I had not far to go before a mile of the open water was before me. But there was nought on its banks but a row of patient herons, fishing or sleeping, and the sight of them told me that no man had passed this way for many a long hour.

I waited in that place for a few moments, to see if the deer made for the refuge of the water from some cover that as yet hid him from me, but he did not come. It was plain to me then that the hunt had doubled back and that I was fairly thrown out, and I went no farther. By this time Eric might be miles away, and I knew nothing of the lie of the land, save that along the crest of the Ridgeway ran the road from Tenby to Pembroke, and that once on that road I could make my way back in no long time. That, as it seemed to me, was the best thing that I could do, and I headed my horse at once for the hill, going slowly, for it was no great distance, and it was heavy going in the places where the snow had gathered in drifts. I thought that maybe I should cross the track of the horses and hounds, or hear Eric's horn before I had gone far, but I reached the foot of the hill without doing either.

Then I came to a place where the land began to draw upward more sharply, thickly timbered, with scattered rocks among the roots of the trees. Fox and badger and wildcat had their hiding places here, for I could trace them on all sides, and then I saw the track of a wolf, and that minded me, as that track in snow ever must, of Owen and the day when he came to my help at Eastdean. That is the clearest memory I have of my childhood.

Then I thought that I heard the horn, and stopped to listen, nor was it long before what I had heard came to my ears again. It was not the sound of the horn, however, but somewhat strange to me, and for a while I wondered what forest bird or beast had a note like that.

For the third time I heard it, and now it was plainly like the half-stifled cry of some one in pain among the trees to the right of me, and not far distant either. So I rode toward the place whence the cry seemed to come, and as I went I called. At that the voice rose more often, with some sound of entreaty in its tone, and it seemed to be trying to form words. I hastened then, crossing more wolf tracks on the way, and then I struck the trail of many men and a few horses; but these were not Eric's, for the hoof marks were rather those of ponies than of his tall steeds. I followed that track, for it seemed to lead toward the weary voice that I heard, and so I came to a circle of great oaks with a clear space of many paces wide between them, and there I found what I was seeking. It was piteous enough.

A man was tied to the greatest of the trees, with knees to chin, and bound ankles, while round his knees his hands were clasped and fastened so that a stout stake was thrust through, under his knees and over his elbows, trussing him helplessly. The cords that bound him to the tree were round his body in such wise that he could by no means fall on his side and so work himself free from the stake, and round his mouth was a ragged cloth tied, but not closely enough to prevent him from calling out as I heard him. I think that he must have gnawed it from closer binding than I saw now. Across the snow behind him the paws of some daring wolf had left marks as if the beast had sniffed at his very back not so long since, and surely but for the chance of my coming that way nought but his bones had been left in that place by the pack before morning came again.

It was a strange cry that this man gave when he saw me, for in no way could I take it for a cry of joy for rescue. I could rather think that he had raised the same when the wolf came near him. And when I dismounted and led my horse after me toward him he seemed to try to shrink from me, as if I also meant him harm. I thought that the poor soul had surely gone distracted with the fear of the forest beasts on him, so that he no longer knew friend from foe, and I wondered how long he had been bound here in this lonely place. I had seen no house or trace of men between here and Tenby.

I hitched the bridle rein over a low bough, and leaving my horse went toward him to set him loose, wondering who had left him here. And as I drew my seax and went to cut the lashings he writhed afresh and cried piteously for mercy in what sounded like bad Saxon from behind the cloth across his face, as though he deemed that I came to slay him. I did not notice the strangeness of his using my own tongue here in the heart of a Welsh land at the time, but thought he took me for one of those who had bound him.

"Fear not," I said, speaking in Welsh to comfort him.

And if anything, that seemed to terrify him yet more.

"Mercy, good Thane--mercy!" he mumbled from his half-stifled lips.

Then it seemed to me that it was strange that he knew what I was, and before I cut the bonds I took the cloth from his face, and lo! the man was Evan the outlaw, my enemy!

That told me why he feared me in good truth, for he had need to do so, and I stood back and looked at him with the bright weapon still in my hand, and he cried and begged for mercy unceasingly. It seemed but right that he should be bound helplessly as he had bound me, yet he had not the bitterness of seeing a friend look on him without knowing him as had I. It was a foe whom he saw, and that a righteous one.

Then I was minded to turn away and leave him where he was, until the foe from the forest looked on him for the last time, for it was all that he deserved, and I set my seax back in my belt and turned away to my horse with a great loathing of the man in my mind; and seeing that, he begged for mercy again most pitiably.

That is a hard thing to hear unmoved, and I stayed and looked at him again. My first wrath was leaving me as I saw the fullness of the end of his plans, and I do not think that it is in me to be utterly revengeful.

"What mercy can you hope from me!" I said coldly.

"None, Thane--none. But let me go hence with you. Better the rope than these wild beasts. Or slay me now, and swiftly."

"Who, of all your friends, tied you here?" I asked him.

"Howel's men," he answered. "They took my goods at the ford of Caerau yonder, and so brought me here and left me. That was early this morning."

"I marvel that you bided in reach of any who might speak with me," I said.

"My comrades left me, for fear of that same. I must hire ponies to get the goods away. I thought you had died on the wild sea that night."

"It seems to me that this is but justice on you. The goods you have lost were stolen from honest men. And it were just if I left you bound as you bound me."

Then the man said slowly: "Ay, it is justice. But will you treat me even as I treated you, Thane?"

I looked at him in some wonder. The man's face had grown calm, though it was yet grey and drawn, and this seemed as if he would own his fault without excuse. I minded that Nona the princess and her father, ay, and Thorgils, had said that they thought well of Evan the merchant up till this time.

"Supposing I let you go--What then?" I said.

"First of all, I would tell you somewhat for which you will thank me, Thane."

"Tell me that first," I said, not altogether believing that he had anything which could be worth my hearing, but with a full mind now to let him go.

Plainly, he had some sort of faith in me, or in the worth of what he had to say, for he began eagerly:

"Thane, when we took you, it was Owen of Cornwall for whom we waited. We were not minding you at all until we saw that we might hurt him through you."

"That I suppose. I know that you laid wait for Owen the prince."

"Ay, for you know the Welsh and heard all that we said. But listen, Thane, this is it. Eight of the friends of Morgan had sworn the death of Owen that morning, and it was the leader of them who set us on. He was not there, for he waited on another road."

"Were you one of the eight?"

"That I am not," he said. "I and my men were but hired, as Morgan was wont to hire us now and then. When we took you methought that it was well for me, for through you I might be inlawed again, even as I told you."

"Who was this leader?" I asked, heeding this last speech not at all.

"Tregoz of the Dart, men call him, for he holds lands thereon. Also there are these of the great men of Cornwall and Dyvnaint."

He called over the names of the other seven, and I repeated them that I should not forget. The only one that I had heard before was that of Tregoz. The outlaws had spoken of him, and now I remembered him as one of those who had seemed loudest in welcome to Owen when he came to Norton. So I told Evan, and he nodded.

"I heard him boast of the same," he said, and I believed him for the way in which he said it.

"How do they think to slay Owen, and wherefore?" I asked, and my blood ran cold at the thought of the treachery that was round him.

Doubtless this Tregoz was back at court.

"In any way that they may compass, and if in such a way as to stir up war with Ina of Wessex so much the better, as they say. It is revenge for the death of Morgan, and hatred of the Saxon, mixed."

"Is there any more that I should know?"

"None, Thane. But I have broken no oath in telling you this, as you might think. We outlaws were not bound, for there seemed no need."

It was strange that he should care to tell me this, being what he was. Once more I minded words of Thorgils--that the knave would beguile Loki himself with fair words. Yet there was somewhat very strange in all the looks and words of the man at this time. But I would not talk longer with him, and I cut his bonds and freed him.

He tried to rise and stretch his cramped limbs, groaning with the pain of them as he did so. And that grew on him so that of a sudden he swooned and fell all his length at my feet, and then I found myself kneeling and chafing the hands of this one who had bound me, so that he should come round the sooner. At last he opened his eyes, and I fetched the horn of strong mead that Howel had bidden his folk hang on my saddle bow when we rode out, and that brought him to himself again. He sat up on the snow and thanked me humbly.

"Now, what will you do?" I said. "Let me tell you that Thorgils is after you, and that Howel has set a price on your head, or was going to do so. And it is better that you cross the sea no more, for if ever any one of the men of Gerent or Ina catch you your life will be forfeit."

"I will get me to North Wales or Mercia, Thane, and there will I live honestly, and that I will swear. Only, I will pray you not to tell Howel that I am free."

"I am like to tell no man," I answered grimly. "For I should but be called a soft-hearted fool for my pains."

"Yet shall you be glad that you freed me. Bid Owen the prince look to the door before ever he opens it. Bid him wear his mail day and night, and never ride unguarded. Let him have one whom he trusts to sleep across his doorway, until Tregoz and his men are all accounted for."

"Well, then," I said, "farewell--as well as you shall deserve hereafter. You best know if you have one safe place left to you in England or in Wales."

"I was not all so bad until the law hounded me forth from men," he said. "I have yet places where I am held as an honest man."

Now I had enough of him, and I would not ask him more of himself yet I will say that my heart softened somewhat toward him, for I knew that here also he had been well thought of. Almost did I forget how he had treated me, for now that seemed a grudge against Tregoz. Maybe that was all foolishness on my part, but I am not ashamed thereof today, as I was then.

"Stay, have you any weapon?" I said, as I was turning away. "There are many ills that may befall an unarmed man in a wild country."

"There was a seax here," he said, rising stiffly. "They left it on the ground, that I might see help out of my reach, as it were. Ay, here it is."

He took it up, and I knew that after all he had felt somewhat as he had made me feel when I saw help close to me and might not have it. I pitied him, for I knew well what his torture had been. Ay, and I will tell this, that men may know how this terror burnt into me. Many a time have I let a trapped rat go, because I would not see the agony of dumb helplessness in anything. It frays me. There is no wonder that I set Evan free.

I said no more, but left him staring after me with the seax in his hand, and rode on my way, thinking most of all of the peril that was about Owen, and longing to be back with him that I might guard him. It seemed likely now that Gerent could take all these men whose names I had heard without the least trouble, for they could not deem that their plans were known. Ina would surely let me bide with my foster father till danger to him was past.

So I came into the road that runs along the top of the Ridgeway, and then I knew where I was. I could see the great ness of Tenby far before me across the hills, and presently at a turn in the road I saw Howel and Eric and his men ahead of me. They had taken the stag, and knew that I should make my way back, and so troubled not at all for me.

There Howel and I parted from the Danes, they going back to Tenby, while we returned slowly to Pembroke. And when we came to the palace yard we found a little train of horses and men there, as though some new guests had come in lately.

"I know who these will be," said Howel. "You will have company in your homeward crossing. Here is Dunwal of Devon, and his daughter, who have been on pilgrimage to St. Davids, for Christmastide. They knew that Nona returned at this time, and have come hither on the chance of a passage home in the ship which brought her. In good time they are, after all."

Presently I met these folk, and very courteous they were. Dunwal was a tall, very dark, man, who chose to hold that he was beholden to myself for the passage home, when he heard why I was sailing so soon. And his daughter was like him in many ways, being perhaps the very darkest damsel I have ever seen, though she was handsome withal. With them was a priest of the old Western Church, a Cornishman, with his outlandish tonsure. He was somewhat advanced in years, and strangely wild looking at times, though silent. He seemed to be Dunwal's chaplain, or else was a friend who had made the pilgrimage with him. His name was Morfed, they told me.

I do not think that I should have noted him much, but that when he heard my Saxon name he scowled heavily, and drew away from me; and presently, when it came to pass that Howel told Dunwal the news I had brought, I saw his eyes fixed on me in no friendly way as he listened. Nor did he join with his friends in the words of gladness for Owen's return, though indeed I had some thought that theirs might have been warmer. It was almost as if something was held back by the Devon man and his daughter, though why I should think so I could not tell. At all events, their way of receiving the news was not like that of Howel and Nona.

By and by, when we came to sit down at table in the largest room of the palace, bright with fair linen, and silver and gold and glass vessels before us, and soft and warm under foot with rugs on the tiled floor which hardly needed them, as I thought, there was a guest I was pleased to see. Thorgils had ridden from Tenby at the bidding of the princess, as it seemed, and his first words to me were of assurance that all went well for our sailing. The good ship would be ready for the tide of the morrow night. Pleased enough also he was with the chance of new passengers, as may be supposed.

I do not think that I have ever sat at a feast whereat so few were present at the high table, and there were no house-carles at all. Truly, the room was not large enough for what we deem that a king's board should be, but we seemed almost in private. There were not more than thirty guests altogether, but it was pleasant for all that. The princess was on the right of her father, and Mara, the daughter of Dunwal, on his left, but I sat next to Nona, and Dunwal to me again. On the other side of the prince were some of his own nobles, and across the room sat Thorgils next to the Cornish priest, among Welshmen of some lower rank. They seemed an ill-assorted pair, but Thorgils was plainly trying to be friendly with every one in reach of him, and soon I forgot him in the pleasantness of all that went on at our table.

However, by and by Howel said to Nona suddenly, in a low voice:

"Look yonder at the Norseman. He must be talking heathenry to yon priest, for the good man seems well-nigh wild. What can we do?"

Truly, the face of Morfed was black as thunder, while that of the Norseman was shining with delight in some long-winded story he was telling. The white-robed servants were clearing the tables at this moment, and the prince's bard, a fine old harper with golden collar and chain, was tuning his little gilded harp as if the time for song had come.

"Make him sing," said Nona. "I bade him here tonight that he might do so. He has some wondrous tale to tell us."

Howel beckoned to the harper, and signed to him, and the old man rose at once and went to Thorgils. It was not the first time that he had sung here, it was plain. Then I noted that the priest was scowling fiercely at myself, and I wondered idly why. I supposed, so far as I troubled to think thereof that he was one of those who hated the very name of Saxon.

Now Thorgils took the harp without demur, smiling at the bard in thanks, and so came forward into the space round which the tables were set, while a silence fell on the company.

"If my song goeth not smoothly in the British tongue, Prince, forgive me. I can but do my best. Truly, I have even now asked my neighbour, Father Morfed, if it is fairly rendered, but I have not had his answer yet."

He ran his hand over the already tuned strings, and lifted his voice and began. It was not the first time that he had handled a British harp, by any means, but if he played well he sang better. I do not think that one need want to hear a finer voice than his; and though he had seen fit to doubt his powers, his Welsh was as good as mine, and maybe, by reason of constant use, far more easy.

And next moment I knew that he was going to sing nothing more or less than of King Ina's Yule feast, and what happened thereat. He had promised to tell the princess the story, and this was her doing, of course. I could not stop him, and there I must sit and listen to as highly coloured a tale as a poet could make of it. Once he saw that I was growing red, and he grinned gently at me across the harp, and worked up the struggle still more terribly. And all the while Morfed the priest glowered at me, until at length he rose and left the room.

I was glad enough when Thorgils ended that song, but Nona must ask him for yet another, and that pleased him, of course, and he began once more. This time he sang, to my great confusion, of the drinking of the bowl, and of my vow, and I wished that I was anywhere but in Pembroke, or that I could reach the three-legged stool on which he was perched from under him. I never knew a man easy while the gleemen sang his deeds, save Ina, who was used to it, and never listened; and I knew not where to look, though maybe more than half the folk present did not understand that I was the hero of the song. Nevertheless, I had to put up with it, till he ended with a verse or two of praise of our host and of the princess who loved the songs of the bard, and so took his applause with a happy smile and went and sat down, while Nona bade her maidens bear a golden cup and wine to him.

Then the princess turned to me with a quiet smile that had some mischief in it.

"This last is more than I had thought to hear, Thane," she said; "you told us nought of yourself and the lady Elfrida when we rode from the hermit's."

And so she must ask me many questions, under cover of some chant which the old bard began, and she drew my tale from me easily enough, and maybe learnt more than I thought I told her, for before long she said:

"Then it seems that, after all, you are not so sure that the lady is pleased with you for your vow?"

And in all honesty I was forced to own that I was not. I suppose I showed pretty plainly that I thought myself aggrieved in the matter, for the princess smiled at me.

"Wait till you see how she meets you when you return, Thane. No need to despair till then."

It came into my mind to say that I did not much care how I was met, but I forbore. Maybe it was not true. And then the princess and the three or four other ladies who were present rose and left the table, and thereafter we spoke of nought but sport and war, and I need not tell of all that. But when I went to my chamber presently, and the two pages were about to leave me to myself some three hours or so after the princess left the board, one of them lingered for a moment behind the other, and so handed me a folded and sealed paper.

"I pray you read this, Thane," he said, and was gone.

It was written in a fair hand, that did not seem as that of any inky-fingered lay brother, but as I read the few words that were written I knew whose it was, for none but Nona would have written it.

"Have a care, Thane. I have spoken with Mara, and I fear trouble. Dunwal her father is, with Tregoz his brother, at the right hand of the men who follow Morgan. Morfed the priest is a hater of all that may make for peace with the Saxon. He is well-nigh distraught with hatred of your kin."

Then there were a few words crossed out, and that was all. And to tell the truth, it was quite enough. But as I came to think over the matter, it seemed to me that until Dunwal knew that it was his brother who had tried to get rid of me I need not fear him. As for the priest, his hatred would hardly lead him to harm the son of Owen.

So I slept none the less easily, but from my heart I thanked the princess for the warning. It should not be my fault if Dunwal had much power for harm when once I met Gerent.

CHAPTER IX
WHY IT WAS NOT GOOD FOR OWEN TO SLEEP IN THE MOONLIGHT.

It needs not that I should tell of the farewell of the next day. I went from Pembroke with many messages for Owen, and a promise that if I might ever come over with him I would do so. The princess was busy with the lady who was to cross with Thorgils, and I did not find one chance of telling her that I thanked her for her warning, but I found the page who gave me the letter, and bade him tell his mistress when we had gone that she had taught me to look in the face of a fellow passenger, which would be token enough that I understood.

Dunwal and his daughter had some few men and pack horses with them, and one Cornish maiden who attended Mara, so that we were quite a little train as we rode from Pembroke toward Tenby in the late afternoon, with a score of Howel's guards to care for us in all honour. Part of the way, too, Howel rode, and when we came to the hill above the Caerau woods, and looked down on the winding waters again, he said to me:

"I have forgotten to tell you that my men took Evan. By this time he has met his deserts. I have done full justice on him."

"Thanks, Prince," I said with a shudder, as I minded what I had saved the man from. "Did your men question him?"

Howel smote his thigh.

"Overhaste again!" he cried in vexation. "That should have been done; but I bade them do justice on him straightway if they laid hands on him. They did it."

I said no more, nor did the prince. It was in my mind that he was blaming himself for somewhat more than carelessness. So presently he must turn and leave us, and we bade him farewell with all thanks for hospitality, and he bade me not forget Pembroke, and went his way.

Then I found Dunwal pleasant enough as a companion, and so also was Mara, and the few miles passed quickly, until we rode through the gates of the strong stockade which bars the way to the Danes' town across the narrow neck of the long sea-beaten tongue of cliff they have chosen to set their place on. The sea is on either side, and at the end is an island that they hold as their last refuge if need is, while their ships are safe under one lee or the other from any wind that blows.

Far down below us at the cliff's foot, as we rode through the town, where the houses had been set anywise, like those at Watchet, and were like them timber built, we could see to our left a little wharf, and beside it the ship that waited us. And the wind was fair, and the winter weather soft as one might wish it for the crossing.

Now, so soon as Thorgils had seen the baggage of the Cornish folk safely bestowed I had time for a word with him, taking him apart and walking up the steep hill path from the haven for a little way, as if to go to the town. And so I told him who this man was, and what possible danger might be.

He heard with a long whistle of dismay:

"'Tis nigh as bad as crossing with Evan," he said--"but one is warned. Let them have the after cabin, and do you take the forward one; it will be safer. Leave me to see to him when we get to Watchet, for it is in my mind that Gerent will want him. Moreover, so long as he thinks that you fear him not he will be careless, and I will watch him. He will want to learn more before he meddles with you. As for the priest, I will tend him."

So we were content to leave the matter. Presently, when we were at sea, I do not think that Dunwal or Morfed had spirit left to care for aught. I know that I had not. I need not speak of that voyage, save to say that it was speedy, and fair--to the mind of Thorgils, at least.

At last I slept, nor did I wake till we had been alongside the wharf at Watchet for two hours, being worn out. Then I found that Dunwal and his party had gone already, and I wondered, with a mind to be angry, whereat Thorgils laughed.

"I have even sent them on to Norton with a few of our men to help him, and they will see that he goes there and nowhere else. You will find him waiting. I did not want him to fall on you on the road."

"What is the news?" I asked. "Have you heard aught?"

"The best, I think. Gerent is hunting Tregoz, and Owen has swept up every outlaw from the Quantocks. Our folk helped him. Some of them told all they knew when they were taken."

"Then," I said gladly, "Owen knows that I am safe."

"Not so certainly," Thorgils said. "None of our folk can say that you crossed with me, and as this is the only ship afloat at this time of the year there is doubt as to where you are. It will be good for Owen to see you again. What a tale you have for him! On my word, I envy you the telling."

"Well, then, ride with me to Norton straightway, and you shall tell all and save me words. Owen shall thank you also for your care for me."

"What, for letting you sit on my deck while the wind blew? Nay, but there are no thanks needed between us. You and I have seen a strange voyage together, and it has ended well. Maybe you and I will see more sport yet side by side, for I think that we are good comrades. Let us be going, then, for it was in my mind that I could not rest until I had seen you safe to your journey's end."

Then I found that he had his own horses ready for us, and two more men, well armed and mounted also, were waiting with them on the green where I had been set down in the litter. So in a very short time Thorgils had told his men all that he would have done about the ship, and we were riding fast along the road to Norton, while the thawing snow told of the going of the frost at last.

I had been gone but these few days, but each of them seemed like a month to look back upon as I rode under the shadow of the hills that I had last seen as a hopeless captive. It grew warm and soft as the midday sun shone on us, and the road was muddy underfoot with the chill water that had filled all the brooks again, but I hardly noticed the change, so eager was I to be back. Glad enough I was when we saw the village and the mighty earthworks above it, and yet more glad when the guards at the gate told us that Owen was even now in the palace.

I left Thorgils and his men to the care of the guard for the time, while I went straightway to the entrance doors and asked for speech with him.

"It is the word of the king that you shall have free admittance into the palace and to himself at any time, Thane," the captain of the guards said.

So I passed into the great chamber of the palace that was used as audience hall for all comers, and also as the court of justice.

The place was full of people, and those mostly nobles, so that I had to stand in the doorway for a moment to see what was going on. It was plainly somewhat out of the common, for there were guards along one end of the room. It seemed as if there were a trial.

Gerent sat in the great chair which one might call his throne at the upper end of the room, and beside him was Owen. I thought that my foster father seemed pale and troubled in that first glance, but I had every reason to know why this was so. Before these two stood a man, with his back to me therefore, and for the moment I did not recognise him. On either side of this man were guards, and it was plainly he who was in trouble, if any one. Gerent was speaking to him.

"Well," he said, "hither you have come as a guest, and as a guest you shall be treated. But you must know that here within the walls of the place you shall abide. If you will give your word to do that I shall not have to keep you so closely."

"This is not what I had looked for from you, King Gerent," the man said.

I knew the voice at once, for it was that of Dunwal, my fellow passenger. So the treachery of his brother must be known, and he was to be held here as a hostage, as one might say. Gerent's next words told me that it was so.

"If there is any fault to be found, it is in the ways of your brother. Blame him that I must needs have surety for his behaviour. It cannot be suffered that he should go on plotting evil against us, unchecked in some way."

Dunwal shrugged his shoulders, as if to say that all this was no concern of his.

"Shall you hold my daughter as well?" he said. "I trust that your caution will not make you go so far as that."

Gerent's eyes flashed at the tone and words, but he answered very coldly:

"She will bide here also, and in all honour."

Then he beckoned to a noble who stood near him, and spoke to him for a moment. It chanced that this was one of the very few whom I knew here. His name was Jago, and I had often seen him at Glastonbury, for he was a friend of our ealdorman, Elfrida's father, holding somewhat the same post in Norton as my friend in our town. Owen liked him well also, and he was certainly no friend to Morgan and his party.

"Jago's wife will give your daughter all hospitality in his house," Gerent said, turning again to Dunwal. "Have I your word as to keeping within bounds during my pleasure?"

"Ay, you have it," answered Dunwal curtly.

Then I slipped out of the door quietly, and went to that room where Owen and I waited on our first coming here, and I sent a steward to tell him of my arrival. There is no need for me to tell how he greeted me, or how I met him.

Then when those greetings were over I heard all that had been going on, and my loss had made turmoil enough. My men had brought back the news, having missed me very shortly, but it was long before they found traces of me. The first thing that they saw was my hawk, as I expected, and after that the bodies of the slain. As I was not with them, they judged that I had escaped in some way, but they lost the track of the feet in the woodlands, and so rode back to Owen in all haste.

Then was a great gathering of men for the hunting of the outlaws, for it would take a small army to search the wild hills and woodlands of the Quantocks to any effect. The whole countryside turned out gladly, and the Watchet Norsemen helped also.

In the end, on the next day they penned the outlaws into some combe, and took most of them, and then all was told by them, so far as they knew it. Gerent laid hands on four of the men who had sworn the oath Evan told me of, that evening after some leading outlaw had given their names, but Tregoz had escaped.

He had been one of the most active in the matter of the hunt, to all seeming, and had ridden out with Owen and Jago and the rest. Then he took advantage of some turn in the hills, when men began to scatter, and was no more seen. Presently it was plain enough why this was, when those who were taken were made to speak. Yet it seemed that he was not so far off, for already an attack had been made on Owen as he rode beyond the village, though it was no very dangerous one. Now it was to be hoped that the danger from him was past, for his brother had been taken the moment he rode into the gate, and he would suffer if more harm was done.

Then I asked if our king had been told of all this, and I learnt that he had heard at once, and had written back to Owen to say that he would pay any ransom that might be asked for me if I yet lived, as was hoped. The outlaws had told of Evan's plan, but it was not known if I had been taken out of the country yet.

"All is well that ends well," Owen said; "but I asked Ina not to say aught of the matter yet for a while. There is one at least in Glastonbury who might be sorely terrified for you."

He laughed at my red face, for I knew that he meant Elfrida. It was in my mind, however, that I wished she had heard, for then, perhaps, she would have been sorry that she had not been kinder to me--unless, indeed, she was glad that I was out of the way, in all truth.

Then there was my own long tale to be told, and of course I told Owen all. It was good to hear him say that he himself could have done nought but free Evan.

Thereafter we sought Thorgils, who was happy in the guardroom, and had seemingly been telling my tale there, for the men stared at me somewhat. I do not suppose that it lost in the telling.

Owen thanked him for his help, and took him to see Gerent; which saved me words, for the Norseman must needs tell how Evan had brought me on board his ship, and so we even let him say all that there was to be said.

After that Gerent loaded him with presents, and so let him go well pleased.

I went out to his horse with him, and saw him start. His last word as he parted from me was that if I needed a good axeman at my back at any time I was to send for him, and so he went seaward, singing to himself, with the men who had brought Dunwal hither behind him.

After that there was more to say of Howel and his court. It seemed that Gerent and Owen liked him well, and I wondered that Owen had not sought him when the trouble fell on him. I think he would not go to Dyfed as a disgraced man, for I know he could not clear himself at the time.

Now at supper, presently, there was Dunwal, looking anxious, as I thought, but trying not to shew it. His daughter Mara was there also, and as it happened she sat next to me. I suppose the seneschal set her there as we had crossed from Dyfed together, unless she had asked it, or gone to that seat without asking. She was very pleasant, talking of the troubles of the voyage, and so went on to speak sadly enough of the greater trouble that had waited her.

"I am glad the king has kept us, however," she said. "I can be content with the court rather than with our wild Dartmoor, as you may guess. But all these things are too hard for me, and how any man can plot against so wonderful looking a prince as Owen passes me. I cannot but think that there is some mistake, and that my uncle has no hand in the affair. That will be proved ere long, I do believe."

I answered that indeed I hoped that it would prove so, and then asked for Morfed, the priest who had crossed with us, as I did not see him among the other clergy at the table. She told me that he had left them, on foot, at the gate of Watchet, making his way westward, as she believed. He had only joined their party for easier travelling in Dyfed.

Then she must needs ask me questions about Thorgils' song, and specially of Elfrida. I had no mind to tell her much, but it is hard to refuse to answer a lady who speaks in all friendly wise and pleasantly, so that I had to tell her much the same that I told Nona the princess, and began to wonder if every lady who had the chance would be as curious to know all about what story there was. And that was a true foreboding of mine, for so it was, until I grew used to it. But all this minded me of Nona and her warning, and I was half sorry that the priest had not come here, to be taken care of with Dunwal.

After that night we saw little of these two. Mara went to the house of Jago, and Dunwal kept to himself about the palace boundaries within the old ramparts, and seemed to shun notice. As for me, word went to Ina that all was well, and he sent a letter back to say that it would please him to know that I was with Owen for a time yet. So I bided with him, and for a time all went well, for we heard nought of Tregoz in any way, while another of his friends was taken and imprisoned in some western fortress of Gerent's. Nor were there any more attacks made on Owen, so that after a little while we went about, hunting and hawking, in all freedom, for danger seemed to have passed with the taking of Dunwal as hostage.

Then one day a guard from the gate brought me a folded paper, on which my name was written in a fair hand, saying that it had been left for me by a swineherd from the hill, who said that it was from some mass priest whom I knew. The guard had let the man go away, deeming that, of course, there was no need to keep him. Nor had they asked who the priest might be, as it was said that I knew him.

I took the letter idly and went to my stables with it in my hand, and opened and read it as I walked.

"To Oswald, son of Owen.--It is not good to sleep in the moonlight."

That was all it said, and there was no name at the end of it. I thought it foolish enough, for every one knows that the cold white light of the moon is held to be harmful for sleepers in the open air. But I was not in the way of sleeping out in this early season with its cold, though, of course, it was always possible that one might be belated on the hills and have to make a night in the heather of it when hunting on Exmoor or the Brendons. There was not much moon left now, either.

So I showed the note to Owen presently, and he puzzled over it, seeing that it could not have been sent for nothing. At last we both thought that whoever wrote it, or had it written, knew that some attack would be made on us with the next moon, when it would be likely that we might be riding homeward by its light with no care against foes. That might well be called "sleeping in the moonlight" as things were; and at all events we were warned in time. The trouble to me was that it seemed to say that danger was not all past.

However, when there was no moon at all I forgot the letter for the time, no more trouble cropping up, and but for a chance word I think that it had not come into my mind again until we were out in the moonlight at some time. As we sat at table one evening when the moon was almost at the full again, some one spoke of moonstruck men, and that minded me, and set me thinking. He said that once he himself had had a sore pain in the face by reason of the moonlight falling on it when he was asleep, and another told somewhat the same, until the talk drifted away to other things and they forgot it. But now I remembered how that at our first coming here I had waked in the early hours and seen a patch of moonlight from a high southern window on the outer wall of the palace passing across Owen's breast as he slept. Then I was on the floor across the door, but now I slept in the same place that Owen had that night, while he was on the couch across the room and under the window. It was possible, therefore, that the light did fall on my face, but I was pretty sure that if so it would have waked me.

At all events, if the letter had aught to do with that, it was a cumbrous way of letting me know that my bed was in a bad place for quiet sleep. The only thing that seemed likely thus was that the good priest who wrote had left the palace before he had remembered to tell me how he had fared in that room once, and so sent back word. There were many priests backward and forward here, as at Glastonbury with Ina. Then it seemed plain that this was the meaning of the whole thing, and so I would hang a cloak over the window by and by.

And, of course, having settled the question in my own mind, I forgot to do that, and was like to have paid dearly for forgetting.

Two nights afterward, when the moon was at the full, I woke from sleep suddenly with the surety that I heard my name called softly. I was wide awake in a moment, and found the room bright with moonlight that did indeed lie in a broad square right across my chest on the furs that covered me. I glanced across to Owen, but he was asleep, as there was full light enough to see, and then I wondered why I seemed to have heard that call. In a few moments I knew that, and also that the voice I heard was the one that had come to me in sore danger before.

Idly and almost sleeping again I watched the light, to see if indeed it was going to cross my face, and then a sudden shadow flitted across it, and with a hiss and flick of feathers a long arrow fled through the window and stuck in the plaster of the wall not an inch above my chest, furrowing the fur of the white bearskin over me, so close was it.

In a moment I was on the floor, with a call to Owen, and it was well that I had the sense to swing myself clear from the light and leap from the head of the bed, for even as my feet touched the floor a second arrow came and struck fairly in the very place where I had been, and stood quivering in the bedding.

Then was a yell from outside, and before Owen could stay me I looked through the window, recklessly enough maybe, but with a feeling that no more arrows would come now that the archer was disturbed. It needed more than a careless aim to shoot so well into that narrow slit. Across the window I could see the black line of the earthworks against the light some fifty paces from the wall of the palace, with no building between them on this side at all; and on the rampart struggled two figures, wrestling fiercely in silence. One was a man whose armour sparkled and gleamed under the moon, and the other seemed to be unarmed, unless, indeed, that was a broad knife he had in his hand. Then Owen pulled me aside.

"The sentry has him," he said, after a hurried glance. "Let us out into the light, for there may be more on hand yet."

Now I hurried on my arms, but another look showed me nothing but the bare top of the rampart. No sign of the men remained. I could hear voices and the sounds of men running in the quiet, and I thought these came from the guard, who were hurrying up from the gate.

"The men have rolled into the ditch," I said. "I can see nothing now."

Then we ran out, bidding the captain of the guard to stand to arms as we passed through the great door of the palace, and so we went round to the place whence the arrows had come. A score of men from the gate were already clustered there on the earthworks, talking fast as Welshmen will, but heedful to challenge us as we came. I saw that they had somewhat on the ground in the midst of them.

"Here is a strange affair, my Prince," one of them said, as he held out his hand to help Owen up the earthworks.

The group stood aside for us to look on what they had found, and that was a man, fully armed in the Welsh way of Gerent's guards, but slain by the well-aimed blow of a strong seax that was yet left where it had been driven home above the corselet. There was a war bow and two more arrows lying at the foot of the rampart, as if they had been wrested from the hand of the archer and flung there. The men had not seen these, but I looked for them at once when I saw that there was no bow on the slain man.

"Who is this?" Owen said gravely, and without looking closely as yet.

"It is Tregoz of the Dart, whom the king seeks," one or two of the men said at once.

I had known that it must be he in my own mind before the name was spoken. There fell a silence on the rest as the name was told, and all looked at my foster father. There was plainly some fault in the watching of the rampart that had let the traitor find his way here at all.

"Which of you was it who slew him?" asked Owen.

"None of us, Lord. We cannot tell who it may have been. Even the sentry who keeps this beat is gone."

"Doubtless it was he who slew him, and is himself wounded in the fosse. Look for him straightway."

There they hunted, but the man was not to be found. Nor was it his weapon that had ended Tregoz.

Then Owen said in a voice that had grown very stern: "Who was the sentry who should have been here?"

The men looked at one another, and the chief of them answered at last that the man was from Dartmoor, one of such a name. And then one looked more closely at the arms Tregoz wore, and cried out that they were the very arms of the missing sentry, or so like them that one must wait for daylight to say for certain that they were not they.

It was plain enough then. In such arms Tregoz could well walk through the village itself unnoticed, as one of the palace guards would be, and so when the time came he would climb from some hiding in the fosse and take the place of his countryman on the rampart, and the watchful captain would see but a sentry there and deem that all was well.

Yet this did not tell us who was the one who had wrestled with and slain him, and Owen told what had been done, while I went and brought the bow and arrows from the foot of the rampart, in hopes that they might tell us by mark or make if more than Tregoz and the sentry were in this business. Then I looked at my window, and, though narrow, it was as fair a mark in the moonlight as one would need. Without letting my shadow fall on the sleeper, it was possible to see my couch and the white furs on it, though it would be needful to raise the arm across the moonlight in the act of shooting. It was all well planned, but it needed a first-rate bowman.

"It was surely Tregoz who shot," one of the men said. "The sentry who was here was a bungler with a bow. None whom we know but Tregoz could have made sure of that mark, bright as the night is. Well it was, Lord, that you were not sleeping in your wonted place."

Owen glanced at me to warn me to say nothing, and bade the men take the body to the guardroom. They were already cursing the sentry who had brought shame on their ranks by leaguing himself with a traitor, and it was plain that there was no need to bid them lay hands on him if they could. That was a matter that concerned their own honour.

So we left the guarding of the place in their hands, and they doubled the watches from that time forward. Then we went and spoke with the captain of the guard, who yet kept his post at the doors, as none had called him.

"Maybe I am to blame," he said, when he heard all. "I should not have left a Dartmoor man from the country whence Tregoz came to keep watch there. I knew that he was thence, and thought no harm."

"There is no blame to you," Owen said. "It is not possible to look for such treachery among our own men."

Then we went into our room to show the captain what had been done. And thence the two arrows had already been taken. The hole in the plaster where the first struck was yet there, and the slit made by the second in the tough hide of the bear was to be seen when I turned over the fur, but who had taken them we could not tell. Only, it was plain that here in the palace some one was in the plot and had taken away what might be proof of who the archer had been, not knowing, as I suppose, that the attempt had failed so utterly. For an arrow will often prove a good witness, as men will use only some special pattern that they are sure of, and will often mark them that they may claim them and their own game in the woodlands if they are found in some stricken beast that has got away for a time. It was more than likely that Tregoz would have been careful to use only such arrows as he knew well in a matter needing such close shooting as this. Indeed, we afterwards found men who knew the two shafts from the rampart as those of the Cornishman, without doubt.

This I did not like at all, for the going of these arrows brought the danger to our very door, as it were. Nor did the captain, for he himself kept watch over us for the rest of that night, and afterwards there was always a sentry in the passage that led to our room.

We were silent as we lay down again, and sleep was long in coming. I puzzled over all this, for beside the taking of the arrows there was the question of who the slayer of Tregoz might be, and who had written the letter that should have warned us.

In all truth, it was not good to sleep in the moonlight!

Somewhat of the same kind Owen was thinking, for of a sudden he said to me: "Those arrows were meant for me, Oswald. Did you note what the man said about my not sleeping in my wonted place?"

"Ay, but I did not know that you had slept on this side. Since I came back, at least, you have not done so."

Owen smiled.

"No, I have not," he said; "but in the old days that was always my place, and you will mind that there I slept on the night we first were here together. That was of old habit, and I only shifted to this side when you came back, because I knew that you would like the first light to wake you. Every sentry who crosses the window on the rampart can see in here if it is light within, but he could not tell that we had changed places, for the face of the sleeper is hidden."

Then he laughed a little, and added:

"In the old days when I was in charge of the palace this face of the ramparts was always the best watched, because the men knew that if I waked and did not see the shadow of the sentry pass and repass as often as it should, he was certain to hear of it in the morning. Tregoz would know that old jest. I suppose Dunwal may have had some hand in taking the arrows hence."

"It is likely enough," I answered. "He will have to pay for his brother's deed tomorrow, in all likelihood, also. But who wrote the letter, and who slew Tregoz?"

Owen thought for a little while.

"Mara, Dunwal's daughter, is the most likely person to have written," he said. "It would be like a woman to do so, and she seems at least no enemy. Maybe the man was the sentry, after all, and fled because he had given up his arms, and so was sharer in the deed that he repented of. Or he may have been some friend of ours, or foe of the Cornishman, who would not wait for the rough handling of the guard when they found him there where he should not be. No doubt we shall hear of him soon or late."

But we did not. There was no trace of him, or of the writer of the letter. One may imagine the fury of Gerent when he heard all this in the morning, but even his wrath could not make Dunwal speak of aught that he might know. But for the pleading of Owen, the old king would have hung him then and there, and all that my foster father could gain for him was his life. Into the terrible old Roman dungeon, pit-like, with only a round hole in the stone covering of it through which a prisoner was lowered, he was thrown, and there he bided all the time I was at Norton.

By all right the lands of these two fell again into the hands of the king, and he would give them to Owen.

"Take them," he said, when Owen would not do so at first: "they owe you amends. If you do not want them yourself, wait until you sit in my seat, and then give them to Oswald, that he may have good reason for leaving Ina for you."

So Owen held them for me, as it were, and was content. Some day they might be mine, if not in the days of Ina, whom we loved.

But Gerent either forgot or cared not to think of Mara, Dunwal's daughter, and she bided in the best house in the town, with Jago's wife, none hindering her in anything. There was no more sign of trouble now that Tregoz and his brother were out of the way.

CHAPTER X
HOW THE EASTDEAN MANORS AND SOMEWHAT MORE PASSED FROM OSWALD TO ERPWALD.

I bided at Norton with Owen until the Lententide drew near, and then I must needs go back to my place with Ina. Maybe I should have gone before this, seeing that all was safe now, but our king had been on progress about the country, to Chippenham, and so to Reading and thence to London, and but half his guard was with him, so that I was not needed. Now he was back at Glastonbury, and I must join him there and go back to royal Winchester with him for the Easter feast.

Owen and I also had been far westward at one time or another, in this space, though there is little worth telling beyond that we went even to the lands of Tregoz that had passed to him, and so took possession of them. I could not see that any of the folk on those lands, whether free or thrall, seemed other than glad that Owen was their lord now. It was said that Tregoz was little loved. We left a new steward in the great half-stone and half-timber house, with house-carles enough to see that none harmed either him or the place, and so came back to Norton.

Now, one may say that all this time, seeing that Glastonbury was but so short a distance from Norton, I was a laggard lover not to have ridden over to see Elfrida, and maybe it would be of little use for me to deny it. However, I would have it remembered that there was always fear for Owen in my mind if I was apart from him at the first, and then there was this westward journey, and the hunting in new places, and many other things, so that the time slipped by all too quickly. Also, when it is easy to go to a place one is apt to say that tomorrow will do, and, as every one knows, tomorrow never comes. Nor had we said much of that damsel; if Owen had not altogether forgotten my oath, he never spoke of it, nor did I care to remind him. Nevertheless, whenever we spoke of Howel and his daughter, Owen's godchild, I minded that the princess had bidden me see how Elfrida greeted me when I came back, and it was in my mind that she would be no less glad to see me after a long absence.

That I should find out very shortly, but the thought troubled me little. I will say that the parting from Owen was all that was of consequence to me, for it was hard enough. I could not tell when we should meet again, for I must go east and he west now, and presently all Devon, and maybe Cornwall, would lie between us, even when our court was at Glastonbury. It would be hard to see him at all in the coming days, for not often was Gerent here. However, partings must needs be, and we made the least of it, and so at last we rode together to the old bridge that crosses the Parrett, and there bade our last farewells, and went our ways, not looking back.

It was a lonesome ride onward for me after all these days with him, and I had not a word for my house-carles, who had ridden from Glastonbury hither to meet me, for the first few miles. Then I bethought myself, and drew rein a little and let them come up with me, for I had ridden alone at their head for a while, and so heard all the news of the court and whatever talk was going about the place, and my mind left Norton and went on, as it were, before me to Glastonbury and all that I should see there.

There was a warm welcome waiting for me from the many friends, and best of all from the king himself. With him I sat long in his chamber telling of my doings and of Owen, and hearing also of what had been going on. At the last, when I was about to leave his presence, he said:

"There is one matter that we must speak of tomorrow, for it is weighty and needs thought. Let it bide now, for it is nought unhappy, and so come to me at noon and we will speak thereof. Now your friends will seek you, and I will not say more."

I left him then with a little wonder as to what this business might be, but thought little of it, as it would very likely be a matter of taking some men on some errand or the like house-carle work, and then I bethought me that I would even go and see how fared Elfrida. It was not unpleasant to think of taking her by surprise, for I did not suppose that she had heard of my return yet. At all events, she would have no chance of making up some stiff greeting for me. Wherefore I went down the street with my head in the air, making up my mind how I would greet her, and maybe I thought of a dozen ways before I reached the ealdorman's door.

His welcome was hearty enough at all events, but before I could make up my mind to ask for Elfrida, who was not to be seen at first, though I had counted on finding her at her wheel in the great hall of the house, as was her wont in the afternoon, he had wasted a long hour in hearing all that he could of my affairs, as may be supposed. There had been some strange rumours flying about since I was lost. I began to wish that I had brought Thorgils home with me, for it was plain that I should have to go over all this too often, and he cared not at all how many times he told the same tale.

At last I was able to find a chance of asking how fared the lady Elfrida, and at that the ealdorman laughed.

"What, has not all this put that foolishness out of your head?" he said.

"No, it has not," I answered pretty shortly.

But all the same, the old thought that I had remembered her less than I would have it known did flash across me for a moment.

"Well, I will send for her, and she will tell you for herself how she fares."

He sent, and then in about half an hour she came, just as I was thinking I would wait no longer. And if she had been stiff with me in the orchard it was even more so now, and I did not seem to get on with her at all. She said, indeed, that she was glad to see me back, but in no way could I think that she looked more so than any one else I had met.

So we talked a little, and then all of a sudden her father said:

"Ho!--Here comes that South Saxon again."

Then at once a blush crept slowly over her fair face, and she tried not to look toward the great door in vain, though no one came in, and presently she was gone with but a few words to me. I did not like this at all, but the ealdorman laughed at her and then at me, the more that he saw that I was put out.

"Never mind, Oswald," he said. "That vow of yours pledged you to no more than duty to any fair lady."

"Maybe it is just as well that it did not," I answered, trying to laugh also.

"Ay, that is right. You were bound to say somewhat, and you did it well. But it has not pleased the girl, nevertheless."

"I did think, at least, she would have been more glad to see me."

"Trouble yourself not at all about the ways of damsels for the next five years, or maybe ten, Oswald, my friend," said the ealdorman. "So will you have an easier life, and maybe a longer one."

Discontented enough I went away, and that same discontent lasted for a full half-hour. At the end of that time I found myself laughing at the antics of two boys who were sporting on a flooded meadow in a great brew tub, while their mother threatened them with a stick from the bank. It was my thought that a cake would have fetched them back sooner than the stick, but maybe she knew best. It was like a hen with ducklings.

Then I grew tired of loitering outside the town and nursing my wounded pride, and when it began to rain I forgot it, and went back to the palace and talked about the British warriors with Nunna and some of the other young thanes until supper time.

Next morning I waited on the king as he had bidden me, finding him in his chamber with a pile of great parchments and the like before him. He bade me be seated, and I sat in the window seat opposite him.

"It is no light matter that I have to speak of," he said, "but I will get to the point straightway. What do you remember of your old home, Eastdean?"

Now the thoughts of old days there that had sprung afresh in my mind in the parting with Owen, made me ready to answer that at once.

"Little, my King. I was but ten years old when we fled," I answered therefore.

"That is likely. But would you go back there? As the Thane of Eastdean, I mean; for I know that you would wish to see the place where your father lies."

I could not answer him this at once, for it was indeed a matter that needed thought. So I said, and he turned to his writings with a nod and left me to myself.

In all these thoughts of mine, pleasant as they were with some memories, it had never come to me to wish that the lands were mine again. Save for that one thing of which Ina spoke, and for the pleasantness of seeing old scenes again, I had never cared to go back. Owen had not spoken of the lands that should have been mine for years, and even as he talked with me and Gerent he had not seemed to remember that old loss at all. Gerent had done so, saying that I should be back there, but even that did not stir me now. I was of the court, and here I had my place, and all my life was knit with the ways of the atheling guard and the ordering of the house-carles under Owen. If I were to turn from all this to become a forest thane it would be banishment.

And then I thought of Owen, and how this would take me yet farther from him. I would sooner, if I must be sent from Ina, go to him and find what home I might on the lands of Tregoz in wild Dartmoor. And then the thought of leaving Ina, who had cared for me since I was a child, was almost as terrible.

"I would not leave you, my King," I said at last.

Ina looked up at me with a smile, but was silent, stroking his beard as was his way when thinking, looking past me out of the narrow window to the great Tor that towered beyond the new abbey buildings.

"Think!" he said at last--"partings must come, and lands are not to be had lightly. Erpwald's brother, who held Eastdean, is dead."

"I need no lands," I answered. "The ways of a captain of your house-carles are good to me, and I need no more. If I took those lands from your hand, my King, needs must that I gave up all the life with you. Sooner would I let the land go and bide with you. Yet if I must needs take them, be it as you will."

"It is a great thing that you speak so lightly of giving up," he answered gravely; "Erpwald, the heathen, was willing to risk his life for those lands, and he held them dear. And a captain of the king's house-carles will always look to be rewarded for service with lands. In time you will seek the same."

"That time has not yet come to me, King Ina."

"Eastdean lies in my hand here," he said, taking up a parchment with a great seal on it. "I may give it to whom I will, but you are the lawful heir who should hold it from me. If it goes not to you, it may be that one whom you would not shall have it."

Then I said, not seeing at all what the king would have me do, but thinking that he deemed me foolish for not taking the lands straightway:

"Let me bide with you even yet for a while. When the time comes that I must leave you I must go to Owen, and neither he nor I care for aught but to be here. He must leave you because of duty, and if this is indeed choice with me, let me choose to stay. It is nought to me who holds the lands, save only that it might be one who will tend the grave of my father."

Then said Ina, looking into my face and smiling, as if well pleased:

"The choice is free, my Thane, and I should be wrong if I did not say that I am glad to hear you choose thus. I have missed you in these days, and I have work here for you yet. It was in my mind that thus you would choose, and I am glad. Let it be so. I need one to take the place of Owen, as second in command of the household, as one may say, and that you must do for me henceforward.

"Nay," he said quickly, raising his hand as I tried to find some words of thanks for this honour; "you know the ways of Owen, and men know you, and it will be as if there had been no change, and that will mean that we shall have no grumbling in the palace, and the right men will be sent to do what they are best fitted for--and all that, so that there will be quiet about the court as ever. It is a matter off my mind, let me tell you, and no thanks are needed."

So he laughed and let me kiss his hand, patting me on the shoulder as I rose, and then bade me sit down again. He had yet more to say.

"With Erpwald who is dead, men would hold that you had a blood feud. That is done with; but his son yet lives. I do not think it is your way, or

Owen's, to hold that a feud must be carried on in the old heathen way of our forefathers."

"Most truly not," I said. "What ill has a son of Erpwald done to me or mine?"

"None! Nay, rather has he done well, for I know that he has honoured the grave of your father, and even now is ready to do what he can to make amends for the old wrong. He brought me this."

He took up the parchment that he had shewn me before. It was a grant of the manors of Eastdean to Erpwald, gained by those means of utmost craft whereby the king thought that indeed the last of our line had perished by other hands than those of the heathen thane.

"Honest and straightforward and Christian-like is this young Erpwald," the king said. "Well brought up by his Christian mother, if not very ready or brilliant in his ways. Now he has learned how his father came into the lands, and though he might well have held them after his uncle on this grant, he has come hither to set the matter in my hands. 'It is not fair,' quoth he, 'that I should hold them if one is left of the line of Ella. I should not sleep easily in my bed. Nevertheless, I will buy them if so be that one is left to sell them to me.' So he sighed, for the place is his home."

"All these years it has been no trouble to me that Erpwald's brother has held the place, my King. It will be no trouble to think that a better Erpwald holds them yet."

"I do not think that he will be happy unless he deems that he has paid some price--some weregild {ii}, as one may say; for slow minds as his hang closely to their thoughts when they are formed. See, Oswald, I have thought of all this, and the young man has been here for a fortnight. I brought him here from Winchester, where he joined me. Let me tell you what I think."

"The matter is in your hands altogether, my King."

"As you have set it there," he said, smiling gently. "Now all seems plain to me, and I will say that this is even what I thought you would wish to do. How shall it be if we bid Erpwald, for the deed of his father, to build a church in Eastdean and there to keep a priest, that all men shall know how that the martyr is honoured, and the land be the better for his death?"

Nought better than this could be, as I thought, and I told the king so.

"Why, then," he said, "that is well. I shall have pleased both parties, as I hope. I know you will meet him in all friendliness."

Then he let me go, and it was with a light heart that I parted from him. Now I knew that my father's grave and memory would be held in more than common honour, and I was content.

Men would miss Owen sorely here, but, save for that, I had so often acted for him in these last two years that my being altogether in his place made little difference to any one, or even to myself in a few days. That last was as well for myself, as it seems to me, for I was not over proud, as I might have been had the post been new to me. As it was, I do not think that there was any jealousy over it, or at least I never found it out. My friends rejoiced openly, and if any one wondered that the king should so trust a man of my age, the answer that I had saved Ina's life was enough to satisfy all.

My men drank my health in their quarters that night, and after I got over the little strangeness of sitting on the high place next to Nunna, things went on, save for the want of Owen about the court, even as when he was the marshal and I but his squire, as it were.

I saw young Erpwald for the first time soon after the king had spoken of him to me, and I liked the look of him well enough. He was some few years older than I, square and strong, with a round red face and light hair, pleasant in smile, if not over wise looking. One would say that he might be a good friend, but one could hardly think of him as willingly the enemy of any man. Some one made me known to him as the son of Owen, as was usual, and as such would I be known to him for a while; but for some time I saw little of him, not caring to seek his company, as indeed there was no reason for me to do so.

The next thing that I heard of him was that he had made a great friend of the ealdorman since he came here, being often at his house. It was not so long before I met him there, though my pride, which would not let me risk another rebuff, kept me away for some days. I had an uneasy feeling that I should fare no better, and I could find good reason enough to justify the thought in some ways, as any one may see from what had happened before.

Maybe that was a token that my first feelings were cooling off, and I do not think that there is much wonder if they were. It would have been strange, and not altogether complimentary to the fair damsel if, after the deed at the feast and the vow that I had to make, I had not thought myself desperately in love with her at last, after a good many years of friendship. But now there had befallen the long days of peril and anxiety which had set her in the background altogether, and I had had time to come to more sober thoughts, as it were. Men have said that I aged more in that short time than in the next ten years of my life, and it is likely. Nevertheless, it needed but a word or two of kindness to bring me to Elfrida's feet once for all, and but a little more coldness to send me from her altogether.

So at last I went to her home to find out how I should fare, thinking less of the matter than last time, and there she sat in the hall, chatting merrily with Erpwald. That pleasantness stopped when I came in, and after the first needful greetings Elfrida froze again, and Erpwald fell silent, as if I was by no means welcome. I could see that I was the third who spoils company. However, the ealdorman came in directly, and I talked to him, and as we paid no heed to those two they took up their talk once more, and presently their words waxed low. Whereon the ealdorman glanced at them with a sly grin and wink to me, and I understood.

So I went away, for that was enough. Of course, I was very angry, by reason of the scratch to my pride; for it does hurt to think that one is not wanted, and for a while I brooded over it just as I had done the other day. Then it came to me that at least I had no reason to be angry with Erpwald, who could know little or anything about me, being a newcomer, and it was not his fault if the girl made a tool of him to scare me away, and after that I found my senses again, rather sooner than before, perhaps. It was plain that the ealdorman took it for granted that I had no feeling now in that direction, and so others would do the same, which was comforting. So I supposed that there was no more to be said on the subject by any one, unless Elfrida chose to have the matter out, and set things on the old footing of frank friendliness again.

There I found that I was mistaken at once. Some one was coming down the lane after me quickly, and then calling my name. I turned, and there was Erpwald, with a very red face, trying to overtake me, and I waited for him.

"A word with you, Thane," he said, out of breath.

"As many as you will. What is it?"

"Wait until I get my breath," he said. "One would think that you were in a desperate hurry, by the pace you go. Plague on all such fast walkers!"

That made me laugh, and he smiled across his broad face in return.

"It is all very well to grin," he said, straightening his face suddenly to a blankness; "but what I have to say concerns a mighty serious matter."

"Well, then, get it done with," I answered, trying not to smile yet more.

"I don't rightly know how to begin," he said in a hesitating kind of way. "Words are as hard to manage as a drove of forest swine, and I am a bad hand at talking. Can you not tell what I have to say?"

"Not in the least," I answered.

It flashed across me that he might have found out who I was, however, and wanted to speak of the old trouble.

"Well," he said at last, growing yet redder, "the Lady Elfrida is angry that her name has been coupled with yours pretty much lately."

He stopped with a long breath, and I knew what he was driving at.

"She has told me as much herself already," I said solemnly.

He heaved a sigh of relief.

"But she did not tell me that," he said in a puzzled sort of way. "Well, it must not go on, or--or else, that is, I shall have to see that it does not."

"The worst of it is that I cannot help it," said I. "Did the lady ask you to speak to me of the matter?"

"Why, no; she did not. Only, I thought that some one must. Of course, I mean that I will fight you if it goes on."

"Of course," I said. "But I can in no wise stop it. Do you know how it began?"

"Not altogether. How was it?"

"Really, that you had better ask some one else," I said, keeping a grave face. "I think that it would have been fairer to me to have done so first. But if there was any real blame to me, do you think that the ealdorman would have been glad to see me just now? I think that it was plain that he was so."

"I am an owl," Erpwald said. "Of course, he would not have been. But did you come to see the ealdorman, or the lady?"

"Why, both of them, of course. I have known them for years."

He looked relieved when he heard that, and I thought that he must be badly smitten already.

"Well, I will go and ask the ealdorman all about it," he said. "Where shall I find you in an hour's time?"

"In my quarters," I answered; "but, of course, if you want to fight me you will have to send a friend to talk to me."

"I will send the ealdorman himself."

"Best not, for he is the man who is charged with the stopping of these affairs if he hears of them. Any atheling you meet will help you in such a matter. It is an honour to be asked to do so. But don't ever ask me to be your second if you have another affair, for I also have to hinder these meetings if I can."

"Is there any one else I must not ask?" he said in a bewildered way.

"Best not ask the abbot," I said, and I could not help smiling.

"Now you are laughing at me, and that is too bad. How am I to know your court ways?"

"Well, you will not have to fight me unless you really want to pick a quarrel. So it does not matter. Get to the bottom of the question, and then come and talk it over, and we will see what is to be done."

He nodded and left me, and I had a good chuckle over the whole business. It was not likely that Elfrida had set him on me, in the least; but I suppose he had heard some jest of her father's, who was one of those who will work anything that pleases them to the last.

So I went my way, and saw to one or two things, and sat me down in the room off the hall that had been Owen's, and presently Erpwald came in, and I saw that he was in trouble.

"Well," I said, "how goes the quarrel?"

"I am a fool," he replied promptly. "The lady should be proud of the affair, and the more it is talked of the better she should like it. You are right in saying that it cannot be stopped. Why, there is a gleeman down the street this minute singing the deeds of Oswald and Elfrida. As for the vow you made, the ealdorman says that it could not have been better done. Forgive me for troubling you about it at all."

He held out his broad hand, and for a moment I hesitated about taking it. He bore his father's name, but in a flash it came to me that I was wrong. We were both children when the ill deed was wrought, and I was no heathen to hold a blood feud against all the family of the wrongdoer. He did not even know that one of us lived, and, as the king had told me, I knew that he was prepared to make amends.

So I took his hand frankly, and he had not noticed the moment's slowness or, if he did, took it for the passing of vexation from my mind.

"You will laugh at me again," he said, "but now I am in hot water in all sooth. The lady will not speak to me at all."

I did laugh. I sat down on the edge of the table and tried to stop it, but his red face was so rueful that I could not, and at last he had to smile also.

"Why, what have you done?" I asked. "Now it is my turn to know reasons why. Here is a new offence to be seen into."

"I only told her that I had spoken to you on the subject, and was going to talk to the ealdorman, her father, if she would not save me the trouble by telling me herself all about it."

"And then?"

"She got up and went away, tossing her head, without a word. So I had a talk with the ealdorman, and learnt all; but after that I tried to see her, and that black-haired Welsh maiden of hers told me that she would not see me."

"It seems to me that you have had a bad day," I said. "But what does it matter? You have done what seemed right, and if it is taken in the wrong way you cannot help it."

"It does matter," he said. "If she is wroth with me, I don't mind telling you that I am fit to hang myself. Could you not set things right for me, somehow? You are an old friend."

"No, hardly; for I am not in favour there just now."

"Well, I shall go and try to get round the Welsh girl to speak for me."

Now, that was a servant I had never heard of, and I thought I knew all the household. So I could not tell him if that would be of use, and he left me in some sort of desperation to try what he could. He was very much in love.

Next day he came back beaming. Somehow the Welshwoman had managed things for him, and all was well again. I had my own thought that Elfrida was by no means unwilling to meet him halfway, but I did not say so. I think I had fairly got over my feelings by this time, but I must say that I felt a sort of half jealousy about it. But the more I came to look on the South Saxon's round face, and to think of him as Elfrida's favoured lover, the less I felt it. It became a jest to watch the going of the affair, and I was not the only one who found it so in a very short time.

Erpwald made no secret of his devotion. He minded me of a great faithful stupid dog, whose trust was boundless and whose love was worth having. One could lead him anywhere, but he was true Sussex--he would not be driven an inch.

So Elfrida had a hopeless slave at her beck and call, and by and by I was on the old footing, and we used to make much of my vow of service to her.

"I would that I had made that vow," Erpwald said once.

"It is not too late now," answered the ealdorman, with his great laugh; "but I do not think it is needed."

After me went Erpwald when he was not at the ealdorman's, and Ina told me that he was glad to see that I harboured no thought of revenge.

"Presently you will want to go to Eastdean to see that your father's grave is well honoured, and this friendliness will help you," he said. "And for his friend such a man as Erpwald will do much. The church at Eastdean will be no poor one, and you will help him choose the place. We could not have asked him to do anything that has pleased him more."

One thing I feared was that when he found out who I was he would be ill at ease with me, and I asked the king to tell him in the way that seemed best to his wisdom, lest the knowledge should come by chance from some one else.

So he did that, and in a day or two Erpwald came to me and told me that he knew at last who I was, and we had a long talk together. It was in his mind to try to make me take the lands again, and I had hard work to make him believe that I was in earnest when I said that I did not want them. And at the end I made him happy by telling him that the king would let me go to Eastdean with him before long, so that we could see to things together.

"Well," he said, "this is all very pleasant for me, and it is common saying that you will be some sort of prince in West Wales before long; but I shall ever feel that my family owes yours more than I can repay."

After that he was a little uneasy with me for a time, but it soon wore off, and we used to talk of our ride to Eastdean often enough.

And then happened a thing that set me back into trouble about Owen again. I had had many messages from him, as may be supposed, and in all of them he said that there was no sign of danger, or even of plotting against him.

One of my men brought me a written message one evening. A thrall had left it at the gate for me. And when I asked from whom it came I had the same answer that was given me when that other writing warned me not to sleep in the moonlight, for it was said to come from a priest whom I knew.

So when I glanced at the writing I was not surprised to see that it was the same, though the sight of it gave me a cold shudder. Somewhat the same also was the form in which the message ran:

"To Oswald, son of Owen.--It is not good to take wine from the hand of a Briton."

Now, I had some reason to believe that Mara had written the first note, as she seemed the only possible person to warn us of the plots of her kin, and that was a very plain warning to Owen rather than to myself, as it seemed. So I thought this might come from the same hand, and be meant for him also, and that all the more that there was not a stranger left in Glastonbury, now that the feasting was over, much less a Welshman. But Owen had none but Welsh round him, and it seemed to say that there was some plot among them again. Maybe he would know who was meant by the "Briton." Men have nicknames that seem foolish to any but those who are in the jest of them. We used to call Erpwald the "Saxon" sometimes, because he was not of Wessex, although we were as much Saxon as he, or more so, according to our own pride.

I went straight down the street to the house of a man whom I knew well, an honest franklin who had a good horse and knew the border country from end to end, and I bade him ride with all speed to Owen at Norton with the paper. He was to give it into his own hand, and I made shift to scrawl a few words on the outside of it that he might shew to my friend the captain of the guard, and so win speedier entry to the palace. I did not send one of my own men, because he would have been known as coming from me, while this man was often in Norton about cattle and the like, and none would wonder at seeing him.

I was easier when I saw him mount and ride away, but I was ill content until the morning came and brought him back with tidings that all was well, and that Owen would be on his guard.

Also, the franklin was to tell me that Gerent's court went to Isca, which we call Exeter, in two days' time, and that Owen would fain see me before he went westward, if I could come to him. There seemed to be difficulty in persuading Gerent to let him return to our court, even for a day now.

Whereon I went to Ina and told him of this new trouble, and he bade me go. He thought that some fresh plot was being hatched in Exeter, but both he and I wondered that the warning was not sent direct to my foster father, rather than in this roundabout way through my hands. He said the same thing to me that Howel had spoken when I parted from him.

"These plotters will not think twice about striking at Owen through you, if it seems the only way to reach him. And you mind that the princess told you to have a care for yourself. Evan said that if strife was stirred up between us and Gerent they would be glad. If they slew you, my Thane, it is likely that there would be trouble, unless Gerent is as wroth as I should be."

So I went with a few guards and spent the day and night with Owen at Norton. I knew it was the last chance I should have of seeing him for a long time, but we talked of the coming summer, promising ourselves that journey together to see Howel. I told him how things went with Elfrida and me, and he did not seem to wonder much, nor to think it of any consequence. He laughed at me, and told me to get over it as soon as I could, and that was all.

But this last warning he could no more understand than I. It was his thought that it was meant for me rather than himself.

"You will have to take heed to any Welshman you meet," he said, "and as you are warned that should be no very difficult matter. No Briton can ever pretend to be a Saxon."

I do not think that there is more to be said of that meeting, though indeed I would willingly dwell on it. Mayhap it will be plain why I would do so presently, for I left him bright and happy in his old place, with nought but the distance from the foster son whom he loved to trouble him.

But when I rode away again the sorrow of that parting fell heavily on me, and I could not shake it off. It seemed to me that I would not see Owen again, though why it so seemed I could not tell. If I had any thought of danger to myself I should have cared little, so it was not that. I wonder if one can feel "fey" for another man if he is dear to you as no other can be?

CHAPTER XI
HOW ERPWALD FELL FROM CHEDDAR CLIFFS; AND OF ANOTHER WARNING.

In the coming week, after I had thus taken leave of Owen, my friend Herewald, the ealdorman, would have a hunting party before we all left him and Glastonbury for Winchester, and so it came to pass that on the appointed day a dozen of us rode with a train of men and hounds after us along the westward slopes of the Mendips in the direction of Cheddar, rousing the red deer from the warm woodlands of the combes where they love to hide. We had the slow-hounds with us, and that, as it seems to me, is better sport than with the swift gaze-hounds I rode after on the Welsh hills with Eric. It is good to hear the deep notes of them as they light on the scent of the quarry in the covers, and to see them puzzle out a lost line in the open, and to ride with the crash and music of the full pack ahead of one in the ears, as the deer doubles no longer, but trusts to speed for escape.

Those who were with us were friends of mine and of the ealdorman, and there were three ladies in the party--one of these being, of course, Elfrida.

Erpwald was in close attendance on her, a matter which was taken for granted by every one at this time. He was to go with the court to Winchester, and thence he and I would ride to Eastdean.

So we hunted through the forenoon, taking one deer, and then rode onward until we came to the place where the great Cheddar gorge cleaves the Mendips across from summit to base, sheer and terrible. The village lies at the foot of the gorge on the western side of the hills, half sheltered between the first cliffs of the vast chasm, but on the hillside above is a deep cover that climbs upward to the summit, and it was said that a good deer had been harboured there.

So presently, while the hounds were drawing this wood below us, I and Elfrida and Erpwald found ourselves together and waiting on the hilltop at the edge of the gorge. I was almost sorry to make a third in that little party, but Erpwald knew nothing of the country, and Elfrida had no more skill in matters of time and place and distance than most ladies, which is not saying much, in all truth, though I hardly should dare to set it down, save by way of giving a reason for my presence with so well contented a party of two.

Now, if there is one who has not seen this Cheddar gorge, I will say that it is as if the mighty hills had been broken across as a boy breaks a long loaf, or as if some giant had hewn a narrow gap with the roughest pick that ever was handled. Our forefathers held that Woden had indeed hewn it so, and we have tales that the evil one himself cleft it in a night, and that the rocky islands of Steep and Flat Holme, yonder in the mid channel, are the rubbish which he hewed thence and cast there. Maybe the overhanging cliffs are full four hundred feet high from the little white track which winds at their foot, and from cliff top to cliff top is but a short bow shot.

From where we waited one could look sheer down on the track below us, and a man who was coming slowly along it seemed like a rat in its run, so far off did he appear. At least, so said Erpwald, who looked over, riding to the very edge. I had no wish to do so, having been there before, and not altogether liking it.

Then he wanted Elfrida to look over also, and that frightened her, and so we rode back and forth a little, for the wind was keen on the hill, listening for sound of horn or hound in the cover.

One reason why we were so near the edge of the cliffs was that Erpwald had not seen the place before, and had heard much of it; and another was that as no deer could cross the gorge we should be sure to have the hunt before us when one broke. There are tales of hunted deer, ay, and of huntsmen also, going over the cliffs at full speed, but that is likely only when the pace has been hot and the danger is forgotten. I had no mind, either, to see some of Herewald's young hounds cast themselves over in eagerness if they chose to follow, as young ones will, the scent of some hill fox who had his lair among the rocks and knew paths to safety on the face of the cliffs, so that was yet another reason why we were in that place, and I tell this because it is likely that some one may ask how it was that I suffered my friends to bide in so perilous a spot, seeing what happened presently.

It was not long before those two forgot me, and rode side by side talking. Maybe I forgot them, for the last time I was on the cliff tops was across the channel, and I minded the two with whom I rode then--Howel and Nona.

Then suddenly the ringing of the horn roused us, and Erpwald came toward me, thinking that, of course, Elfrida was close after him, but with his eyes too intently watching the place where I had said a deer was most likely to break cover to notice much else. I was some twenty paces farther from the edge than they. The horses pricked up their ears at the well-known sound, and stood with lifted heads watching as eagerly as we.

Then there came a little cry from Elfrida as she bade her horse stand, and I heard it trampling sharply, as if restive, behind us. I turned in my saddle to see what was amiss, and what I saw made my blood run cold, and the sweat broke out on my forehead in a moment.

With the sound of the horn and the moving away of Erpwald the horse had waxed restive, as horses will at a cover side when the time to move on seems near. I think that it had probably reared a little and that she had tried to check it, for now it was backing slowly and uneasily toward the edge of that awesome cliff that was but ten paces from its heels. Even now the girl was backing him yet more in her efforts to make him stand still, and I dared not make a move to catch the bridle lest he should swing round at once from me and go over.

"Spur him, Elfrida. Let his head go, and spur him," I said as quietly as I could, but so that she must needs hear.

It was all that I could do.

She spurred him, and then as he made a little leap forward, checked him, and that was yet worse. Then I saw Erpwald, with an ashy face, dismount and go hastily toward the edge behind her, sidelong, and I swung my horse away from him, so that by chance hers might follow me out of danger.

But that was useless. The brute was yet backing, and his heels were almost on the brink. It seemed that his rider did not know how near she was.

"Get off!" I said hoarsely. "Get off at once!"

Then she knew, but could only turn and look. The hinder hoofs lost hold on the rocky edge as the horse made its first slip backward, and even as the loosened stones rattled down, and it lurched with one leg hanging over the gulf, Erpwald leapt forward and tore Elfrida from the saddle, and half threw her toward me. I do not remember when I dismounted, but I was there and grasped her hand and dragged her back out of the way of the lashing fore feet.

Then Erpwald was gone. The horse struggled wildly in one last effort to save itself, and swept my friend over with it. There was a rattle of stones, a silence, and then a dull crash in the depths below.

One moment later and all three would have gone. I heard the shout of the man on the track below, and I wondered in a dull way if he had been killed also.

And now I had Elfrida to tend, for she had fainted. What she had seen I could not tell, but I hoped that at least she knew nought before Erpwald went. It was as if she had lost consciousness when he reached her, for I saw the hand on the rein loosen helplessly. I carried her back from the cliff and tried to bring her to herself, vainly, though indeed I almost wished that she might remain as she was until we were back in Glastonbury.

Then I wound my horn again and again to bring some to my help, and I tried not to think of that which surely lay crushed on the road below. There could be no hope for either man or horse.

Then came the sound of swift hoofs, and there was the ealdorman and one or two others, coming in all haste to know what the urgent call betokened, but by the time that he had dismounted and asked if there was any hurt to his daughter I could only gasp and point downward. My mouth was dry and parched, and I did not know how to put into words the thing that had happened; but he saw that Elfrida's horse was not there, and that Erpwald's ran loose with mine, and he guessed.

"Over the cliff?" he said, whispering, and I nodded.

"Go and look," he gasped, and he knelt down and took Elfrida from me.

The two who were with him were trying to catch the loose horses, and we were alone for the moment. So I crept to the edge and looked over, fearing what I should see. But I saw nothing but the bare track winding there, and I remembered that the cliff overhung.

Then, as I scanned every rock and cranny below me a man came out from under the overhang at the foot of the cliff and looked up. For a moment my heart leapt, for I thought it was Erpwald. But it was only the traveller we had seen, and he must have been looking at what had rolled into the hollow that hid it from me. He glanced up and caught sight of me.

"How did it happen?" he called up to me.

"Dead?" I called back, with a terror of what I knew would be his answer.

Then he laughed at me.

"Do you expect a horse to be leather all through, Master? Of course he is.-- Saddle and all smashed to bits."

Then a dull anger took me that he thought of the horse only, as it seemed, unless he was mazed as I was with it all.

"The man--the man," I said.

"There is no man here, Master. Did one fall?" he said in a new voice, and he crossed to the other side of the gorge and scanned the face of the cliff.

"He is not to be seen," he said. "Maybe he has caught yonder."

He pointed to a ledge that was plain enough to me, but nowhere near the place whence the fall was. There were no ledges to be seen as I looked straight down, and I knew that this place was the most sheer fall along all the length of the gorge.

Now three more of our party came up, and at once they rode down to the village and so round to where the man stood. It seemed a long time before they were there and talking to him.

"Ho, Oswald!"

Their voices came cheerfully enough, and I looked down at them.

"There seem to be clefts here and there, and in one of those he must needs be," they said. "We are going to the village to get a cragsman with a rope, and will be with you anon."

There was at least hope in that, and I watched them ride swiftly away. The ravens were gathering fast now, knowing that what fell from above must needs be their prey, and two great eagles were wheeling high overhead, waiting. I heard the kites screaming to one another from above the eagles, and from the woods came the call of the buzzards. They knew more than I.

Now the ealdorman could not bring Elfrida round, and he thought it best to take her hence. So he had her lifted to him on his horse, and went slowly and carefully down the hill toward the village with her. I had told him all that had happened by this time, and I was to bring word presently to him of how the search went.

So I and those two friends who had first come sat there on the cliff top waiting in silence for the coming of the man with his ropes. All that could be said had been said.

Here and there on the face of the cliff some yew trees had managed to find a holding, and their boughs were broken by the passage of the horse at least through them. But there were no shreds of clothing on them, as if Erpwald had reached them. That might be because the weightier horse fell first. It seemed to me in that moment of the fall that he was between the horse and the cliff as he went over the edge, for the forefeet of the horse struck his legs and threw him backward, and the last thing that I minded was seeing his head against the horse's mane in some way. That last glimpse will bide with me until I forget all things.

It seemed very long before our friends came back with the ropes. Backwards and forwards in front of us flew untiringly two ravens, now flying across the gorge, and then again almost brushing us with their wings as they swept up the face of the cliff from below. We thought they had a nest somewhere close at hand, for it was their time.

"If Erpwald were dead," I said presently, "those birds would not be so restless. It is hard to think that they know where he is and how he fares; but at least they tell us that he is not yet prey for them."

Backward and forward they swept, until my eyes grew dazed with watching them, and then suddenly they both croaked their alarm note, wheeled quickly away from the cliff's face, and fled across the gorge and were gone.

Then was a rattle of stones, and a shout from some one in the track below, and I started and saw a head slowly rising above the edge of the cliff as if its owner had climbed up to us. White and streaked with blood was the face, but it was not crushed or marred, and it was Erpwald's.

"Lend me a hand," he said, as we stared at him, as one needs must stare at one who comes back as it were from the grave. "My head swims even yet."

I grasped his hand and helped him to the grass, and once there he stood upright and shook himself, looking round in an astonished way as he did so.

"No broken bones," he said. "Where is Elfrida? Is she all right? I was rough with her, I fear, but I could not help it. Could I have managed otherwise?"

"In no way better," I said, finding my tongue at length. "She has gone to the village. But where have you been!"

"In a long hole just over here," he answered. "But how long has she been gone?"

"How long do you think that you have been in your hole?"

"A few minutes. It cannot be long. Yet it must have been longer than I thought, for the shadows are changed."

It was a full hour and a half since he fell, but I did not say so, lest it should be some sort of shock to him. So I bade him sit down while I saw to a cut there was on his head--the only sign of hurt that he had.

"I thought that I was done for at first," he said.

"So thought I, until we found that you were not at the bottom. Even now some of us have gone for ropes that we might search the cliff for you. We could not see you anywhere, and there does not seem to be any ledge here that could catch you."

"Why, you could have touched me with a spear all the time, if you had known where to thrust it. I think I fainted, or somewhat foolish of the sort. My head hit the rock as I went over. Also the horse ground me between it and the cliff, so that all my breath went. But that pushed me into the hole, and I will not grumble. At least, I think that was it, but I cannot be sure. My senses went."

He began to laugh, but suddenly turned to me with a new look on his face.

"Oh, but was Elfrida feared for me?--What did she think?"

"She saw nought of it," I said. "I believe that she had fainted with terror when you laid hold of her. The ealdorman came and took her to the village, and I do not suppose she knows that you have been lost."

"That is well," he said, with his great sigh. "Look over and see my hole."

I did not care to look over again, and, moreover, knew that I could not see it. I mind every jutting stone and twisted yew that is on the cliff there, to this day. However, one of the others went a little to one side, where Erpwald had appeared, and swung himself to the tiny ledge that had given him foothold as he came up, and so looked at the place. There was a long cleft between two layers of rock which went back into the cliff's face for some depth, with a little backward slope that had saved the helpless man from rolling out again, and there was a raven's nest at one end of it. One may see that cleft from below and across the gorge if one knows where to look, but not by any means from above, by reason of the overhang of the brink. It was plain that, as he thought, the horse's body, or maybe its shoulder, thrust him into the cleft, but it was well that he was senseless and so could not struggle, or he would have surely missed it. It is his saying that he had no trouble in getting into the place, but more in climbing out.

Now we called the good news to some of our people and the villagers who were on the road below, and they broke into cheers as they heard it. They could hardly believe that the man they had seen on the edge just now was Erpwald himself. Then we went down to the village, meeting the men with the ropes halfway, and so came to the first houses of the street, where the ealdorman was standing outside one of the better sort. He came to meet us, and I never saw anything like the look on his face when he saw Erpwald and heard his cheerful greeting. I told him how things ended.

"I have given a lot of trouble, as it seems" Erpwald said humbly; "but I could not help it."

"Trouble!" said the ealdorman. "Had it not been for you there would have been nought but trouble for me all the rest of my life."

He took Erpwald's hand as he spoke and pressed it, but he would not say more then. Maybe he could not. So he turned to me.

"It is all right, Oswald, for Elfrida is herself again, and she saw nothing after she looked into the gulf below her. I have told her nothing."

"Do not tell her anything, Ealdorman," Erpwald said. "No need to say what a near thing it was, or that I handled her like a sack of oats. She would never forgive me. But Oswald says it was all that I could have done. It was a good thing that he was there to take her."

"How are you going to account for the broken head, then?"

"Say I was thrown from my horse afterward, or somewhat of that kind," he said. "Or, stay, these will do it. I have been birds' nesting. I thought these would please her. One gets falls while scrambling after the like."

He put his hand into his pouch as he spoke.

"Plague on it, one is broken," he said, bringing out a raven's egg. "There were two in that place where I stopped falling."

The ealdorman and I stared at him in wonder. It amazed us that in such a moment a man should think of this trifle. And now he was turning his soiled pouch inside out and wiping it with a tuft of grass, grumbling the while. It was plain that the danger had made no impression on him.

"Were not you frightened when you found how nearly you had fallen from the cliff?" I asked him.

"No; why should I be? I did not fall from it. I was feared enough when I thought that I was going, and I thought I was at the bottom when I came to myself. But as I had not gone so far, there was an end."

I minded the story of the Huntsman's Leap, and how I had felt when I knew my escape. It was plain that this forest-bred Erpwald, with his cool head, and lack of power to picture what might have been, would make a good warrior, so far as dogged fearlessness goes, and that is a long way.

Now the ealdorman kept what else he might have to say until we were at home, for it was time for us to be off. So we brushed Erpwald down and hid his cut under a cap that the good franklin of the house lent him, for his own was gone, as he said, to make a bird's nest somewhere on the cliffs; and then Elfrida came from the cottage, looking a little white and shaken with her fright, but otherwise none the worse, and we started.

Erpwald kept out of her sight for a little while, but as we were fairly on the way home it was not long before he found his way to her side, and we let those two have their say out together.

One by one the friends who had joined us dropped out of the party as their way led them aside, until by the time we reached the ealdorman's house only half a dozen of us were left. Then Herewald would have us come in for some cheer after the long day, but we were tired and stained, and I must be back at the guardroom, and so he bade his folk bring somewhat out here to us. There was a cask of ale already set on the low wall by the gate for the men, and we sat on our horses waiting, with a little crowd of thralls and children round us, looking at the two good deer that we brought back. Then the steward and some of the women of the house brought horns of ale from the house for us.

One of the women came to me, and without seeing who she was, or thinking of doing so, I reached out my hand for the horn that she held up, and at that moment some one from behind seemed to run against my horse's flank, and he lashed out and reared as if he was hurt. My rein was loose, and I was bending carelessly over to take the horn, and it was all that I could do to keep my seat for the moment. As for the girl, she dropped the horn and ran from the plunging horse into the doorway for safety.

Then I heard the sharp crack of a whip, and the voice of the head huntsman speaking angrily:

"Out on you for a silly oaf!--What mean you by going near the thane at all?"

The whip cracked again, and the long lash curled round the shoulders of a ragged thrall, who tried in vain to escape it.

"On my word, I believe you did it on purpose!" the huntsman cried, with a third shrewd lash that found its lodgment rightly.

"Mercy, Master," mumbled the man, writhing; "it is this terrible crossing of the eyes. I do not rightly see where I go."

I had quieted the horse by this time, and I held up my hand to stay the lash from the thrall. Some one picked up the horn that the girl had let fall.

"Let him be," I said. "It could but have been a chance, and he is lucky not to have been kicked. See, he does squint most amazingly."

"Ay," growled the huntsman, "so he does; but I never knew a cross-eyed man before who had any trouble in walking straight enough."

The thrall slunk away among his fellows. He was a round-shouldered man with hay-coloured hair and a stubby beard of the same, and he rubbed his shoulders with his elbows lifted as he went. Then the steward gave me a fresh horn, and we said farewell to our host and hostess, and Erpwald and I went our way.

"I thought that the horse would have knocked the Welsh girl over," he said presently. "She was pretty nimble, however. That churl must have kicked your horse sharply to make him plunge as he did."

"Trod on his fetlock most likely," I answered. "Clumsy knave."

"Well, that huntsman knows how to use a lash, at all events, and he will have a care in future. But how my head does ache!"

"That is likely enough," I said, laughing. "It was a shrewd knock, and it kept you in that hole for the longest hour and a half I have ever known."

"It does take somewhat out of the common to hurt me much," he said simply.

"Well, by tomorrow you will be famed all over Glastonbury as the man who fell over Cheddar cliffs and escaped by reason of lighting on the thickest part of him," I answered.

It was a poor jest enough, but it set him laughing. I did not wish him to say more of what had just happened, for I was puzzled about it, and wanted to get my thoughts to work. He had spoken of the very thing that I had been warned of, for almost had I taken the horn from the hand of a Briton--the Welsh girl of whom he spoke once before. I had forgotten her, for I do not think that I had ever seen her since she came here, until now. But at this moment I seemed to have a feeling that her face was in some way familiar to me, though only in that half-formed way that troubles one, and I was trying to recall how this might be.

Erpwald went off to the guest chamber where he was lodged, and presently I found our old leech and took him to see after him. He went comfortably to sleep after his hurt had been dressed, and so I left him. I will say at once that he felt no more trouble from it.

Then I went to the stables to see how fared my horse after the day's work, and found him enjoying his feed after grooming. I looked him over, but I could see no mark to show where the man might have hurt him. But as I was running my hand along the smooth hock to feel for any bruise, my groom said to me:

"Have you had a roll in a thorn bush, Master?"

"No.--What makes you think I might have had one?"

"I found this in his flank when I rubbed him down, and it was run thus far into him."

He held out a long stiff blackthorn spine, marking a full inch on its length with his thumbnail.

"Enough to set a horse wild for a moment," he went on. "And unless you had fallen, I could not think how it got there."

"In which flank was it?" I asked, taking the thorn from him.

"The near flank, Master."

That was where the thrall ran against him, and surely the huntsman was not so far wrong when he said that he did so on purpose. If so, it was done at the right moment to give me a heavy fall, save for a bit of luck, or maybe horsemanship. It was a strange business.

"I was through a thicket or two today," I said carelessly. "Maybe I hit a branch in just the right way to drive it in. If we were galloping he would not have noticed it. These little things happen oddly sometimes."

Then the man began to tell me some other little mishaps to horses that could not be explained, bustling about the while. And before long I left the stables and went to my own quarters, with the thorn yet in my hand. It had been cut from the bush, and not broken, just as if it had been chosen. Now, if these hidden plotters wanted to frighten me, I am bound to say that they succeeded more or less. Was the giving of the horn by the Welsh girl to be a signal to the thrall in some way? If there is one thing that a man need not be ashamed to say that he fears, it is treachery, and I seemed to be surrounded by it. Hardly could a house-carle come to my door but it seemed to me that he must needs bring one of these unlucky notes. It was just as well that I had some unknown friend to write them to me, though I cannot say that I had profited by them so far.

Now I sent two of my men to see if they could find the cross-eyed thrall, but of course he was not to be laid hands on. Only the people who had been at the ealdorman's door seemed to have seen him, and they could not tell who or whence he was. He was so easily known, however, that I thought I should be certain to have him sooner or later. Such a squint as he had is not to be hidden, and that made the wonder that he had dared to do this all the greater.

I slept on it all, and woke with fewer fears on me, for I was overwrought yesterday after all the terrible waiting on the cliff and what went before. It was Sunday, moreover, and the early services in the new church helped mightily to set a new face on things. So when I had seen to the few duties of the morning, I went down the street to ask after Elfrida, being anxious to hear that her fright had done her no hurt. Erpwald had been there before me, but I had missed him since.

Elfrida was well, and glad to see me. We sat and talked of yesterday, and I found that Erpwald had said nothing of how he saved her, and it was pleasant to tell her of it, while she listened with eyes that sparkled. It was plain that I could have found nothing that would please her better than to talk of him. So I even told her how he had gone over the edge into the cleft, but without saying that we feared for his life for so long. Then her father came in, and at once she asked after some sick person.

"How goes it with him now," she said.

"Well enough, says the leech; but he had well-nigh died in the night."

"What is it that ails him?--Can the leech tell that yet?"

"He has taken somewhat that has poisoned him," the ealdorman answered. "The leech asked if he had eaten of mushrooms, or rather toadstools, by mistake."

"But there are none about as yet."

Now I asked who the sick man was, and Herewald told me that he was such an one who was with us yesterday. I minded him as one who stood near me at the door when my horse reared. I thought that he was the man who picked up my dropped horn, and I was sorry for him. However, that was not much concern of mine, so we passed to other talk for a little, and then Elfrida said:

"Are there any tidings of my maiden? I fear for her."

"None at all," the ealdorman said. "Here is a strange thing, Oswald; for that girl whom you so nearly rode over last evening is as clean gone as if she had never been. None saw her go, but when supper time came she was nowhere to be found. Nor is there any trace of her now."

I felt as if I had expected to hear that the Welsh girl had gone as well as the thrall, and I cannot say that I was surprised; though as they had failed in whatever they meant to compass this time, I could not see why they should not have tried again.

"Whence came she," I asked as carelessly as I could. "Maybe she has only gone home, fearing blame for dropping that horn."

"She has no home to go to, that we ken. She came from Jago at Norton only a little while ago, and she would hardly try to get back there across the hills alone. She is an orphan serf of his, and I fear that she has been stolen away."

"She has not been here long, then?"

"She came when you were with Owen. Jago sent to ask if Elfrida would take her in, she being worth having as a maid. His wife had no place for her, but would that she was well cared for. So she came with the first chapman who travelled this way."

Now as I thought of this girl, in a moment it flashed across me where I had seen her before. It was on board the ship at Tenby, and she came with Dunwal and his daughter Mara. I was certain of it, though I had only seen her that once, for there I was in a strange land, and so noticed things and people at which I should hardly have glanced elsewhere. The Danish and British dress over there was strange to me also.

Then, as soon as I had a chance I asked the ealdorman for a few moments of private speech, and we went into his own chamber that opened on the high place of the hall where we had been sitting. There I told him all the trouble, for surely I needed all help that I could find, and at the last I said:

"Mara, the daughter of Dunwal, was at guest quarters with Jago."

Then I saw the face of my friend paling slowly under its ruddy tan, and he rose and walked across the room once or twice, biting his lip as though in wrath or sore trouble. I could not tell which it was, but I thought that he was putting some new thought together in his mind.

"It is plain enough," he said at last, staying his walk at a side table. "I saw my sick man pick up that horn the girl dropped, and he looked into it and laughed and drank from it, saying that it was a pity to waste good stuff. See, here it is. The curl of it may have kept a fair draught in it for him."

There were several horns standing in their silver or gilded rests on the table at his elbow, and he held up that one which had been brought to me, and then dropped it.

It fell with its mouth upward, rocking on the bend in its midst, so that it might well have had a gill or two left in it, for it had a twist as well as the curve in its length, which was somewhat longer than usual.

"Poison!" he said in a low voice. "That a friend should be thus treated at my own door, by my own servant! What shall I say to you?"

"It is hard on you as on any one, Ealdorman," I answered. "But the girl did not come from Jago. Mara sent her in some way. I am sure it was she whom I saw at Tenby."

"Ay," he said, "one could not dream that a message seeming to come from honest Jago was not in truth from him. The trick was sure to be found out, and that soon, though."

"Not until the deed was done, maybe. This is the first chance that the Welsh girl has had to hand me aught."

The ealdorman held his peace for a moment, and then he broke out suddenly:

"By all the relics in Glastonbury, that thrall saved your life! He is no fool either, for he knew that the horn must be spilt in one way or the other, and it was worth while for you to run the risk of a fall rather than that you should drink it. How had he knowledge of what was to be done?"

"Whoever wrote the warning told him. It was a chance, however, that we did not come into the house."

"There is some friend watching these traitors," said Herewald. "I did not know the thrall, but so often men from the hill who have followed us come here for the ale that they know will be going, that I thought nothing of a stranger more or less. But why choose my house for this deed?"

I knew well enough, and it was plain when I minded the ealdorman that my vow was well known, and told, moreover, by Thorgils in Mara's hearing. This was a house where I should often be, and when Mara found out that Jago was a friend of Herewald of Glastonbury the rest was easy.

"Well, I will send to Jago today, and find out what he knows. That Cornish damsel must be better watched. Come, let us go and tell the king."

So we went, and when Ina heard what we had to say he grew very grave, and asked many questions before he told us what his thoughts were.

"They have struck at Owen through you, my Thane, even as I feared," he said. "I think that the matter of the land of Tregoz has saved you, for I seem to see in this thrall one of his men who hates him and will thwart his plans. There are yet men who will carry out what he planned ere he died. Now I am glad that we soon shall be gone from hence, and that is the first time that I have been ready to leave Glastonbury."

Now I will say that when Herewald's messenger came back from Norton it was even as we thought. Jago had no knowledge of the Welsh girl, or her sending. But Mara was gone a fortnight or more since, for Gerent had sent her father for safer keeping to the terrible old castle of Tintagel on the wild shore, and she had followed to be as near him as she might. Doubtless the girl might be found there also in time.

So I had no more warnings, and in a few days the strain on my mind wore off. I sent a message through Jago to Owen to tell him what had happened, so that he should have less anxiety for his own comfort, while he knew that I was shortly to be far hence.

Before that came about, however, Erpwald and Elfrida were betrothed with all solemnity in the new church, for their wedding was to be held here also in the summer, when all was ready for a new mistress at Eastdean. So Erpwald rode with us to Winchester a proud man, and by that time I thought I had forgotten that I ever held myself entitled to the place he had won.

But I did not forget the plotting, and as the days wore on, and my thoughts of it grew a little clearer, I began to wonder if the thrall who saved me from the poisoned horn might not be the man who slew Tregoz on the ramparts at Norton in the moonlight. I must say that it went against the grain for me to believe that Mara had aught to do with contriving my end through her maid, but unless there was some crafty hand at work in the background, all unsuspected, it seemed that there could be none else.

And then one day I found the little letter that Nona had sent me. In that I was warned against Morfed the Cornish priest, and I had forgotten him.

Now I will confess that two days after the Cheddar business I took that little brooch that Elfrida had given me, and dropped it into three fathoms of water as I rode by the mere one day. There are foolishnesses one does not care to be reminded of.

CHAPTER XII
OF THE MESSAGE BROUGHT BY JAGO, AND A MEETING IN DARTMOOR.

As one may be sure, there was no danger for me at Winchester, and if I had any anxiety at all it was for Owen, who had dangers round him which I did not know. I had sent him word by that old friend of his, Jago of Norton, how the last warning was justified, and had heard from him that with the imprisonment of Dunwal his last enemies seemed to have been removed or quieted. So I was more at ease concerning him, and presently rode with Erpwald to Eastdean in the fair May weather to see the beginning of that church which should keep the memory of my father.

And all I will say concerning that is that when I came to visit the old home once more I knew that I had chosen right. The life of a forest thane was not for me, and Eastdean seemed to have nought of pleasure for me, save in a sort of wonderment in seeing how my dreams had kept so little of aught of the true look of the place. In them it had grown and grown, as it were, and now I was disappointed with it. I suppose that it is always so with what one has not seen since childhood, and for me it was as well. I felt no shadow of regret for the choice I had made.

So after the foundation was laid with all due rites, I went back to the king and found him at Chippenham, for he was passing hither and thither about his realm, as was his wont, biding for weeks or maybe months here, and so elsewhere, to see that all went well. And I knew that in Erpwald and his mother I left good and firm friends behind me, and that all would be done as I should have wished. Ay, and maybe better than I could have asked, for what Erpwald took in hand in his plain single-heartedness was carried through without stint.

Through Chippenham come the western chapmen and tin traders, and so we had news from the court at Exeter that all was well and quiet, and so I deemed that there was no more trouble to be feared. It seemed as if Owen had taken his place, and that every foe was stilled.

And yet there grew on me an uneasiness that arose from a strange dream, or vision, if you will, that came to me one night and haunted me thereafter, so soon as ever my eyes closed, so that I grew to fear it somewhat. And yet there seemed nothing in it, as one may say. It was a vision of a place, and no more, though it was a place the like of which I had never seen.

I seemed to stand in a deep hollow in wild hills, and round me closed high cliffs that shut out all but the sky, so that they surrounded a lawn of fair turf, boulder strewn here and there, and bright with greener patches that told of bog beneath the grass. In the very midst of this lawn was a round pool of black, still water, and across on the far side of that was set a menhir, one of those tall standing stones that forgotten men of old were wont to rear for rites that are past. It was on the very edge of the pool, as it seemed, and was taller than any I had seen on our hills.

And when in my dream I had seen this strange place, always I woke with the voice of Owen in my ears calling me. That was the thing which made me uneasy more than that a dream should come often.

Three times that dream and voice came to me, but I said nought of it to any man. Then one day into the courtyard of the king's hall rode men in haste from the westward, and when I was called out to meet them the first man on whom my eyes rested was Jago of Norton, and my heart fell. Dusty and stained he was with riding, and his face was worn and hard, as with trouble, and he had no smile for me.

"What news, friend?" I said, coming close to him as he dismounted.

"As they took you, so have they taken Owen. We have lost him."

"Is he slain?"

"We think not. He was wounded and borne away. We cannot trace him or his captors. Gerent needs you, and I have a letter to your king."

I asked him no more at this time, but I took him straightway to Ina, travel stained as he was. He had but two men with him, and they were Saxons he had asked for from Herewald the ealdorman as he passed through Glastonbury in haste.

So Ina took the letter, and opened it, and as he read it his face grew troubled, so that my fear that I had not yet heard the worst grew on me. Then he handed it to me without a word.

"Gerent of the Britons, to Ina of Wessex.--I pray you send me Oswald, Owen's foster son, for I need him sorely. On my head be it if a hair of him is harmed. He who bears this is Jago, whom you know, and he will tell my need and my loneliness. I pray you speed him whom I ask for."

That was all written, and it seemed to me that more was not needed. One could read between the lines, after what Jago had said.

"What is the need for you?" Ina asked, as I gave him back the letter.

"To seek for Owen, my father," I said. "Jago must tell what we have to hear."

Then he told us, speaking in his own tongue, so that I had to translate for the king now and then, and it was a heavy tale he brought.

Owen had gone to some house that belonged to Tregoz, in the wild edge of Dartmoor north of Exeter, and there men unknown had set on the house and burnt it over him, slaying his men and sorely wounding himself. Only one man had escaped to tell the tale, and he was wounded and could tell little. And the deed was wrought in the night, and into the night he had seen the men depart, bearing the prince with them. But who and whence they were he could neither tell nor guess.

Then Gerent had ridden in all haste to the house, and found even as the wounded man had told, for all was still as the burners left it. But no man of all the village, nor the shepherds on the hills, could tell more. Owen was lost without trace left.

Then said Ina: "What more could be done by Oswald?--Will men help a Saxon?"

"This must be between ourselves, King Ina," Jago said plainly. "It is in my mind that if Oswald and I or some known lord of the British will go to that place and sit there quietly with rewards in our hands, we may learn much; for men fear Gerent the king in his wrath, and they fled from his coming."

"So be it," said Ina. "Oswald shall go, and it seems to me that every day is precious, so that he shall go at once. Is there thought that Owen may be taken out of the country, as Oswald was taken?"

"Every port and every fisher is watched, and has been so. For that was the first thing we feared. And word has gone to Howel of Dyfed and Mordred of Morganwg, farther up the channel, that they should watch their shores also. Nought has been left undone that may be done."

So it came to pass that on the next morning Jago and I rode away together along the great road that leads westward to Exeter and beyond, asking each train of chapmen whom we met if there was yet news, and hearing nought but sorrow for the loss of the prince they had hailed with such joy again. Nor did we draw rein, save to change horses, till we clattered up the ancient paved street of the city on its hill, and dismounted at the gates of the white palace where Gerent waited me.

There the first man who came out to greet me was one whom I was altogether glad to see, though his presence astonished me for a moment. Howel of Dyfed passed from the great door and bade me welcome.

"It is a different meeting from that which we had planned, Thane," he said, somewhat sadly. "I am here to help you if I can; for when we heard that Owen was lost much as you were, we came over straightway, there being reasons of her own which would not let Nona rest till we had sailed. Presently you will hear them from herself, for she is here. Glad am I to see you."

"There is no fresh hope?" I asked, as we went in.

"None; but we hope much from you. At least, your coming will cheer the old king, for he is well-nigh despairing."

Now I was prepared to see some change in Gerent by reason of all this sorrow and trouble, but not for all that was plain when I first set eyes on him presently. Old and shrunken he seemed, and his voice was weary and dull. Yet there came a new light into his eyes as he saw me, and he greeted me most kindly, bidding me, after a few words of welcome, to rest and eat awhile after the long ride, before we spoke together of troubles.

So in a little time I sought him again, and found him in a room with warm sunlight streaming into it, making the strange pictured walls bright and cheerful, and yet somewhat over close for one who loves the open air or the free timbered roof that loses itself in the smoke wreaths overhead, with the wind blowing through it as it blows through the forest whence it was wrought, and with twitter of birds to mind one of that also. Nevertheless, the old king in his purple mantle with its golden hem over the white linen tunic, and his little golden circlet on his curling white hair, seemed in place there, even as I minded thinking that Owen in his British array seemed in place.

Now Howel stood where Owen was wont to stand, and the only other in the room was the lady, who rose from the king's side to greet me.

And if her smile was a little sad, it was plain that Nona the princess was glad as her father to see her guest again, and I will say that to me the sight of her was like a bright gleam in the grey of sadness that was over all things. It did not seem possible that she and trouble could find place together.

So I greeted her, and she went back to her place quickly, for hardly would Gerent wait for us to speak a few words before he would talk of that which was in all his thoughts; and then came Jago and stood at the door, guarding it as it were against listeners.

Now the old king told me all that I had heard from his thane already, and I must tell what I thought thereof, and that was little enough beyond what I have said, and at last, when he seemed to wait for me to ask him more, I put a question that had come into my mind as I rode, and asked if there might be any chance of Morfed the priest having a hand in the matter.

And at that the king's frown grew black, and he answered fiercely:

"Morfed, the mad priest?--Ay, why had not I thought of him before? Look you, Oswald, into my hall of justice he came, barefoot and ragged from his wanderings, but a few days before Owen left me; and before all the folk, high and low, who were gathered there he cried out on all those who spoke for peace with the men who owned the rule of Canterbury, and who held traffic with the Saxon who has taken our lands. And Owen was for speaking him fair, seeing that he was crazed, but I bade him be silent, telling the priest that what was lost is lost, and there needed no more said thereof; and that if the men of Austin and we differed it was not the part of Christian men to make the difference wider, even as Owen and Aldhelm were wont to say. And at that he raved, and threatened to lay the heaviest ban of the Church on Owen, and on all who held with him, and so he was taken from my presence, and I have seen him no more. But he was a friend of Morgan."

"That is the priest who was with Dunwal, surely," Howel said.

"The same," I answered--"and I was warned of him," and I looked toward the princess, and she smiled a little and flushed.

"I mind how he glared at Oswald across my table," Howel said. "But one need fear little from him, as I think. Who will heed a crazy priest?"

"Many," answered Gerent. "The more because they deem him inspired. I will have him taken and brought to me."

There fell a little uneasy silence after that outburst of the king's, but I felt that I had not yet heard all that they would tell me. So we waited for the old king to speak, and at last he turned suddenly to the princess, setting his thin white hand on her shoulder, and said:

"Now tell Oswald what foolishness brought you here, Nona, daughter of Howel, that he may say what he thinks thereof."

"Maybe he also will think it foolishness, King Gerent," she said in her low clear voice. "But however that may be, I will tell him, for in what I have to say may be help. I cannot tell, but because it might be so I begged my father to bring me hither. It was all that I could do for my godfather."

There was just a little quiver in her lip as she said this, and the fierce old king's face softened somewhat.

"Nay," he said, "I meant no unkindness. I forgot that it is not right to speak to a child as to grown warriors. It is long since there was a lady about the place who is one of us."

Then Nona smiled wanly, and set her hand on that of the old king, and kept it there while she spoke.

"Indeed, Thane, it may be foolishness, and now perhaps as time goes on it begins to seem so to me. Once, as I know now, on the night when Owen first slept in his new house on the moor, I dreamed that he was in sore danger, for I seemed to see shadows of men creeping everywhere round the house that I have never set eyes on; and again, on the next night, and that was the night of the burning, I saw the house in flames, and men fought and fell around it among the flickering shadows, but I did not seem to see Owen. And then on the next night, soon after I first slept, I woke trembling with the most strange dream of all. I think that the light had hardly gone from the west, but the moon had not yet risen. I dreamed that I stood at the end of a narrow valley, whose sides were of tall cliffs of rough grey stone, and in the depth of the valley I saw a great menhir standing on the farther side of a black pool. And all the surface of the pool was rippling as if somewhat had disturbed it, and set upright in the ground on this side was a sword, like to that which King Ina gave you, Thane--ay, that which you wear now, not like my father's swords. And I thought that I heard one call on your name."

Now I heard Jago stifle a cry behind me, and as for myself I stood silent, biting my lip that I might know that I was not dreaming also, and I saw that Howel was looking at me in a wondering way, while Gerent glowered at me. All the time that she had been speaking, Nona had looked on the ground, in some fear lest we should smile at this which had been called foolishness, and I was glad when the king broke the silence with a short laugh.

"Well, Oswald, what think you of this? On my word, it seems that you half believe in the foolishness that some hold concerning dreams."

"I would not hold this so," said Howel,--"seeing that she has dreamed of things that did take place, as we know too well."

"Fire and fighting? Things, forsooth, that every village girl on the Saxon marches is frayed with every time she sleeps."

So said Gerent, and I answered him:

"Foolishness I cannot call this, either, Lord King. I also have seen the same in the night watches. I have seen pool and menhir, and the cliffs that hem them, even as the princess saw them. And I woke with the voice of Owen in my ears."

"Dreams, dreams!" the old king said. "Go to, you do but tell me these trifles to please me, and as if to give me hope that in such an unheard-of place we shall find him whom we have lost. Say no more, but go your ways on the morrow and search. And may you find your dream valley and what is therein."

He rose up impatiently, and Howel gave him his arm from the room. Jago followed him, and when the heavy curtain fell across the doorway, Nona, who had risen with Gerent, turned to me.

"I am sure now that there we shall find Owen," she said, with a new light of hope in her eyes. "And also I am sure that at the bottom of all the matter is Morfed the priest."

"It was a needed warning against him that I had from your hand, Princess," I said; "now let me thank you for it."

"I am glad you had it safely, for indeed I feared for you with those people on the ship with you. What has become of them?"

I told her the fate of Dunwal, so far as I knew it. I did not then know that Gerent had put an end to his plotting once for all two days after Owen was lost. As for his daughter, I knew no more than Jago told the ealdorman.

Then she said: "Now I would ask you to speak to my father, that he would let me go with you to Dartmoor, that I may help you search. I do not like to be far from him, but he says there may be danger. Which makes me the more anxious not to leave him, as you may suppose."

She smiled, but as I made no answer she went on:

"And maybe Owen will need nursing when you find him. They say he was sorely wounded. Ay, I am sure we shall find him, else why did we have these strange visions? And I think that were he not disabled altogether he would have won to freedom in some way."

"It is that wounding that makes me fear the worst," I said in a low voice; for indeed the thought of Owen as hurt, in the care, or want of care, of those who hated him, was not easy to be borne. "It is my fear that we shall be too late."

"Nay, but you must not fear that," she said quickly. "That is no sort of mind in which you have to set to work. I will think rather that they have carried him to some safe tending. There will be time enough to dread the worst when it is certain. There was nought in the dreams to make us think that he was dead."

The bright face and voice cheered me wonderfully, and for the moment, at least, I felt sure that our search would not fail. Then I tried to persuade her not to come with us. One could not say that there was any safety, even for her, among the men who would harm Owen, though I thought that none would be in the least likely to fall on Howel. Rather, they would keep out of his way altogether. In my own mind I wished that I was going alone, or with none but Jago, though, on the other hand, it might be possible that men would speak to him if they would not to me. And at last I did persuade her to bide here until we had news, promising that if need was she should come and see the place herself when all was known.

"Well, maybe it is not so needful that I should go now," she said. "I thought that I alone could tell my father when that valley was found, but you know as much of it as I, and will be sure when you stand in it."

And so we fell to talk of these visions which were so much alike, and there was but one difference in them. In the dream of the princess the pool had been ruffled, and mine was still as glass. And that seemed strange, and we could make nothing of it. Then Howel came back, and there is little more to say of the doings of that evening. There was no feasting in Gerent's house now.

Very early in the next dawning Howel and I rode westward with five score men of Gerent's best after us, into wilder country than I had ever yet seen; and late in the evening we came to where the countless folds of Dartmoor lie round the heads of Dart River. And there Tregoz had set his house, and I think that it was the first that had ever been in those wilds, save the huts of the villagers. Only the hall of the place had been burnt, and there yet stood the house of the steward on the village green, if one may call a meadow that had a dozen huts round it by that name, and we bestowed ourselves in the great room of that, while our men found places in stables and outhouses and the huts. Every man of the place had fled as they saw us coming, for the fear of Gerent was on them; but the women and children remained, and they had heard of the son of Owen, at least, since he and I were in Dartmoor in the spring. I had some of them brought to me when we were rested, and told them that none need fear aught, knowing that they would tell their menfolk.

And so it was, for after we had been quietly in the place for two days the men were back and at their work again. I do not think that even our Mendip miners were so wild as these people, and their strange Welsh was hard for me and Howel to understand. I will say that the whole matter seemed hopeless for a time, for no man would say anything to us about it. If we spoke to a man, questioning him, and presently wished to find him again, he was gone, and it would be days ere he came back.

Some of our guards knew the country as well as most, and with them we rode many a long mile into the hills during the first few days, searching for the deepest valleys, and ever did I look to see the great menhir before me as we came to bend after bend of the hills. Circles of standing stones we found, and cromlechs, ruins of ancient round stone huts where villages had been before men could remember, and once we saw a menhir on the hillside; but that was not what I sought, and none could tell us of the lost valley.

Yet it was in my mind as I questioned one or two that their looks seemed to say that the description of the place was not unknown to them, and if they would they could tell me more. At last, when I came to know the speech better at the end of a week, I thought that I would try another plan; I would trust to the shepherds, and ride alone for once across the hills. I thought that, even were I set upon, my horse would take me from danger more quickly than hillmen could run, and Howel, unwillingly enough, agreed that it seemed to be the only chance. Maybe the men would speak more openly with me on the hillside and alone.

So I asked if there was any one could tell me where there were menhirs in the valleys, and a shepherd said that he knew two or three. So I rode with him at my side to one of these, but it was not that which I sought; and, as I hoped, the man was more willing to speak, and we got on well enough. We had not met with a soul all day, but my hawk had taken two bustard after I saw the stone and was disappointed. One of these as a gift to the shepherd had opened his lips wonderfully, and we were talking as we rode in the dusk, and were not so far from the village, of another stone that I was to see next day, when I asked him if he had ever heard of the lost valley of pool and menhir.

He did not answer, but shrunk to my side, looking round him fearfully.

"What comes, Lord," he said, whispering;--"see yonder?"

He pointed across the bare hillside, and I looked but saw nothing.

"I saw nought," I said. "Is it unlucky to speak of the place?"

"I saw somewhat leap from yonder rock," he whispered; "it went behind that other."

Plainly the man was terrified, and I asked him what he feared.

"The good folk, Lord."

"Pixies?--Do they come when one speaks of the lost valley?"

"Speak lower, Lord,--lower! Look, yonder it is again!"

Then I also saw in the dusk the figure of a man who crept softly from one great boulder to another, and without thinking of the terror of the shepherd

I spurred my horse, and rode straight for the rock behind which the figure disappeared, having no mind to have an arrow put into me at short range by one of the men of Tregoz--or of Morfed--unawares.

The shepherd howled in fright when he was left, but I did not heed him, and in a moment I was round the rock and almost on the cowering man whom I had seen. He turned to fly, and I cried to him to stop, but he only got another rock between me and him, for the hillside was covered with them, and shrank behind it, so that I could only see his wild eyes as he glared at me across it. He said nothing, and I did not think that he was armed, so far as the dim evening light would let me see.

"Why are you dogging me thus?" I cried; "come out, and no harm will befall you."

I rode round, and he shifted as I did, so that he was between me and the shepherd, and then I called to the latter that this was but a man, and bade him come and help me to catch him. Whereon the man looked swiftly over his shoulder and saw that he was fairly trapped.

"Keep him back, Master," he said in a strange growling voice, which was not that of a Dartmoor savage either in tone or speech. "Keep him back, and we will talk together; I mean no harm."

But I had no need to tell the shepherd not to come, for he bided where he was, being afraid; but I held up my hand to him as if to bid him be still, lest the man should know that he would not help me.

"Come out like a man," I said. "One would think that you were some evildoer."

"Master, I will swear that I am not. Let that be, for I have somewhat to tell you that you will be glad to hear."

"If that is true, why did you not come openly, instead of waiting till I had you in a corner? Every one knows that there is reward for news from any honest man."

"There are those who would take my life if they caught me, Master. I have been seeking for speech with you alone all this day; I hoped the shepherd would leave you hereabout for his home, and then I would have come to you."

"Well," I said, "if you could tell me what I need to hear I will hold you safe from any."

"Master, will you swear that?" said the man eagerly.

Then it came across me that maybe this was one of those who fell on Owen, for one might well look for a traitor among so many.

So I answered cautiously: "Save and except you are one of those who have wrought harm to the prince you shall be safe. If you are one who has him alive and in keeping you shall be safe also."

"Master, you have promised, and it is well known that you keep your word. I am your man henceforward, by reason of that promise. I will give you a token that I have not harmed the prince."

"What have you to tell?"

"Master, they say that you seek the lost valley, of which none will speak."

"That seems true; but speak up, and mouth not your words so."

"Here was I born and bred, Master," said the man, still in the same growling voice. "I know where the lost valley is hidden, though none may go there save at peril of life. It is unlucky so much as to speak thereof."

"Can you take me within sight of its place, so that I can find it?" I asked, with a wild hope at last springing up in me.

"I can; and, Master, unluckier than I am I cannot be, so that life is little to me. Into that place I will even go for you, and risk what may befall me, if only you will find pardon for me. Only, I do not know if you will find aught of Owen the prince there."

"You must be in a bad way, my poor churl," said I, "if things are thus with you. But if you will help me to that place, and there let me find what I may, there is naught that may not be forgiven you. Even were it murder, I will pay the weregild for you, and you shall have cause to say that the place has no ill luck for you."

"Thane," said the man, in a new voice that was strangely familiar to me, "you have spoken, and forgiven I shall surely be."

Then he rose from behind the rock and came to my side, and took my hand and kissed it again and again, and surely I had seen his form before.

"Thane, I am Evan the outlaw, and my life is yours because you forgave me a little once, and saved me from the wolves, giving that life back to me when I knew it well nigh gone."

I looked at the pale hair and beard of the man, and wondered. Evan's had been black as night.

"It is Evan's voice," I said; "but you have changed strangely."

"Needs must I, Thane, with every man's hand against me, if I would serve you and Owen the prince for your sake."

Then I looked round for my shepherd, but he had fled.

"Come to the house with me," I said. "I think that none will know you, and if they do so I will answer for you."

"No, Thane; after tomorrow, seeing that even Howel sets such store on finding the valley, as men tell me, I shall be safe even from him. I think that you are the only one who will trust me yet."

There I knew that he was most likely right. Had I not been certain that he could have kept me from knowing him even yet, I think that I might have been doubtful of him myself.

"As you will," I answered. "We can meet tomorrow. Now give me that token by which I am to know that you have not harmed Owen."

"It is right that you should not yet trust me," Evan said, as if he read my thoughts, "for I do not deserve it. Here is one token: 'It is not good to sleep in the moonlight.' And I will give you yet another, if I may, for, indeed, I would have you know that the words I spoke yonder were true when I said that you should be glad that you freed me, and that I have tried to serve you. That may be known by the token of the blackthorn spine and the dog whip."

I reined up my horse in wonderment and stared at him, and he came close to my side, so that I could see him plainly. And, lo! his shoulders grew rounded, and his eyes crossed terribly, and they bided so, and he mumbled the words he had said when the whip of the huntsman fell on him.

Then he straightened himself again and looked timidly at me. He was not like the man who had bound me so cruelly in Holford combe on the Quantocks.

"Evan," I cried, "what you did for me at the ealdorman's gate is enough to win any pardon you may need."

"It is wonderful that, after all, pardon should come from you, Thane. Do you mind how I said to you that I hoped to win it otherwise through you when we took you on the Quantocks? It is good to feel as a free man once more."

"Free, and maybe honoured yet, Evan," I said; for I knew that he had risked his life for me and Owen. "Presently you shall come with me to Wessex, where none know you, and there shall be a fresh life for you. It is in my mind that what you brought on me was as a last hope."

"Ay, that is true, Thane."

And then I asked him to tell me all he knew of Owen, and of what had happened here, and how it came about that he knew aught. And as he told me it was plain that this was a true tale, for one could feel it so.

He had followed Owen, keeping himself hidden, after I went to Winchester, for there he knew that I was safe, and yet he would serve me if he could. So from the hillside where he lay he had seen the burning and the fight; and after Owen fell he followed them who bore him away, till he lost them in a grey mist that rolled from the hills and hid them in the darkness. Nor had he been able to find trace of them again, though he had hunted far and wide.

And so he waited for my coming, being sure that I would not be long. But he knew that they had gone toward what he called the lost valley, if it was not likely that they would dare so much as look into it.

"But," he said, "there was a priest with them, seeming to lead them. Maybe he would dare."

Into my mind at once came the certainty that this must be Morfed, but Evan knew nought of him. He had no more to tell me of this.

CHAPTER XIII
HOW OSWALD AND HOWEL DARED THE SECRET OF THE MENHIR, AND MET A WIZARD.

So we two rode on together over the wild hills, and talked of what chance there might be of finding Owen on the morrow. He could not tell me if his wounds were deep, for he was far off and helpless, but he told me how he had fought, and that was even as I had known he would.

Now the soft June darkness had fallen, and we were not a mile from the first houses of the village. Soon, if they were alert, we should meet the first outpost of our men who guarded us, and mayhap it were better that Evan came no farther tonight. Yet I would know somewhat of himself and the way in which he had helped me thus. So I stayed my horse and dismounted for a few minutes.

"Tell me, Evan," I said, "how came you into trouble at the first?"

"It is easy, Thane," he answered. "I was Evan the chapman, and well known near and far in Cornwall and Dyvnaint as an honest man, even as I have seemed yet beyond the water. Two years ago I slew the steward of this Tregoz in the open market place of Isca, and there was indeed little blame to me, for I did but protect my goods which he would have taken by force, and smote too hard. Little order was there in that market if the king was not there, and Morgan and his friends were in the town. Men have taken heart again since the coming back of Owen, for it was bad enough, as you may suppose by what happened to me. So I fled, and then Tregoz had me outlawed, with a price on my head, so that, being well known, I had to take to Exmoor and herd with others in the same case. I knew that no weregild, as the Saxon calls it, would be enough to save me from the Cornishman.

"There I was the one who could sell the stolen goods across the water, being held in good repute there, and I traded with the Norse strangers who ferried me across. So it was that when Owen came I was in Watchet, and there Tregoz saw me and laid hands on me. Then he needed men to carry out that which he would do, and he had me forth and spoke to me, saying that if I would manage the Quantock outlaws for him he would forgive me and have me inlawed again. I was to have been hanged that day, Thane, and so you will see that I had no choice. Owen's coming saved me then."

Evan was not the first man whom I had known to be driven into evil ways by misfortune and powerful enemies. I had little blame for him. A man will do much to save his neck from the rope. But this did not tell me how he knew the plans of Tregoz after I set him free in Dyfed.

"Then you came back to the Cornishman after I freed you?" I asked.

"That I did not, Thane, for the best of reasons. He would have hanged me at once if he were in power, and I had not meant to let him set eyes on me again in any case, for he was treacherous. I came back round the head waters of the Severn, through Wessex, where I was only a Weala, though, indeed, that is almost the same as an outlaw there; and there, by reason of Gerent's seeking for me, I changed my looks and watched for Tregoz, for I found that he was yet about the place in hiding. Thralls know and tell these things to men of their own sort, though they seem to know nothing if you ask them, Thane."

"Then you wrote the letters?"

"I had them written by the old priest of Combwich by the Parrett River, who will tell you that he did so. I took them myself to the palaces for you."

"And was it you who slew Tregoz?"

"Ay, with that seax you gave me back at the Caerau wolf's den. I heard that he had been speaking with a sentry, and thereafter I followed him and heard his plan. I saw him change arms with the sentry, and presently I fell on him, but the arrow had sped and I feared I was too late. I had to cross the trench from the bushes where I was hidden."

"But the poisoning at Glastonbury?--How did you know of that?

"Easy it was to know of, but less easy to prevent. I lurked round Glastonbury until I saw the girl, and knew that some fresh trouble was on hand for you. I knew her, for I had seen to that at Norton, that I might learn somewhat, if I could, while she attended on the lady, the daughter of Dunwal. She met her master there once or twice with messages, and it was by following her that I found his hiding in the hills. It was not hard for me to get her to tell me all that she had to do, for I made her think that I was in the plotting. Then she found it harder than had been expected to serve you, for she was kept about the lady. So she asked me, and I told her to wait. I thought she would most likely lose her chance altogether, and maybe but for your staying at the gate that day she would have done so."

"It was not the first time that we have had half the household outside serving a hunting party," I said.

"And each time I have been there, Thane, lest this should happen. The girl told me that such times were her only chance, and I said she had better wait for such a one again. I knew that in the open I could in some way spill the horn, so that she would be helpless and harmless afterward. Therefore I bade her not to try to harm you in the house, for my own reasons, but told her that it were safer for herself to wait for some stirrup cup chance, as it were. That day I saw that it had come, and I cut a thorn from the nearest bush and was ready. I could not reach the girl to stumble against her."

I minded that Thorgils had said that this Evan could beguile Loki himself with fair words, and I could well believe it. But he did not do things by halves when he set himself a task, and I felt that but for him I should certainly have been a victim--to Mara, or to whom?"

"Who wrought this plot? Was it Mara, the Cornish lady?"

"I do not think so," he answered, shaking his head. "There is one thing that the girl would never tell me. In no wise could I get the name of the one who gave her the poison. I do not know where she fled to, but it is likely that it was to that one."

"Some day you shall know how grateful I am for this, Evan," I said. "Now I must go. Only one thing more.--Where do you sleep?"

"Wheresoever I may, that I may be near you, Thane. Now meet me tomorrow at this place, and we will go to the lost valley. After that let me serve you for good and all if I may. I can do many things for you, and you had my life in your hand and gave it back to me; though indeed I know that it was hard for you to do so, seeing that a thane is sorely wronged by being bound by such as I."

"I can give you little, Evan; but I can, as I have said, find you a place in the court, whence you may rise."

"Let me serve you, Master," he said earnestly. "I have served myself for long enough, and it has not turned out well. If I please you not, I will go where you bid me, but in anywise let me try."

"As you will," I said. "I owe you well-nigh aught you can ask, and this is little enough."

Then I shook hands with him and parted. It was a strange meeting.

I went back to Howel with a mind that was full of what I might find on the morrow, but with little hope that there would be anything of sign that Owen yet lived. Howel was growing anxious for me as the darkness fell, and was glad to greet me, and I suppose my face told him somewhat.

"Why," he said, as I stepped into the firelight on the hearth of the little house, "what is this? Have you heard news at last?"

"I have found one who will take us to the lost valley, but nothing more. I have heard nought fresh, but that there was indeed a priest with the men who took Owen away."

"Well, we guessed as much as that; but I tell you plainly, Oswald, that I fear what may be in store for us in that place. Nona is not the girl to fancy things, and I know that her dreams must have been terrible to her. And then you also--"

"I fear, too," I said. "But I do not think that anything will be worse than this long uncertainty. Well, that is to be seen. Now I must tell you who it is that is to guide us, and maybe you will say that it is a strange story enough. Have patience until you hear all, however."

So I told him, beginning with the certainty that I had had some friend at work for me, and then telling him at last that I had found the man who had indeed saved me from these two dangers, and would also have saved Owen if he could.

"Why, how is it that he kept himself hidden all the time?"

"For good reason enough, in which you have some share," I answered, laughing. "It is none other than Evan the chapman."

"Evan!--How did he escape the Caerau wolves? I tell you that I had him tied up for them--and hard words from Nona did I get therefore when she knew. I was ashamed of myself for the thing afterwards, and on my word I am glad he got away. But when I am wroth I wax hasty, and things go hard with those who have angered me. But he was a foe of yours."

"Laugh at me as you will," I said; "I made him my friend when I cut his bonds in your woods."

He stared at me in wonder, and I told him what the hunting led to. And then I also told of what had sent Evan among the outlaws, and how he came to fall in with me.

"You are a better man than I, Oswald," he said thoughtfully, when I ended. "I could not have let him go. I am glad that you did it, and that for other reasons than that the deed has turned out to be of use."

Then he would hear more, and when it came to the way in which Evan had beguiled the Welsh servant he laughed.

"Surely he laid aside the squint when he made up to her, else from your account he would not have been welcome. But he could hardly have kept it up, lest the wind should change and it should bide with him, as the old women say. Well, I used to like the man, and so did Nona, and it is good to think that one was not so far wrong."

Now we thought that on the morrow we would go with but half a dozen men to the valley, if that would seem good to Evan. If he thought more were needed it would be easy to call them to us from the place where we were to meet him; and so we slept as well as the thought of that search would let us, and it was a long night to me. I think it was so for Howel also, for once in the night he stirred and spoke my name softly, and finding that I waked he said:

"I know why that girl of Mara's would not tell who set her on you. It is not like a maid to be sparing with her mistress' secrets, and Morfed is at the back of it. It is his work, and he laid a curse on the girl if she told who sent her. About the only thing that would keep her quiet."

"Why would Morfed want to hurt me?"

"Plain enough is that. If you were slain, Gerent would hold Ina responsible for Owen's sake, and Ina would blame Gerent, and there would be a breach at the least in the peace that your bishop has made."

Then we were silent, and presently sleep came to me, until the first light crept into the house and woke me.

In an hour we were riding across the hills with Evan, for whom we had brought a horse, and there were fifty men with us. We should leave them at a place which Evan would show us, and so go on with him without them. It was not so certain that we might not run into the nest of the men who had taken Owen, though this would surely not be in the lost valley.

Many a long mile Evan led us into the hills northwestward, and far beyond where I had yet been. I cannot tell how far it was altogether, for the way was winding, but I lost sight of all landmarks that I knew, and ever the bare hills grew barer and yet more wild, and I could understand that there were places where even the shepherds never went.

At first we saw one or two of these watching us from a distance, but soon we passed into utter loneliness, and nought but the cries of the nesting curlew which we startled, and the wail of the plover round our heads, broke the solemn stillness of the grey rocks on every side. Even our men grew silent, and the ring of sword on stirrup seemed too loud to be natural at last. We were all fully armed, of course.

Then we came to a place where the hills drew together, and doubled fold on fold under a cloud of hanging mist that hid their heads, and as we rode, once Evan pointed silently to a rock, and I looked and saw strange markings on it that had surely some meaning in them, though I could not tell what it was. And when I looked at him in question I saw that his face was growing pale and anxious, so that I thought we must be near the place which we sought. So it was, for after we had left that stone some two score fathoms behind us, as we passed up a narrow valley, there opened out yet another, wilder and more narrow still, and at its mouth he would have us leave the men and go on with him.

Now, we had seen no man, but when it came to this, Howel said:

"By all right of caution, we should have an outpost or two on those ridges. If we are going into this place it will not do to be trapped there."

So without question Evan pointed out places whence men could watch well enough against any possible comers, but he told me that we were close to the place we would see, and a call from our horns would bring help at once if it were needed. Howel sent men by twos to the hilltops, and the rest dismounted and waited where we stayed them, while we three went on together up the valley. I bade one of the men give Evan his spear, for he had none.

Grey and warm it was there, for the clouds hung overhead, and no breeze could find its way into the depths of this place, and it was very silent, but it was not the lost valley itself. And now Howel, who had not yet so much as seemed to know Evan, rode alongside him for a moment, and spoke kindly to him, telling him that he was glad of all that I had told him, and at last asking him to forget that which he had done to him in the woods of Dyfed. And that was much for the proud prince to ask, as I think, and I held him the more highly therefor in my mind.

And Evan replied by asking Howel to forget rather that he had ever deserved death at his hands.

"It shall be seen that I am not ungrateful to the Thane, my master, hereafter--if I may live after seeing this place," he said.

"Is it so deadly, then?" asked Howel, speaking low in the hush of the valley.

"It is said that those who see it must die--at least, of us who ken the curse on it. I do not think that it will harm you or the thane to see it, for you are not of this land at all. I have known men see this valley by mischance, and they have died shortly, crying out on the terror thereof. Yet none has ever told what he saw therein."

Now it seemed to me that it was possible that such men died of fear of what might be, as men who think they are accursed, whether by witchcraft or in other ways, will die, being killed by the trouble on their minds, and so I said to Evan:

"I will not take you into this place. Show us the way, and I will go alone."

"No, Master," he said, in such wise that it was plain that there was no turning him. "I am a Christian man, and I will not let old heathen curses hold me back, now that there is good reason why I should stand in that place. I will not be afraid thereof."

"Is the curse so old?" I asked.

"Old beyond memory," he said. "As old as what is in that place."

"As the menhir, therefore."

"I do not know that there is a menhir, Thane. How know you?"

I reined up, and told him shortly. It was only fair that I should do so. Then he said:

"The prince is dead, and maybe that he lies there will end the curse. Come, we will see."

A few paces more, and suddenly the hillside seemed to open in a ragged cleft that made another branching valley into the heart of the left-hand hillside, so deep that it seemed rather to sink downward from the mouth than to rise as a valley ever will. In all truth, none would ever have found that place unless he sought for it with a guide. I had not guessed that we were so near its entrance.

I looked round the hills, but from here I could see not one of our men on their watch posts, though one would have thought that where they stood it would have been impossible to lose sight of all. We were almost at the head of the wider valley along which we had ridden.

Now I had thought to be the leader into the lost valley when we came to it, but this Evan would not suffer. There was not room for us to ride abreast into its depths, for the narrow bottom of the cleft in the hills was littered with fallen boulders from the steeps that bordered it, and through these we had to pick our way. There was no path, nor was it possible to trace any mark of the foot of man or horse that might have been there before us, and the valley turned almost in a half circle, so that we could see no distance before us.

Now, I know that Evan had a hard struggle with his fears, but nevertheless, without drawing rein he led on, only turning to me with one word that told me that we had found the place; and as he turned I saw that his face was ashy pale, and as he rode on he crossed himself again and again, and his lips moved in prayer.

Down the long curve of the valley we rode, and it ever narrowed under rocky hills that grew at last to cliffs, and I knew that this must be but the bed of a raging torrent in the winter, for the stones that rattled under the horse hoofs were rounded, and here and there were pools of clear water among them. Any moment now might set us face to face with what I longed to see.

And when I saw Evan, ten paces ahead of me, straighten himself in the saddle as if he would guard a blow from his face, and draw rein, I knew that we were there, and I rode to his side and looked.

Suddenly the valley had ended in the place which I had seen in my vision--a rugged circle of cliffs, in whose only outlet, to all seeming, we stood. And in the midst of that circle was the pool of still, black water, and across that towered the tall menhir from a green bank on which it stood facing me. All round the pool was green grass, bright with the treacherous greenness that tells of deep bog beneath it, and then fair turf, and beyond the turf the rocky scree from the cliffs again. The menhir was full thrice a man's height.

It was even as I had seen it. I knew every rock and patch of green, and the very outline of the edge of the beetling crags that had been so plain to me in the dream light ere Owen called me.

But I did not heed these things at the first. My eyes went to the place where Nona the princess had seen the sword in the long grass on the hither side of the pool's edge, but I could not see it now. Then I must ride forward and search for it, and at that time Howel was close to me, and together we rode yet a little farther into the circle that the cliffs made, and as we drew closer to the edge of the pool I scanned every inch of the ground, seeking the sword which it seemed impossible that I should not find.

"It has gone," said Howel in a hushed voice.

And at that moment I saw a sparkle among the new grass at the very edge of the bog that surrounded the pool, and I threw the reins to the prince and sprang from my horse and went toward it. The light was very dull here, though it was nigh midday now, and indeed so high and overhanging were the cliffs that I do not think the sun ever reached the surface of the pool, save at this high midsummer, and then but as it passed athwart the narrow entrance, which faced south. Then it would send its rays across the pool full on the face of the menhir, as it seemed.

So I could see nought again until I was close to the spot whence the spark shone, and then I caught it once more, and hastily I cleared aside the rank grass with my spear butt, and lo! even as she had seen it in dreams the sword of Owen was there, and it was the gleam from the gem in its hilt, which no damp could dim, which had caught my eye. But a little while longer and we should never have seen even that, for the weapon was slowly sinking into the bog in which its scabbard point had been set, and even as I stepped forward a pace to reach it the black ooze rose round my foot, and Evan, who was behind me, caught my hand and pulled me back from its edge.

Then I turned with the sword in my hand, and I saw that his face had found its colour again, and that his fears had left him, for he had looked on the valley of the mighty curse and yet lived. His horse was at his side, and he had sprung to help me, but I hardly heeded him, for I had what I sought in my hand, and I held it up to Howel without a word, and a sort of fresh hope began to rise in my heart. Owen might not be so far from us.

"How came it there?" Howel said, wondering.

"Who can tell," I answered, turning over many possibilities in my mind.

"One thing is certain," Evan said,--"no man set it in that place meaningly, for there he must have known that it would be whelmed soon or late."

"Nor could it have been dropped there," I answered. "None would go so near the edge of the bog. It was surely thrown there. One thought to hurl it into the pool. Yet if so he could have done it, or would have tried again."

"Come, let us search the place," said Howel.

I hung the sword to my saddle bow, while Evan took the horses. The leather scabbard was black with the bog water of the turf where it had been set, but the blade within it was yet bright and keen.

Then I and the prince together walked slowly round the edge of the black pool on the broad stretch of grass between the bog around it and the loosely piled stones of the cliffs' foot. Here and there even this turf shook to our tread, as if it too were undermined with bog, and we went warily, therefore, wishing that we had not left our spears by the horses.

"One would call such a place as this 'the devil's cauldron' in our land," said Howel. "I mislike it altogether."

Then he sprang back with a start, and clutched my arm and pointed to the ground at his feet. The skull of a man grinned up at us, half sunk in the green turf, and the ends of ribs shewed how he to whom it had belonged lay. There went a cold chill through me as I looked; but I saw that the bones were old, very old. They had nought to do with our trouble, and what had been to others about the loss of him who had died here was long past and forgotten, or amended. But for the sake of what had been I was fain to unhelm for a moment as we stepped past them.

So we went on silently until we were halfway to the menhir, and then we saw that there was yet another way into this place, for across the water a jutting wall of rock had hidden a gorge that had surely been cleft by water, for down it came a little stream that seemed to sink into the turf so soon as it reached it.

"That is what fills the pool," said I, "and it must find its way hence underground like the stream at Cheddar. The pool may be fathomless. I would that I could look into its depths."

"What may not be in yonder gorge?" said Howel. "We must go and see."

So we came to the menhir's foot, and though the bog came almost to it there was yet a little mound of turf on which it stood, and I went to that to see if thence I could peer deeper into the dark water, but I could not.

"Come," Howel said, "it is midday, and I for one would not be on these hills on Midsummer Eve. Call me heathenish if you like, but this is an unlucky night whereon to walk in the haunts of the good folk."

I had forgotten that so it was, and even now I only smiled at the prince, for my mind was full of other things as I followed him toward the glen whence the stream came. And now I was sure that here was growing more clearly a trace as of a seldom trodden path toward its mouth. We passed a great flat rock, whereon were strange markings and a hollowed basin, which stood behind the menhir near the cliff, and to this the path led, but not beyond, from the glen. Now we were almost in the opening, when both of us stopped and looked at one another.

Surely there were footsteps coming among the rocks of the water course before us. Steep and crooked as this was, we could hear them, though as yet if it were a man or men who came we could not see. I pulled the prince back into cover, where the rocks hid us from any one who came down the stream, and I loosened my sword in its sheath, for I could not be so sure that it might not be sorely needed.

The rattle of stones came nearer, and I saw Evan hurrying to us. He also had heard, and he had made shift to tie the horses to some point of rock, and he ran with our spears in his hand to join us.

"Get to the other side of the pool, Thane," he said. "It may be the band of men who wrought the burning."

"No," I answered. "Listen. Maybe there are three or four men, not more. I want to take one if I can. He shall tell me all he knows of this place."

For I had made up my mind that one who would come here freely must needs be of those who had brought Owen.

Then from the narrow portal of the glen passed quickly, looking neither to the right nor left, a tall man, followed by two others, and they seemed not to see us, but went straight toward the menhir along that path I thought I had traced, and Howel and I stared at them, speechless and motionless, for the like of them we had never seen.

As for Evan, he reeled against the rock, and stared after them, clutching it with both hands, so that his spear fell rattling along the rocks.

"The Druids!" he gasped. "We are dead men."

At the sharp rattle the leader of the three men turned, and I knew him. He was clad in a wonderful gold and white robe that swept the ground, priest-like, but not that of any Christian, and his hair was bound with a golden fillet with which oak leaves were twisted, and in his ears were large earrings. On his bare right arm was a coiled golden bracelet, and a heavy golden torque was round his neck, and a great golden brooch knit up the folds of his flowing white cloak on his right shoulder. But for all this strange dress I knew him, and he was Morfed the priest, and I heard Howel mutter the name also.

Then a word from Morfed caused the other two to turn, and they saw us, and there flashed from under their robes--which were like those of their leader, save for golden ornaments--a long knife in the hand of each, and they made as if to fly on us.

Morfed held up his hand, and they stayed, glaring at us. I listened for the coming of more of his followers down the water course, but I heard none.

Then Morfed spoke a word or two to his men, and came toward us, leaving them standing where they were, some twenty paces or less behind him, and as he came his pale face shewed no sort of feeling of any kind. His strange bright eyes seemed to look past us, as if we were but stones at the path side.

"So it is the Saxon," he said, staying close before us. "Well, I have waited for you, if I did not look to see you here. And this is Howel of Dyfed. Surely a Briton knows that to break in on the rites of the Druid is death? But Howel ever was rash. And this is the outlaw. It is a true saying that he who sees this place shall die, Evan."

Then said Howel boldly: "Briton I am, and therefore I know that the rites of the Druid are banned by Holy Church. Wherefore does one of her priests come in this heathen robe to such a place as this on the eve of midsummer?"

"Seeing that none but the initiated may know what truth the ancient faith holds, it is not for you to say that this is heathenry, Prince," Morfed answered more quietly than I expected. "Ask yon Saxon if his Yule feast is less sacred to him now because it is not so long since that it was Woden's. Is tomorrow less Midsummer Day because it is the day of St. John? Hold your peace thereon, and go hence while I suffer you."

At that I glanced at the mouth of the valley whence we came, half looking to see it blocked by men, but it was not. There was nothing to stay us three armed men in this place, with but three against us, and they well-nigh defenceless. Morfed saw that glance and laughed.

"The Druid has other arms than those of steel," he said, and he drew slowly from the wide cincture round his waist a little golden sickle and balanced it in his hand before me, flashing it to and fro.

Now I was sure that he was crazed in all truth, and I would speak him fair that I might learn what he would tell me. Howel was silent, seeming to look curiously at the golden toy in the priest's hand, as it shifted restlessly backward and forward.

"We have come hither to pry into no ancient rites, Morfed," I said. "Tell me what you know of Owen the prince, my foster father, and we will go hence. I have seen that which tells me that he is near, but there are yet things that I must learn of how he came and where he lies."

But Morfed seemed to heed me not at all as I spoke. Only, he kept moving the little sickle which Howel watched, and its glancings drew my eyes to it in spite of myself, for overhead the sky was clearing somewhat and the sun was trying to break through, and the gold shone brightly.

"Midday," muttered the priest, "nigh midday, and what is to be done against the morrow must be done, else will the tale of many a thousand years be marred, and by me. Lo! the sun comes, and time passes swiftly."

The sun did indeed shine out now as some cloud passed, and I saw that its rays came slanting through the gap in the cliffs across the pool, passing the menhir without lighting on it, but falling now on the flat rock that was behind it, though not fully yet. Half thereof was still in the shadow thrown by the hills.

Morfed glanced at that shadow, and his face changed, for I think that he knew the time for some midday rite which we might not see was near, and at that he seemed to make some resolve. He did not turn from us, but he lifted his voice in a strange chant, and said somewhat in Welsh that I could not understand, and as they heard it his two followers placed themselves on either side of the flat rock three paces behind him, and stood motionless. Then Morfed lifted his arm and began to sing softly, swinging the sickle in time to the song, with his eyes on us.

I thought that maybe he would sing to us the end of Owen, as would Thorgils, but the tongue in which the words were spoken was not the Welsh that I knew. I think now that it was the tongue of the men who reared the menhir, and that which was the mother of the tongue of Howel and Gerent alike. It was an uncanny song, and I waxed uneasy as it went on, and the flashing sickle waved more quickly before my eyes.

Soon the murmur of the song seemed to get into my brain, as it were, and the sparkle of the gold in the sunlight wove itself into strange circles of light before my eyes, widening and narrowing in mystic curves that dazzled me, until at last I would look no longer, and with an effort I turned my head and glanced at Howel to ask if this foolishness should not be ended.

But he shook his head.

"Let him be," he said in a whisper. "It is ill to anger a crazed man. Surely he will tell what we need soon."

But beside him Evan seemed to be shrinking as in terror. I suppose the Briton has old memories of the Druids of past days which yet bid him fear them.

"Hearken to me, and heed them not," sang Morfed in words that I could understand. "Hearken, for you have much to learn."

That was true, and I turned to him. I supposed that he was in truth about to speak to me as I would, and straightway the look of Morfed was on my face, and the song went back to its old burden, and the flashing sickle held my eyes with its circling, and I knew that if I looked long I also must pass as it were from myself, as had those two, and I wrenched my eyes from him.

Then a movement on the stone caught my gaze, and I saw that the two men yet stood motionless, but across the sunlit patch which had crept nearer the centre where the hollowed bowl was, a great adder, greater than any I had ever seen, thick and spade-headed, had coiled itself in shining folds peaceably and seeming not to heed the men. Only its head was raised a little, and it swayed as in time to the chant of the priest, while the long forked tongue flickered forth now and then restlessly.

But Morfed went on with his song and his waving, seeming to try to draw my look back to him, and I noted, as I glanced again at him, that a shade of doubt crossed his face, and at that a new thought came to me. Maybe if he saw that I feared him not he would speak. So I looked in his eyes and bade him be silent and hearken to what I said to him.

Some wave of anger flushed his face then, and he drew a pace nearer to me, but he was not silent, and the waving sickle was not still. Neither of these things troubled me any longer, and I looked past them, in such wise that he might see that I meant him to obey me, even as one will look at a sullen thrall who delays to carry out an order given. A captain of warriors will know what signs to watch for in a man's face well enough, and slowly and at last I saw the look for which I waited steal across the face of the man before me, and then I raised my hand and said:

"Be still, and answer me."

The song stopped, and the lifted sickle sank with the hand that held it, and the eyes of Morfed left mine and sought the ground.

"What will you?" he said. "Let me go, for it is time."

"When you have answered," I said sternly. "Tell me, where is Owen?"

"In yonder pool," he said, as a child will answer its teacher.

But if he answered as a child, his face was sullen as of a child that is minded to rebel, and I knew that he would try not to tell me aught.

"You lie," I said coldly. "Neither Christian priest nor Druid would dare set a prince of Cornwall in an unhallowed grave. Tell me the truth."

"Ay, I lied," he said, speaking in a strange voice that seemed to come from him against his will. And then he spoke quickly, without faltering or excuse. "I led the men who should slay the despiser of the faith of his youth and friend of the Saxon, and we came to the house and destroyed it, but they slew him not. Sorely wounded he was, and yet they would not do my bidding and make an end, but murmured at me. Then they bore him away into the hills, saying that they would heal him of his hurts and thereafter win his pardon, for he was ever forgiving, and it is true that I told them not who it was they were to slay. I said that it was Oswald the Saxon, who slew Morgan, and they were glad. I do not know how it has come to pass that you are here. I hate you!"

"Speak on, Morfed," I said, for he had stayed his words on that, and I bent all my mind into that command as it were, so that he knew that I meant to be his master in this.

"Why should I not speak," he said dully. "Let me end quickly. Ay, I went with them, thinking that he would die on the way, for he was sorely wounded, and I mocked them and threatened them in vain. I led them to this place, and when they knew it they fled, and left him to me. Wherefore I brought him here, that I might see him die--I and these two carried him on the litter the men made. Then will I bury him in no hallowed grave, for I myself spoke the uttermost ban of Holy Church against him, for that he had herded with the men of the Saxons who follow Canterbury, and has wrought for peace with them."

Then I knew at last that Owen was not dead, and I think that in my gladness I lost my hold on Morfed, as it were, for I half forgot him. And at that moment there came a little cry from one of the men who waited by the flat altar stone, and both of them looked to Morfed for some command, as if a time had come. The stone was in full light now, and I noted that the shadow of the menhir was creeping toward its base, but not yet quite pointing to it.

But Morfed did not answer the cry, and the great adder, roused by it, moved restlessly in its coils, darting its long forked tongue into the hollow of the stone as if it sought somewhat. Then one of the men who seemed the younger took from under his robe a golden flask and poured what looked like milk into the hollow, and the creature lowered its head and lapped it thence.

At that cry Morfed started and half turned. But I had more to ask him, and I spoke sternly. Behind me was a rattle of arms, as if Howel would have stayed him.

"Morfed," I said, "you have yet to tell me where Owen, the prince, is hidden. If you would finish what you are about here, tell me straightway, or bid one of these men shew me, or we will stay all this wizardry."

Maybe I spoke more boldly than I felt, for indeed the whole business and the place made all seem uncanny. I know that my comrades feared it all.

But now Morfed heeded my word no longer. Slowly at last he turned away, and now he must needs look back toward the altar stone and the menhir in turning, and the sight of them seemed to bring to his mind what work he had here, so that in a moment I was forgotten, and he sprang past me toward his attendants, one of whom was pointing silently, but with a white face, to the shadow of the menhir. And I saw that now it touched the stone and crept up on its surface for an inch or less.

I suppose that tomorrow that shadow would be so much shorter, and would not lie on the flat top of the stone at all. Then for a little space the sun would seem to one at the back of the altar to stand on the menhir's top, while all the stone and the bowl where the adder lay was in full light, even as men say the sun seems to stand on the great stone of Stonehenge on Midsummer Day at its rising. I had seen that wonder once, and this minded me of it.

But what Morfed saw told him that midday had come and was passing; and all that meant to him, beyond that the time for some rite had been forgotten, I cannot tell. There came from his lips a cry that was of terror and of sorrow as I thought, and the adder lifted its head from its lapping and coiled itself menacingly.

He did not heed the creature, but threw abroad his hands sunwards, and began to speak hurriedly in that tongue which I could not follow; and as his words went on the faces of his men grew haggard, and one of them wept openly. The younger threw the golden vessel he had in his hand into the pool, and turned on me a look of the most terrible hate, and his hand stole under his robes as if he sought the knife I had seen him draw when they first came.

Now Howel and Evan were beside me, wondering, but spear in hand, and I was glad. There was more than enmity in the look of these men, and one to three has little chance. Whatever strange fears my friends had felt passed with the sight of danger.

But while Morfed spoke his followers were still, listening to him intently, until at last he seemed to dismiss them; and then they turned from him with a strange deep reverence, and folded their hands on their breasts, and came past where we stood, not looking at us, but with their eyes on the ground as if they were going back, up the water course whence they came. And at that I thought they might be going to where Owen was, and that they would harm him.

"Quick, Evan," I said; "follow them. See where they go."

"Ay, follow them," said Morfed. "Now I care not what befalls."

And with that he raised his voice and called somewhat to the men, and they quickened their pace into the glen. I did not understand what they said in return, but somewhat in the words of the ancient tongue they spoke was more plain to Howel, and he cried to me hastily, hurrying after Evan.

"Guard you the priest here, and beware of him!"

Then he dashed up the water course into which Evan had already disappeared, and I heard the feet of the four on the loose stone as they climbed upward. I had almost a mind to follow them, for I thought that their way led to Owen, but I dared not leave Morfed to go elsewhere. This might only be a plan to lead us astray.

CHAPTER XIV
HOW OSWALD FOUND WHAT HE SOUGHT, AND RODE HOMEWARD WITH NONA THE PRINCESS.

So I was left with Morfed the priest, and he did not offer to follow his men, but stood and faced me with eyes that gleamed with the fire of wrath or madness, or both. We waited, both of us, as I think, to hear if any sound beyond the lessening footfalls came from the water course, but they died away upward, and there was still no word between us. Then I thought that I would try one more plan with him.

"Morfed," I said, "take me to Owen, and I will pledge my word that Gerent shall seek no revenge for what has been done by you."

"What I have done!" he broke out. "I sought to rid the land of a foe, and that was a deed worth doing. Know you what you have done?--Through you is ended the tale of many a thousand years. The time is past when I, the priest and Archdruid of this poor land, should have done what has been done, since time untold, without fail, against tomorrow's rites. That day, therefore, through you shall be unobserved. It is strange that a mere Saxon warrior, with no thought beyond his feasting and fighting, should set his will against mine and prove the stronger. Now I wit well that this is some fated day, and that herein lies some omen of what shall be."

Then he turned a little from me, and looked at the shadow which had passed altogether from the altar stone now, and half to himself he said:

"I had thought that this menhir had fallen when this came to pass. But maybe the old prophecy meant that not until it fell we must cease our rites. But that was not how we read the words of old time. If we read them wrong, what else have we mistaken?"

"Morfed," I broke in on his musings, "end this idle talk, and tell me of Owen. Then I will go hence and leave you to work what you will here. I had no wish to disturb your rites, whatsoever they were. If aught has happened amiss, it was your own fault, not mine. Your own deed brought me here."

But he paid not the least heed to me, and yet I thought that he tried to put me off, as it were, by seeming wrapt in thoughts.

"Surely it should have fallen on this day that sees the end, even as runs the ancient prophecy--'When the pool shall whelm the stone, Druid rite and chant are done.' But it has not fallen, and the end is not yet. But what shall amend this fault?"

I had listened for some sound from Howel and Evan, but since the footsteps passed up the glen I had heard none until this moment. Then came one cry from far upward, and silence thereafter. Morfed heard it and looked up, setting at the same time his hand on the edge of the altar stone.

The golden sickle flashed as he did so, and at that, swift as the flash itself, the adder stiffened its coils, and its head flew back, baring the long fangs, and twice it struck the hand deeply.

"I am answered," Morfed said quietly. "My life shall amend."

But he never moved his hand, and the adder swiftly slid from off the stone and sought some hiding place in the loose rocks at the cliff foot, and the priest watched it go, motionless.

"Look you, Saxon," he said, lifting his eyes to me; "now I must die, and with me ends the line of the Druids of this land of the olden faith. Yonder in the Cymric land beyond the narrow sea whence Howel came it shall not be lost. The hills shall keep it, and there the slow mind of the Saxon shall not slay the old powers as you have slain them in me. Now I know that nought but the power of the cross shall avail on such minds as yours, for the lore of the older days is not for you. See! This is an end, and now you in your simpleness shall do one last thing for me."

I saw that the hand which yet rested on the altar was swelling already, and was waxing fiery red with four black marks where the fangs struck it. And I had a sort of pity for him, seeing him bear this, which he deemed his punishment, bravely. Still, he had answered nothing as to where Owen was.

"Morfed," I said, therefore--"if it is indeed the last hour for you, make amends for another ill by telling me where Owen is, and I will do what you ask me, if it is what I may do honestly and as a Christian."

"Grave me a cross on yonder menhir in token that the days of the Druid are numbered," he said softly, sitting down on the stone with his head bowed, as if in deadly faintness.

Two steps took me to the menhir, and I drew my seax that I might do as he asked me. It was a little thing, and Christian, and I thought that maybe he had come to himself from the madness of which men spoke. Yet though it seemed long that Howel was away, and I longed to follow him, I dared not leave this man, seeing that for all I knew Owen was somewhere close at hand, and it was not to be known what this priest might do in his despair. Howel and Evan might be following the men yet into some hiding place.

I set the point of my weapon to the stone and went to work, graving the upright stem of the cross first, thinking that Morfed would speak when he saw that I was indeed doing as he asked me. The stone was softer than I expected, and surely was not of the granite of the cliffs around, but had been brought from far, else I could not have marked it at all. Yet I had to lean heavily on my seax as I cut, and it was no light task, as I stood sidewise that I might not lose sight of Morfed.

"I die," he said presently. "There will be none left who may bring back the ancient secrets hither from the land of the Cymro. See, this is an end."

He rose up, staggering a little, and cast the golden sickle from him into the pool with a light eddying splash, as if it skimmed the surface ere it sank, but I did not look at it, and that was well for me. I saw his hand fly to his breast, as the hands of his men had gone for their weapons when they first saw us, and I knew what was coming.

Hardly had the golden toy touched the water when out flashed a long dagger from his robes, and he flew on me, thinking, no doubt, that I must needs turn my head to watch the fall of his sickle, and I was ready for him. He was no warrior, and his hand was too high, but he was a priest, and on him I would not use my weapon. I swung aside from him, striking up his arm, and his blind rush carried him against the menhir, so that the blow which was meant for me fell thereon, scoring the stone deeply; and lo! his own hand ended with that blow what I had begun, marking the cross-beam I had yet to make, so that the holy sign was complete.

And I saw that in a flash, even as he reeled back from the menhir and staggered. His foot splashed into the ooze of the bank and went down; and with that he lost his footing altogether and fell headlong into the pool, swaying as he went, across the front of the menhir.

Now there was a shout and the sound of hurrying footsteps behind me, but it was Howel's voice, and I did not turn. I leaned on the menhir to try to catch the white robes that swirled below me, and then I felt a heave and quaking in the turf on which I knelt as I reached over the black water, and Howel cried out and dragged me back roughly for a long fathom.

The menhir was falling. Slowly at first, and then more swiftly, it bent forward over the pool, and then it gathered way suddenly, and with a mighty crash it fell with all its towering height across it--and across the last flash of the white robes of the man who yet struggled therein.

For a moment the cross looked skyward, and then the wave swept over the stone, and it was gone into the unknown depths that maybe held so many secrets of the strange rites of those who had reared it. Only where its foot had been planted was a pit to shew that somewhat had been there, and that was slowly filling with the black bog which had undermined the stone at last. The old prophecy had come to pass, and there was indeed an end.

But I saw for a moment into that pit before it was filled, and in it was laid open as it were a great stone chest, where the base of the menhir had been to cover it, and in that were skulls and bones of men, and among them the dull gleam of ancient gold and flint.

The wild tumult of the water died away, and the ripples came, and then the pool was glassy as before, but there was no sign of movement in it, and now it was clear no longer. And still Howel and I stared silently at that place whence the great stone had passed like a dream.

"Nona saw it troubled," Howel said at last.

But I answered what was in my mind, with a sort of despair:

"He never told me where Owen lies."

"But I think we have found him, or nearly," Howel answered. "Come with me. This is no place for us to bide in. Did you hear those voices?"

I had heard the echoes from the rocks after the great crash, and they were strange and wild enough, but I heard nothing more.

"I heard one shout some time since," I said, rising up from where I still sat as Howel had left me.

"Nay, but the wailing when the stone fell," he said. "Wailing from all around. Wailing as of the lost. Come hence, Oswald."

I do not know if the man of the more ancient race heard more than I, mingled with those wild echoes, but I know that Howel the prince feared little. Now he was afraid, even in the bright sunlight, and owned it.

But the first shock had passed from me, and I looked for our horses. They had gone. I think that the fall of the menhir scared them, for they were yet tied where Evan left them, just before that.

"Howel, the horses have broken loose and gone," I cried.

"Let them be," he said; "they will but go to the men down the valley, and will be caught there. Come, we must get hence."

He fairly dragged me with him towards the glen, and it was not until we were out of the circle of cliffs round the pool and picking our way among the boulders of the water course, that he spoke again.

"That is better," he said,--"one can breathe here. I do not care if I never set eyes on that place again, and indeed I hope we need not. Now we have to find Owen as quickly as we may."

"What of the two men?"

"One turned on us, and we slew him perforce. The other Evan has tied up safely, though it took us all our time to catch him. I left Evan trying to make him speak."

I wondered in what way he was trying, but the path grew steeper and steeper, and the plash of water falling among the stones made it hard to hear. We went on and on, ever upward, until the walls of the narrow glen widened, and at last we were on a barren hillside, across which the little stream found its way in a belt of green grass and fern and bog from farther heights yet, and there I looked for Evan. The path reappeared here again, and it went slanting across the hill and over its shoulder, hardly more than a sheep track as it was. And here lay the body of the slain man.

"Over the hill crest," Howel said, noting my look around. "The man ran across this track. Did you hear what Morfed said to them?"

"No, I heard him call, of course, but his tongue is unknown to me."

"It was the ancient British, I think. I heard a word or two here and there, but few of those we use yet. I heard more that are written in our oldest writings, and few enough of them. But what he said to his men was plain enough, happily. He bade them kill the captive to amend the wrong done. I do not know what the wrong was."

I knew then that Owen had had a narrow escape, and but for the fleetness of foot of Evan he would surely have been slain. I told Howel of what had passed while he was absent, and so we came to the hilltop, and I saw a little below me the white robes of the captive, and Evan sitting by him, resting on his spear. He rose up as we came to him.

"Has he spoken, Evan?" I said.

"Ay, Master," he answered, with a grin that minded me of other days with him. "He says he will take us to the place where Owen lies, if we will promise to spare his life."

"We will promise that," I answered. "We will let him go his own way after we have seen all that we need."

"Let me rise, then," the man said quietly. "I will shew you all."

"Do not untie his hands, Evan, but let him walk," I said. "He is not to be trusted, if he is like his master."

It was the elder of the two whom we had before us, and he seemed downcast and harmless enough as we let him rise, though he was unhurt. He had run on while the younger turned to stay the pursuers, but Evan had caught him. He led us along the path, which I suppose his own feet and those of Morfed had worn, unless it was old as the menhir itself, and on the way he said suddenly:

"Let me ask one thing of you. Has the menhir fallen?"

"Ay, with the cross graven on it," I answered; and my words checked a laugh that was on Evan's lips.

"I knew it. I heard the crash," the man said. "That is an end therefore."

But Howel told the whole story as he had seen it take place, from the time when Morfed flew at me, to the time when the waters were still again; and as he heard, the man clenched his hands and bowed his head and went on quickly, as if that would prevent his hearing. After that he said nothing.

Then the path took us round the shoulder of a hill, and before us was a rocky platform on the sunward slope which went steeply down to another brook far below us. Far and wide from that platform one could see over the heads of three streams, and across three hill peaks that were right before us, and at the back of the level place was a great cromlech made of one vast flat stone reared on three others that were set in a triangle to uphold it. Seven good feet from the ground its top was, and each of the three supporting stones was some twelve feet long, so that it was like a house for space within, and the two foremost stones were apart as a doorway. And again beyond the cromlech was a hut, shaped like a beehive of straw, built of many stones most wonderfully, both walls and roof. There were things about this hut that seemed to tell that it was in use, and even as our footsteps rang on the rocky platform, out of its low doorway crept an ancient woman and stared at us wildly.

"What is this?" she screamed. "How should these unhallowed ones come hither?"

"Silence, mother," our captive said. "All is done, and these men come to take away the prince."

Then she saw that he was bound with Evan's belt, and at that she screamed again, and a wild look came into her face, and with a bound that was wonderful in one so old and bent she fled to the cromlech, and climbed up the rearward stone in some way, perching herself on the flat top, whence she glared at us.

"We will not harm you, mother," I said, seeing her terror.

And even as I spoke, from within the stone walls of the cromlech came the voice that I longed to hear again, weak, indeed, but yet that of Owen:

"Oswald, Oswald!"

Then I paid no more heed to the hag, but ran into the dark place, and there indeed was my foster father, swathed in bandages, and lying white and helpless on a rough couch, but yet with a bright smile and greeting for me, and I went on my knees at his side and answered him.

I will not say more of that meeting. Outside the old woman cursed and reviled Howel and Evan and the captive in turns unceasingly; but I heeded her no more than one heeds a starling chattering on the roof in the early morning. I had all that I sought, and aught else was as nothing to me.

After a little while Howel's face came into the doorway, and Owen called him in. I saw the look of the prince change as he marked the many swathings that told of Owen's sore hurts.

"Nay, but trouble not," Owen said, seeing this. "I am cut about a bit, for certain, but not so badly that I may not be about again soon. The old lady overhead has a shrewd tongue, but she is a marvellous good leech. I have not fared so badly here, and I knew Oswald would not rest until he found me."

"Now we must take you hence," I said. "Our men wait, and we can no doubt get them here."

He smiled, being tired with the joy of seeing us and the speaking, and I went out to Evan. The old woman still sat on the cromlech, and when she saw me her voice rose afresh with more hard words, which I would not notice.

"Evan," I said, "how shall we take the prince hence?"

"The litter they brought him on stands behind the hut yonder," he answered; "for this man tells me so. Also he says that we are not half a mile from our men, and that we can see one from just above here."

So I sent him to bring them, telling him how the horses were gone, so that we had no need to go back into the valley. To tell the truth, I was as much relieved in my mind that we need not do so as it was plain that he was. Then when he was gone I went back to Owen, and he asked me if we had seen Morfed. I did not tell him more than that we had done so, but that he was not here, one of his two men having guided us, for the tale we must tell him by and by might be better untold as yet.

"It does not matter," he said. "I cannot understand the man. At one time I think that he was at the bottom of all the trouble, and at another that he rescued me from the men who fell on the house. I have seen little of him here until yesterday and today. There is a man whom he calls 'the Bard,' who has tended me well enough with the old dame, and another whom he names 'the Ovate,' whom I have seen now and then--a younger man. I have set eyes on none but these four since the men of the burning left me to them in the hills."

We asked him how all that went, and he told us what he could remember. He had waked from some sort of a swoon while he was being carried, in the midst of many men, and again had come to himself when his litter had been set down. At that time there was seemingly a quarrel between Morfed and his two followers and these men, and it ended by the many departing and leaving him to the priest. That was, as I knew, when the hillmen would not come into the lost valley.

"They set my sword beside me," he said. "Presently in the dark I saw the gleam of a pool, and I made shift to throw it into the water, so that no outlaw or Morgan's man should boast that he wore it. Ina gave it me. One of the men saw me throw it, and was for staying, but the other said he had heard the splash and that it was gone. Morfed was not near at the time, having gone on. I heard him singing somewhere beyond the water."

"I have found it, father," I said. "It was on the edge of the pool, in long grass, and it helped us somewhat, for we knew you were near. Now say if it is well to move you yet. We can bide here with the men if not."

He laughed a little.

"I think so, but that is a question for the leech. Ask the dame. Maybe she will answer if you speak her fair."

Howel went to do that, saying that maybe she would listen to a Briton, for most of her wrath was concerning my Saxon arms. So presently I heard her shrill voice growing calmer as Howel coaxed her, and then there was a sound as if she climbed from her perch, and Howel came back to us.

"We may take you, she says. Hither come the men in all haste also, and we may get away from this place at once. These hills are uncanny on Midsummer Eve, and I am glad that we have long daylight before us."

Then said Owen:

"Oswald, I have not withal, but I would fain reward the bard and the old woman for their care of me. I think that even at Glastonbury there are none who would have healed these hurts of mine more easily than she."

I had my own thoughts about the bard, but I said that I would see to this, and went to him. The men were close at hand, and I saw that they led our horses with them.

"Bard," I said, "Owen the prince speaks well of you. Is it true that you would have slain him had you not been stayed on your way?"

"I do not know, Lord," he answered. "When I was with Morfed, needs must I do his bidding, even against my will. Yet, away from him, I think that I should not have harmed the prince. I am a Christian man, for all that you have seen."

"There was somewhat strangely heathenish in what I did see," I said. "But I suppose that is all done with?"

"I might go across the sea to the British lands in the north or in the south and learn to attain to druidship," he said. "But I will not. What I know shall die with me. He who was the next to me above, even Morfed, is gone, and he who was next below is gone also. Druid and Ovate both. I am the only one of the old line left, and I will be the last. Call me Bard no longer, I pray you."

"Well," I said, for there was that in the face of the man which told me that he was in earnest, "I will believe you, and the more that Owen trusts you."

I let loose his hands then, and he stretched his cramped arms and thanked me. I minded well what that feeling was like.

"What would Morfed have done with the prince?" I asked.

"I do not know. I have heard him plan many things. I think that if he had won him to his thoughts concerning the men of Canterbury he would have taken him home. If not, I only know this, that he would never have been seen in this land again. There was a thought of carrying him even across the sea to the Britons in the south--in Gaul. But of all things Morfed hoped that he would die here."

So I supposed, but I said no more, for Evan and the men reined up close to us. There was joy enough among them all as Owen was slowly and carefully laid on the rough litter. And we left those two staring after us, silent. But I suppose that the terror of that strange place will still lie on all the countryside, and I hold that since the day when the wizards of old time reared the menhir on that which it covered, with cruel rites and terrible words that have bided in the minds of men as a terror will bide, no man but such as Morfed has dared to pry into that valley lest the ancient curse should fall on them--the curse of the Druid who would hide his secrets. It may be, therefore, that it will not be known by the folk that the menhir has fallen, even yet, for we who did know it told them nought thereof.

As for that falling, it is the saying of Howel that it was wrought by the might of the holy sign, and maybe he is not so far wrong in a way. For if the slow creeping of the bog had at last undermined the base of the tall stone so that it needed but little to disturb its balance, no wind could reach it in that cliff-walled place even in the wildest gale, and it is likely that no hand but mine had touched it for long ages. I began, and the rush and blow of Morfed ended, the work of overthrow, with the sign of might complete. And Evan holds that but for the graving thereof he at least were by this time a dead man.

It was late evening when we came to the village, with no harm to Owen at all beyond tiredness, which a good sleep would amend; and after that there is little that I need tell of Howel's going to Exeter with the good news, and of his bringing back to us a litter more fitted for the carrying of the hurt prince, and then the welcome that was for us from Gerent.

When we were back with him, Owen passed into the loving hands of Nona the princess, and I do not think that he had any cause to regret his older leech of the beehive hut, skilful as she was, for we who loved him saw him gain strength daily.

Now I found means to send a letter to Ina, by the tin traders who were on the way to London, telling him that all was well, and begging him to suffer me to bide with my foster father for a time yet, as I knew indeed that I might, for my new place in the household had few duties save at times of ceremony, and in war, when I must lead the men of the household as the bearer of the king's own banner. And as the days went on it grew plain to me that there was somewhat amiss about the court here.

There was no dislike of myself, as I may truly say, among the men of West Wales whom I met with, but there was a coldness now and then which I could not altogether fathom, and that specially among the priests. It seemed that while Gerent had forgotten that I was aught but the son of Owen, who had brought him back, no one else forgot that I was a Saxon, and that there was more in the remembrance than should be in these times of peace. I could not think that this was due to my share in the death of Morgan either, for it was plain that not one of his friends was about the court.

At last I spoke of this to Howel, and found that he also had seen somewhat of the kind.

"I know it," he said. "If I am not very much mistaken, and I ought to know the signs of coming trouble by this time, there is somewhat brewing in the way of fresh enmity with your folk. It comes from the priests."

"There are more of the way of thinking of Morfed, therefore," I answered.

"And if that is so there may be more danger for Owen. It is well known that he is for peace, and that Gerent will listen to him in all things."

We talked of that for some time, not being at all easy yet concerning the matter, after seeing how far some were willing to go toward removing one who was in their way. I could not stay here long, nor could Howel, and it was certain that Gerent could not well guard Owen up to this time.

And at last Howel spoke the best counsel yet, after many plans turned over between us.

"We will even take him to Dyfed, and nurse him to strength in Pembroke. Then if aught is in the wind it will break out at once, lest he should return and spoil all. Gerent will either have to bow to the storm and fight, or else he will get the upper hand and quiet things again. If he can do that last, at least till Owen is back, all will be well. Owen will take things in hand then, and will be master."

That was indeed a way out of the trouble, and therein Nona helped us with Owen, so that at last he consented. I will say that he knew little or nothing of possible trouble here, and we told him nothing, for, in the first place, we had no certainty thereof, and in the next, he was not strong enough to do anything against it if we had.

When we came to ask Gerent if Howel might take him to Dyfed, we found no difficulty at all, which surprised me not a little. I think that the king knew that it was well for him to be across the channel in all quiet.

So it came to pass that in a few days all was ready for our going to Watchet to find Thorgils or some other shipmaster who would take us over. We could wait at Norton until the time of sailing came, if we might not cross at once, and thence I should go back to Ina.

One may guess without any telling of mine what the parting with Owen was for Gerent. As for myself, I was somewhat sorry to bid the old king farewell, for I liked him, and he was ever most kind to me. But I was not sorry to leave his court, by any means, for those reasons of which I have spoken, and of them most of all for fear of more plotting against Owen.

Now I will say that the ride to Watchet, slow and careful for his sake who must yet travel in the litter, and in fair summer weather, is one that I love to look back on. As may be supposed, by this time I and the princess were very good friends, and it is likely that I rode beside her for most of the way. We had many things to talk of.

One thing I have not set down yet is, that it had been easy, after what he had done for us, to win full pardon for Evan from Gerent. Now he rode with me, well armed and stalwart, as my servant, and one could hardly want a more likely looking one. And Nona had some good words and friendly to say to him, which made him hold his head higher yet after a time.

Presently, since I was on my way back to Glastonbury and onwards, we must needs speak of Elfrida, and I told her how I had fared when I came back from Dyfed. She laughed at me, and I laughed at myself also; for now I knew at last that the old fancy had in all truth passed from my mind.

So we came to Norton, and then sought Thorgils, and after that it was a week before he was ready. I mind the wonder on the face of the Norseman when he saw Evan at my heels on the day when his ship came home and I met him on the wharf; but he was glad to see him there.

"Faith," he said, "it has been a trouble to me that a man whom I was wont to trust had turned out so ill. It shook my own belief in my better judgment. I did think I knew a man when I saw him, until then. So I was not far wrong after all. Now I will make a new song of his deeds, and I do not think it will be a bad one."

Then it came to pass that one day, when the wind blew fair for Tenby, I saw the ship draw away from me as her broad sail filled, while on the deck was Owen in a great chair, and from his side Nona waved to me, and Howel shouted that I must come over ere long and fetch Owen home. Thorgils was steering, and he lifted his arm and cried his parting words, and so I turned away, feeling lonely as a man may feel for a little while. And presently I looked again toward the ship, and I think that the last I saw of her was the flutter of Nona's kerchief in the soft wind, and I vowed that nought should hinder me from Dyfed when the time came.

Thereafter I rode to Glastonbury, and told Herewald what I thought of the trouble that was surely brewing in the west; and he said that he also had some reason to think that along his borders men were getting more unruly, as if none tried to hinder them from giving cause of offence to us.

"Well, if they will but keep quiet until this wedding is over it will be a comfort," he said. "I should be more at ease if once Elfrida was safely in Sussex."

Then I learned that the wedding was to be in a month's time or so, and already there were preparations in hand for it. With all my heart I hoped also that nought might mar it.

Then I passed on to the king at Winchester, and glad was he to hear that we had indeed found Owen. But as he listened to what I thought was coming on us from the west, he said:

"It is even what Owen and I foresaw with the death of Aldhelm. This is a matter that not even Owen could have prevented, for it comes of the jealousy of the priests. We will go to Glastonbury and watch, and maybe we shall be in time for the wedding. But I will not be the one to break the peace. If war there must be, it must come from Gerent."

And so he mused for a while, and then said:

"Well, so it will be. And not before West Wales has tried her failing force for the last time will there be a lasting peace."

CHAPTER XV
HOW ERPWALD SAW HIS FIRST FIGHT ON HIS WEDDING DAY.

So we went to Glastonbury in a little time, and now it was as if Yuletide had come again in high summer, so full was the little town with guests who came to the wedding. Erpwald had come soon after us, with a train of Sussex thanes, who were his neighbours and would see him through the business, and take him and his bride home again. Well loved were the ealdorman and his fair daughter, and this was the first wedding in the new church, of which all the land was proud.

Only Ina was somewhat uneasy, though he would not shew it. For on all the Wessex border from Severn Sea to the Channel there was unrest. It seemed that the hand of Gerent had altogether slackened on his people, so that they did what they listed, and it was even worse than it had been in the days of Morgan and his brother, for at least they were answerable for what the men of Dyvnaint wrought of harm. There was none to take their place here, while the old king bided in Exeter or in Cornwall, and never came to Norton at all now. So there was pillage and raiding across the Parrett, and at last Ina had sent messages to Gerent concerning it.

A fortnight ago that was, and now the messengers had returned, bearing word from Gerent that he himself would come and speak to Ina of Wessex and answer him, and it was doubtful what that answer meant. There might well be a menace of war therein, or it might mean that he was only coming to Norton. It would not be the first time that the two kings had met there and spoken with one another in all friendliness concerning matters which might have been of much trouble. And we heard at least of no gathering of forces by the Welsh.

Yet Ina warned all the sheriffs of the Wessex borderland, and could do no more. The levies would come up at once when the first summons came.

All of which the ealdorman spoke to me of, but neither Erpwald nor Elfrida knew that war was in the air. We did not tell them. Thus we hoped to keep all knowledge that aught was unrestful from them in their happiness, until at least they two were beyond the sound of war, if it needs must come.

But it came to pass on the day before the wedding that all men knew thereof in stern truth, and that was a hard time for many.

Erpwald and I sat on the bench before the ealdorman's house in the late sunshine of the long July evening, talking of the morrow, and of Eastdean, and aught else that came uppermost, so that it was pleasant to think of, and before us we could see the long road that goes up the slope of Polden hills and so westward toward the Devon border. Along it came a wain or two laden high with the first rye that was harvested that year, and a herd or two of lazy kine finding their way to the byres for the evening milking. And then beyond the wains rose a dust, and I saw the waggoners draw aside, and the dust passed them, and the kine scattered wildly as it neared them; and so down the peaceful road spurred a little company of men who shouted as they came, never drawing rein or sparing spur for all that the farm horses reared and plunged and the kine fled terror stricken.

I think that I knew what it meant at once, but Erpwald laughed and said: "More of our guests, belike. One rides fast to a bridal, but they are over careless."

But I did not answer, for the hot pace of those who came never slackened, and spurring and with loose rein they swept across the bridge over the stream and so thundered toward us.

"Here is a hurry beyond a jest," said Erpwald, sitting up; "somewhat is amiss, surely."

Never rode men in that wise but for life. In a minute they were close, and one of them spied me and called to me, waving his arm toward the palace and reeling in his saddle as he did so. His arm was bandaged, and I saw that the spear his comrade next him bore was reddened, and that the other two had leapt on their horses with nought but the halter to guide them withal, as if in direst need for haste. Not much longer could their horses last as it seemed.

I sprang up and followed to the king's courtyard, leaving Erpwald wondering, and a footpath brought me there almost as they drew rein inside the gates. One of the horses staggered and fell as soon as he stayed, and his rider was in little better plight. That one who had beckoned to me knew me, and spoke at once, breathless:

"Let us to the king, Thane. The Welsh--the Welsh!"

"An outlaw raid again?" I asked.

"Would I come hither in this wise for that?" the man answered.

He was a sturdy franklin from the Quantock side of the river--one whose father had been set there by Kenwalch.

"I can deal, and have dealt, with the like of them, but this is war. They are on us in their thousands, and I have even been burnt out for being a Saxon, by a raiding party."

"Whence?"

"From Norton," answered another of the men. "Gerent, their king, is there with a host beyond counting. One fled from across the hills and told us, and we believed him not till the raiders came."

With that I took the men straightway to the king, bidding the house-carles hold their peace awhile. And even as we talked with this party, another man rode in from the Tone fenlands, and he had seen the march of the West Welsh men, and knew that Gerent's force was halted at Norton. A swift and sudden gathering, and a swift march that was worthy of a good leader, else had we heard thereof before this.

After that man came another, and yet another, till all the courtyard was full of reeking horses and white-faced men, and the ealdorman was sent for and Nunna; and in an hour or less the war arrow was out, and the news was flying north and south and east, with word that all Somerset was to be here on the morrow to hold the land their forebears had won from those who came.

Presently with the quiet of knowing all done that might be done on us, the ealdorman and I went down to his house.

"Here is an end of tomorrow's wedding," he said sadly. "I do not know how Elfrida will take it, for it is not to be supposed that Erpwald will hold back from the levy, though, indeed, if ever man had excuse, he has it in full."

I knew that he would not, also, and said nothing. He was yet sitting on the settle where I had left him waiting for me, with the level sun in his face as it sank across the Poldens, and he looked content with all things.

"What a coil and a clatter has been past me, surely," he said. "I doubt there must be a raid over the border, from what I hear the men shouting."

"More than that, friend," I said gravely, looking straight at him. "The Welsh are on us in all earnest, and tomorrow we must meet them somewhere yonder, where the sun is setting."

He looked at me, and his face flushed redder and redder.

"What, fighting in the air?" he said, with a sort of new interest.

"War,--nothing more or less," answered Herewald with a groan.

"I am in luck for once," he said, leaping up. "Let me go with you, Oswald; for this is what I have never seen."

"Hold hard, son-in-law," cried the ealdorman. "What of the wedding?"

His face fell, and he stared at us blankly, but his cheek paled.

"Forgive me," he said. "I never can manage to keep more than one thing in my head at a time. Here was I thinking of nought but that, until this news came and drove out all else. Don't tell Elfrida that I forgot it."

"Trouble enough for her without that," answered Herewald. "You cannot hold back, maybe, though indeed, not one will think the worse of you if you do so. We must tell Elfrida what has befallen, however, and she must speak her mind on your doings. Come, let us find her."

"Do you speak first, Ealdorman," I said, and he nodded and went his way.

Erpwald and I followed him into the hall, and there stayed. He was long gone thence to the bower where Elfrida sat with her maidens preparing for the morrow.

"What will she say?" asked Erpwald presently.

"I think that she will bid you fight for the king, though it will be hard for her to do so."

"I hope she will, though, indeed, I should like to think that it will not be easy for her to send me away," said the lover, torn in two ways. "How long will it take to settle with these Welsh?"

"I cannot tell," I said, shaking my head.

For, indeed, though I would not say it, a Welsh war is apt to be a long affair if once they get among the hills.

"If we have the victory, I think that the wedding will not be put off for so very long," I added to comfort him.

He walked back and forth across the hall until Herewald came back, and then started toward him.

"Go yonder and speak with her," the ealdorman said, pointing to the door whence he came.

Then he went hastily, and we two looked at one another.

"How is it with her?" I said.

"In the way of the girl who helped you slay Morgan," he said grimly. "She would hold him nidring if he had not wished to go."

We went to the door and looked out. All the road was dotted with men from the nearer villages who came to the gathering, and as they marched, each after the reeve of the place, they sang. And past the hindmost of them came a single horseman hurrying. Another messenger with the same news, doubtless.

Then there were footsteps across the hall behind us, and Elfrida and Erpwald came to us. I stole one glance at her, and saw that she hid her sorrow and pain well, though it was not without an effort. She spoke fast, and seemingly in cheerful wise, as we turned to her.

"Father, here is this Erpwald, who will go to the war, and I cannot hold him back. What can you say to him?"

"Nought, surely. For if he will not listen to you, it is certain that he will hearken to none else."

She laughed a little strained laugh, and turned to Erpwald.

"You must have your own way, as I can see plainly enough; and our wedding must needs wait your pleasure. Even my father will not help to keep you here."

"But, Elfrida--it was your own saying--" the poor lover went no further, for he was beyond his depth altogether.

It would seem that this was not the way in which she had spoken to him when they were alone. So I went to help him.

"We will take care of him, Elfrida," I said, trying to laugh; "but I think that he is able to do that for himself fairly well."

Then I was sorry that I had spoken, for it was a foolish speech, seeing that it brought the thought of danger more closely to her than was need, or maybe than she had let it come to her yet. She turned into the half-darkness of the hall again, and after her went Erpwald. The ealdorman and I went to the courtyard and left them, feeling that we need say no more.

Then through the dusk that horseman whom we had noted clattered up, and called in a great voice to us, asking if we knew where he should find Oswald the marshal, and I answered him and went out into the road to him. And there sat Thorgils, fully armed, on a great horse that was white with foam, but had been carefully ridden.

"Ho, comrade! have you heard the news?" he said, gripping my hand.

"Twenty times in half an hour," I answered. "But is there somewhat fresh?"

"Have any of your twenty told you that these knaves of Welsh have broken peace with us, tried to burn Watchet town--and had their heads broken?"

"News indeed, that," said I. "What more?"

"If you Saxons will stand by us, your kin, it may be worth your while. Here have I ridden to tell you so."

Then I hurried him to the king, for this was a matter worth hearing. Watchet was on Gerent's left flank, and a force there was a gain to us indeed, if only by staying the force at Norton for a day longer. We should have so much the more time in which to gather the levies.

But, seeing that they were not yet gathered, it did not at first seem possible to Ina that we could help to save the little town, whose few men had beaten off today's attack, but would be surely overwhelmed by numbers on the morrow if Gerent chose. But Thorgils had not come hither without a plan in his head, and he set it before the king plainly.

"Norton is on the southern end of the Quantocks, and Watchet is at the northern end, as you know, King Ina. Between the two on the hills is the great camp which any force can hold, but nought but a great one can storm. If you will give me two hundred men, I will have that camp by morning, and that will save Watchet, and maybe hold back Gerent in such wise that he will not care to pass it without retaking it. He will not know how few of us will be there, and you will be able to choose your own ground for the fighting while he bethinks him. There is but one road into Wessex across the Quantocks, and we shall seem to menace that while we cover the way to Watchet."

"So the camp is held?" asked Ina. "Gerent is before me there."

"Held by the men we beat off from Watchet, King. One we took tells us that they had no business to fall on our town, but turned aside to do it. Gerent has little hold on some of his chiefs. Now they are there with a fear of us and our axes on them, and if we may fall on them unawares we can take the camp without trouble, as I think."

"Oswald," said Ina, after a little thought, "how many horsemen can you raise now?"

The town was full of horses by this time, and I thought that it would not be hard to raise a hundred, and that in half an hour. Maybe if we did go with Thorgils we should meet many more men on the way to the levy also.

"Then you shall go with Thorgils," the king said. "It is a risk, certainly, but it is worth it. We had held that camp, had we had but a day's earlier warning, and that loss may be made good thus. That outlaw of yours will know many a safe place of retreat for you if need is. Good luck be with you."

He shook hands with us both, and we did not delay. His only bidding was that we should hold the camp until we had word from him, if we took it, and he was to learn thereof by signal.

So it came to pass that in an hour and a half Thorgils and I and Erpwald, who would by no means let me go without him, and three of his Sussex friends, rode across the causeway to the Polden hills in the dusk, with a matter of six score men behind us, well armed and mounted all--for these borderers have need to keep horse and arms of the best, and those ever ready.

From the ealdorman's door Elfrida watched us go very bravely, and the glimmer of her white dress was the lodestar that kept the eyes of her lover turned backward while it might be seen. It vanished suddenly, and he heaved a deep sigh, and I knew that she had been fain to watch no longer lest her tears should be seen.

As we went along the Polden ridge we met flying men, and men who came to the levy, and by twos and threes we added to our little force, until we had a full hundred more than when we started.

Thorgils took us to a tidal ford that crosses the Parrett River far below any bridge, which he thought would not yet be watched by the Welsh. There is a steep hill fort that covers this ford, but on it were no fires as of an outpost yet. Then we were a matter of eight miles from the great camp on the highest ridge of the Quantocks which we had to take, and we had ridden five-and-twenty miles. I was glad that we had to wait an hour or more for the fall of the tide before we could cross, for we rode fast thus far.

So we dismounted and watched the slow fall of the water, and we planned what we would do presently; until at last we splashed through the muddy ford, and rode on through dense forest land until the great camp rose above us, a full thousand feet skyward, and we saw the glow of the watch fires of those who held it. It seemed almost impossible to scale this hill as we looked on its slope in the darkness, but we reached its foot where the hill is steepest, and held on northward yet, until we came to where there is a long steady rise up to the very gate of the earthworks.

Now there should have been an outpost halfway along this slope toward the camp, for whatever tribe of the Britons made the stronghold had not forgotten to raise a little fort for one. But we were in luck, for this outpost was not held, and we rode past it, and knew that there was every chance now of our fairly surprising the camp. The first grey of dawn was coming when I passed the word to the men to close up, and told them what we were to do.

"We charge through the earthworks, for there is no barrier across the gate, and spread out across the camp with all the noise we can. Follow a flight for no long distance beyond the earthworks, but scatter the Welsh."

So we rode on steadily until we were but a bow shot from the trench, and yet no alarm was raised, for the foe watched hardly at all, deeming that no Saxon force would think of crossing where we crossed the river, or of coming on them from the north at all.

Then Thorgils and I and Erpwald rode forward, and I gave the word to charge, and up the long smooth slope we went at the gallop, with a heavy thunder of hoofs on the firm turf of the ancient track. And that thunder was the first sign that the Welsh knew of our coming.

I saw one come to the gateway and look, and then with a wild howl throw himself into the outer ditch for safety, and the camp roared with the alarm, and the dim white figures flocked to the rampart, and through a storm of ill-aimed arrows we rode through the unguarded gate and were on them.

"Ahoy!--Out, out!--Holy Cross!"

The war shouts of Norseman and South Saxon and Wessex men were in startling medley together here, and that terrified the Welsh yet more. It must have seemed to them that the Norsemen had called unheard of allies to their help. There was no order or rallying power among them.

We three were first through the gateway, and then we were riding across the camp with levelled spears, over men and through the fires, and a panic fell on the foe, so that without waiting to see what our numbers were, in headlong terror they fled from the charge over the ramparts and into the forests in the valleys on either side beyond whence we came. I had no fear of their rallying thence to any effect, for it would take them all their time to find their leaders in the combes and the thick undergrowth that clothed their sides. Once out of the camp, too, they could not see into it to tell how few we were.

I suppose that there were some five hundred Welsh in the place. I do not think that we harmed many of them in the hurry and the dark, but we scared them terribly. Here and there one rolled under the horses' hoofs, and we paid no heed to such as fell thus, and they rose again and fled the faster. All but one, that is, so far as I was concerned. I charged a man, and my spear missed him as he leapt aside, and he struck at my horse as I passed him, and the next moment I was rolling on the ground with the good steed, and the man behind me had to leap over us as we lay. That was one of the Sussex thanes, and he was no mean horseman or unready, luckily. Then he chased my enemy out of the camp, and came back to see if I were hurt. But I was not, and I bade him go on with the rest. We were almost across the camp at this time.

"Take my horse rather," he said. "See, there is a bit of a stand being made yonder."

There were yet some valiant and cooler-headed Welshmen whom the panic had not carried away, and they were getting together to our right. The camp was full three hundred paces across, and as we spread over it our line had gaps here and there, so that some at least had seen what our numbers were. They had passed into the camp again over the earthworks, or had been passed by in the place by us, and they were gathering round one who wore the crested helm and gilded arms of a chief, and he was raving at the cowards who had left him. Even now he had not more than a score of men with him.

Our men were chasing the flying foe across the open hilltop now, outside the camp, and there were but few left within its enclosure, though I saw the dim forms of some who were turning back without going beyond the rampart, and one of these was Erpwald. He also saw the group of Welshmen, and called the other horsemen to him, and even as the chief saw us two standing alone together, and led his few toward us, the shout of the four or five who charged with my friend stayed them, and they closed up to meet the new attack.

Then the Sussex thane, whose name was Algar, saw this, and again urged me to take his horse, saying that it was not fitting for the leader to be dismounted while work was yet in hand; but I saw a thing that bade me forget him, and set me running at full speed toward the Welshmen. Erpwald had ridden well ahead of his comrades, and as his spear crossed those of the foe one of them stepped forward before his chief and made a sweeping blow at the legs of the horse with a long pole-axe. Down the horse came, and Erpwald flew over its head into the midst of the enemy, overthrowing one or two of them as if he had been a stone from a sling.

In a moment they closed over him, but I was there before they could get clear of one another to slay him. I cut my way through the turmoil before they knew I was on them, and stood over him sword in hand, while the Welsh shrank back for a space with the suddenness of my coming. There was Algar also hewing at them and trying to reach my side, having dismounted, and those who followed Erpwald were on them with their long spears. It was more as a shouting than a fight for a moment or two, but Erpwald never moved, being stunned, as it seemed. It was like to go hard with me for a time, for my men could not reach me. Still, I held the Welsh back from Erpwald and myself.

There was a great shout of "Ahoy," and I saw from beyond the ring round me the rise and fall of a broad axe, and then Thorgils was at my back, and close behind him was Evan. More of our men were coming up fast to where they heard the noise; but the foe were minded to make a good fight of it, and only to yield when there was no shame in doing so.

"It is no bad thing to have a good axe at one's back," quoth Thorgils in a gruff shout between his war cries as he hewed, and with that I heard the said axe crash on a foe again.

Then I had the chief before me, and his men fell back a little to make way for him to me. Our swords crossed, and I took his first thrust fairly on the shield and returned it, wounding him a little, and he set his teeth and flew at me, point foremost, with the deadly thrust of the Roman weapon. That the shield met again, and I struck out over his guard and he went down headlong. And at that his men made a wild rush on me, yelling. At that time I saw Thorgils, with a great smile on his face, smite one man to his right with the axe edge, and another on his left with the blunt back of the weapon as he swung it round, and Evan saved me from a man who was coming on me from behind. That is all I know of the fight, save that it seemed that I heard some cry for quarter, for of a sudden I went down across Erpwald for no reason that I could tell.

It was full daylight when I came round, and the first thing that my eyes lit on was the broad face of Erpwald, who sat by my side with a woebegone look that changed suddenly to a great grin when he saw me stir and look at him. Then I saw Evan also watching me, with his arm tied up, and I was fain to laugh at his solemn face of trouble. Whereon from somewhere behind me Thorgils cried in his great seafaring voice:

"There now, what did I tell you two owls? His head is too hard to mind a bit of a knock like that."

Then he came and laughed at me, and I asked what sent me over.

"The pole-axe man hit you with the flat of his unhandy weapon. It is lucky for you that he was a bungler, however, for there is a sore dint in your helm."

I sat up and looked round the camp. There was a knot of captives in its midst, among whom was the chief I had fought, wounded, indeed, but not badly, and our men were eating the enemy's provender and laughing. A fire of green brushwood and heather was sending a tall pillar of smoke into the air to tell the watchers on the Poldens and at Watchet that we had done what we came to do. But here we had to stay till we heard from Ina that we were to join him, and for Erpwald's sake and Elfrida's I was not sorry.

He had seen his first fight, and nearly found his end therein. I do not know how I could have looked Elfrida in the face again had he indeed risen no more from that medley. But I thought that he made more than enough of my coming to his rescue. It was only a matter of holding back a crowd till help came.

"All very well to put it in that way, comrade," said Thorgils; "but where does my axe come in? You are not fair, for, by Thor's hammer, Erpwald, both of you had been mincemeat but for that."

"Nay," said I, laughing; "you and I were those who held back the crowd. I could not have done it alone."

"But you did, though," the Norseman answered at once. "Nevertheless, it was as well that I happened up in good time."

Now we rode across the nearer hills until we could see into the fair valley which men call Taunton Deane since those days, and we saw the answering fires which told us that all was well at Watchet, for we had saved the little town. Not until Gerent learned how few we were here would he dare to divide his forces. Far off to the southward in the valley we could see the blue reek of his campfires, and it would seem that he had not yet moved on the Wessex border.

All the day we waited and watched, anxious and restless, but no attack came on us here, and the smoke of the camp grew no thinner at Norton. A few Norsemen rode up to us from Watchet, and they said that no move was on hand yet, so far as they could tell. And at last, as the sun was setting, and shone level on the slope of the Poldens, above which the Tor of Glastonbury sent a waving wreath of smoke into the air to bid Wessex gather against the ancient foe, we saw the long line of sparkling helms and spear points as our host marched from hill to causeway to the bridge that spans the Parrett. Ina would hold the heights above Norton before morning.

But that made it the more needful that we should bide here till we were sent for, seeing that we guarded the flank of our advance; and hard it was to sit still and do it, with a battle pending yonder. It was a long night to us, and hungry.

Early in the next morning there was heavy smoke on these hills that told of burning on the line of our march, and there was more away toward the far Blackdown hills, as if there were trouble beyond Tone. And in the afternoon there fell a strange stillness on the woods round us, and I wondered. There was never a buzzard or kite, raven or crow, left in all the woodland, and then I minded that overhead lately the birds of prey had all flown in one direction, and that toward where Norton lay.

It was the cry of the kite and the voice of the songbirds that I missed. The birds of prey had gone, and in the cover their little quarry cowered in fear of the shadow of the broad wings which had crossed them so often. Even now two of the great sea eagles were sailing inland, and from these strange signs we knew for certain that yonder a battlefield was spread for them, where Saxon and Welsh strove for mastery in the fair valley. But we must pace the hill crest, silent and moody, waiting for some sign that might tell us of victory.

That came at last in the late afternoon. Slowly there gathered, over the trees where Norton was, a haze that thickened into a smoke, and that grew into heavy dun clouds which rose and drifted even to the hilltops, for Norton was burning, and by that token we knew that Ina was victor.

Presently there were flying men of the Welsh who could be seen on the open hillsides, and some few came even up to this camp, and we took them, and from them heard how the battle had gone. It had been a terrible battle, from their account, but they knew little more than that, and that they were beaten. I suppose that Ina thought it best for us to hold this camp for the night, for here we bided, chafing somewhat; and but for what we took from the Welsh, hungry, until early morning. Then at last a mounted messenger came to us, and we went to Norton.

There, indeed, was high praise waiting for us from Ina, for it seemed that our work had checked the advance of Gerent, and had given time for full gathering of the levies before he was over the border. But now I learnt that there was another Welsh army in the field, beyond the Tone River, and until we heard how it fared with the Dorset levies in that direction it was doubtful if we might hold that all was well yet. Gerent had not set everything on this one attack, but had also marched on Langport across the Blackdown hills. Thither Nunna had led what men he could be spared, and was to meet the Dorset levies, whose ealdorman, Sigebald, had sent word to Glastonbury, soon after I left there, to tell of this attack.

In the late evening there were beacon fires on the Blackdown hills, and a great one on the camp at Neroche which crowns and guards the hills in that direction. And so presently through the dusk one rode into Norton with word of the greatest battle that Wessex had fought since men could remember, for Nunna had met the foe on the way to Langport, and at last, after a mighty struggle which had long seemed doubtful, had swept them back across the hills whence they came, in full flight homeward. So there was full victory for Wessex, but we had to pay a heavy price therefor. Nunna had fallen in the hour of triumph, and Sigebald, the ealdorman, was lost to Dorset also.

Presently we laid Nunna in his mound on the Blackdown hills where he had fallen. There he bides as the foremost of Saxon leaders in the new land we had won, and I do not think that it is an unfitting place for such a one as he. It is certain that so long as a Wessex man who minds the deeds of his fathers is left the name of Nunna will be held in honour with that of the king; his kinsman.

CHAPTER XVI
OF MATTERS OF RANSOM, AND OF FORGIVENESS ASKED AND GRANTED.

Now I must needs tell somewhat of the way in which Ina won Norton, for that had so much to do with my fortunes as it turned out, seeing that all went well by reason of our holding the hill fort, in which matter, indeed, Thorgils must have his full share of praise.

Gerent halted in his march when the flying men from the camp came in to him, telling him that we were in strong force on the hill, and so our men crossed the Parrett unhindered, and won to the long crest of the southward spurs of Quantocks, where the Welsh gathered against Kenwalch in the old days and stayed his farther conquest. There was some sort of an advance post by this time in the Roman camp at Roborough, and Ina sent a few men to take it, and that was easily done. Then Gerent heard that Ina was on him, and went to meet him, and so the two armies met on the westward slope of the hills above Norton, and there all day long the battle swayed to and fro until the Welsh broke and fled back to the town itself. Then was a long fight across the ramparts, and at last Ina took the place, and so chased his enemy in hopeless rout across the moorland westward yet, until there was no chance of any stand being made.

But Gerent escaped, though it was said that it was sorely against his will. I was told that the old king came to the battle in a wonderful chariot drawn by four white horses, and that he stood in it fully armed, bidding his nobles carry him to the forefront of the fighting, but that they would not heed him. And presently when they knew that all was lost they hurried him from the field, though he cursed them, and even hewed at them with his sword to stay them as they went.

Now Ina's camp was set within the walls of Norton among the yet smoking ruins of the palace, where not one stone was left on another; and the Dragon banner of Wessex floated side by side with the White Horse of the sons of Hengist, where I had been wont to see the Dragon of the line of Arthur.

All the afternoon of that day Ina sat and saw the long files of captives pass before him, and I was there to question any he would, for he knew little or none of the Welsh tongue.

Many of these captives were of high rank, men who had only yielded when they must, and here and there I knew one of these by sight. They would be held to ransom by their captors, and the rest, freeman or thrall, as they had been, would be the slaves of those who took them, save they also could pay for freedom. It was a sad enough throng that passed under the shadow of the proud banners.

At last I saw one whom I knew well, and whom the king knew, for it was Jago. He stood in the line, looking neither to right nor left, but taking his misfortune like a brave man.

"Here is Jago, the friend of Owen, whom you know, King Ina," I said.

The king glanced up at the Welsh thane. There was no pride of conquest in the face of Ina as he gazed at his captives, and when one came as Jago came he looked little at him, lest he should seem to exult.

"Take him, and do what you will with him, Oswald. We owe you much again; if you see others for whom you would speak, tell me. I will deal with friends of Owen as you will. That is known already, and none will gainsay it."

I thanked the king quietly, but none the less heartily, and I ran my eyes down the line, but I saw no more known faces. So I went after Jago, who had passed on.

"Friend, you are free," I said. "That is the word of our king, for the sake of old friendship."

He could not answer, but the light leapt into his eyes, and he held out his hand to me. Then I took him to the tent which my house-carles had pitched next the king's, where Nunna's should have been, and bade him sit down there. Then I went out and brought up my own prisoners, passing the commoners into the hands of the men who had been with me, but keeping the chief until the last. Two of the house-carles led him up, and his face had as black a scowl on it as I had ever seen, and he looked sullenly at us.

"Who is he?" asked Ina, turning towards me.

I did not know, and, to tell the truth, had forgotten to ask him in the waiting for news of Nunna. So I asked him his name with all courtesy, and could win no answer from him but a blacker scowl than ever. Judging from his arms, which were splendid, and of the half Roman pattern that Howel wore, he might be of some note. I thought Jago might know him, so I asked him.

"Mordred, prince of Morganwg {ⁱⁱⁱ}, from across the channel," he answered, looking from the tent door. "He is a prize for whoever took him. Gerent sent word to several of those princes, and his men are somewhere in the country yet, I suppose. They came at Gerent's invitation."

I went back to Ina, who had set the chief aside for the moment, and when some other man's captives had passed, bound to a long cord, my men brought him forward again.

"Ask him what brought him here," said Ina, when he heard who he was.

"I have a mind not to answer you," Mordred growled, when I put the question, "but seeing that there is no use in keeping silence, I will tell you. I hate Saxons, and so when Gerent asked me I came to help him."

"With your men?"

"A shipload of them. They are up in the hills yonder, where you left them, I suppose; and they will be a trouble to you until they get home, if they can. I am well quit of the cowards."

Now I began to understand how it was that this force went aside to fall on Watchet, and had little heart in the defence of the camp. They were strangers, who hated the name of the Northmen from their own knowledge of them, and could not miss a chance of a fight with them here. After that the men of Gerent who were with them at the camp cared nought for their strange leader.

"Take him, and hold him to ransom, Oswald," Ina said, when I told him all this. "From all I ever heard of Morganwg, he should be some sort of reward for what you have done. I should set his price high also, for he deserves it for coming here."

So I took Mordred to my tent, telling him that I must speak of him of ransom.

"Ransom? Of course, that will be paid. What price do you set on me?"

Now that was a question on which I had no thought ready, seeing that I had never held any man of much rank to ransom before, and I hesitated. At last I remembered what some great Mercian thane had to pay to Owen some years ago, and I named that sum, which was good enough for me and Erpwald and Thorgils to share between us.

Thereon his face flushed red, and he scowled fiercely at me.

"What!--Is that the value of a prince of Morganwg? It is ill to insult a captive."

"Nay, Prince, there is no insult--"

"By St. Petroc, but there is, though! What will the men of Morganwg--what will the Dyfed men say when they hear that the Saxon holds one of the line of Arthur at the value of a hundred cows? Ay, that is how I shall be known henceforth!--Mordred of the cows, forsooth."

He was working himself up into a rage now, and even Jago from the corner of the tent where he sat, dejectedly enough, began to smile. I had spoken of fair coined silver, and I had some trouble myself in keeping a grave face when this Welsh prince counted the cost of cattle therein.

"Will you double the sum, Prince?" I asked in all good faith.

"I will pay the ransom that is fitting for a prince of Morganwg to pay when his foes have the advantage of him. The honour of the Cymro is concerned."

"Ask him his value," said Jago in Saxon, knowing that Mordred did not understand that tongue at all. "Never was so good a chance of selling a man at his own price."

Then I could not help a smile, and Mordred waxed furious. He turned on Jago with his fist clenched.

"Silence, you miserable--"

"Prince, Prince," I cried. "He did but bid me ask you what was fitting."

"Well, then, do it," he cried, stamping impatiently, and glaring at Jago yet.

It was plain that if he did not understand the Saxon he saw that there was some jest.

"It is a hard matter for me to set a price on you, Prince," I said gravely. "I have never held one of your rank to ransom before, so that you will forgive seeming discourtesy if I have unwittingly done what was not fitting in the matter. What would the men of your land think worthy of you?"

"Once," he said slowly, "it was the ill luck of my--of some forebear of mine to have to be ransomed. They paid so much for him."

He named a sum in good Welsh gold that it had never come into my mind to dream of. It was riches for all three of us. And I dared not say that it was too much and somewhat like foolishness, for it was his own valuation. So I held my peace.

"Not enough?" he asked, not angrily, but as if it would be an honour to hear that I set him higher. "What more shall I add?"

"No more, Prince. I see that I have yet things to learn."

Truly, I had always heard that the tale of the golden tribute to Rome from Britain had tempted my forebears here first of all, and now I believed it. I suppose these Welsh princes had hoards which had been carried from out of the way of us Saxons and Angles long ago.

"Ay, you have," Mordred said grimly. "One day it shall be what the worth of a British prince is in good cold steel, maybe. Now let me have a messenger who shall take word to my people and bring back what is needed."

He scowled when I mentioned Thorgils, but he knew him by repute at least, and was willing to trust him, as I would do so. In the end, therefore, it was he who took the signet ring and the letter the prince had written and brought back the gold. Some of the coins were of the days of Cunobelin, but the most of it was in bars and rings and chains, wrought for traffic by weight.

Now I will say at once that neither of my comrades would share in this ransom, though I thought that it was a matter between the three of us, as leaders of the force that day.

"Not I," quoth Thorgils--"the man was your own private captive, for you sent him down yourself. What do I want with that pile of gold? I have enough and to spare already, and I should only hoard it. Or else I should just give it back to you for a wedding present by and by. What? Shaking your head? Well, what becomes of all my songs if they end not in a wedding? Have a care, Oswald, and see that you make up your mind in time."

So he went away, laughing at me, but afterward I did make him promise that if he needed a new ship at any time he would tell me, so that I might give him one for the sake of the first voyage in the old vessel, and that pleased him well.

Now I told Ina this, being always accustomed to refer anything to him, and he was not surprised to hear that the Norseman would not take the gold.

"And if I may advise," he said, "I would not offer a share to Erpwald; for, in the first place, he does not expect it, seeing that the captive is yours only, by all right of war; and in the next, he deems that you have already given him Eastdean, and he is not so far wrong. So it would hurt him. He will be all the happier now that he will know that you have withal to buy four Eastdeans, if you will."

So against my will, as it were, that day made a rich man of me. Presently I gave the wealth into the hand of Herewald the ealdorman, and he so managed it, being a great trader in his way, that it seemed to grow somewise, and I have a yearly sum therefrom in ways that are hard to be understood by me, but which seem simple enough to him.

I handed over Mordred to the Norsemen to keep until Thorgils returned with the ransom, for before we could rest with the sword in its scabbard again it was needful that all care should be taken for the holding of the new land we had won, and Ina would see to that himself. Here and there we had fighting, but the Welsh never gathered again in force against us, and at last we held every town and camp from sea to sea along the line of the hills that run from Exmoor southwards, and there was our new border.

Jago went back to Exeter, seeing that his house was burnt at Norton with the rest of the town, and I heard afterwards that there he had found his wife, whom he had sent away when the certainty of war arose. I was in no trouble for him, as he had houses elsewhere.

But we sent Erpwald back to Glastonbury in all haste, and he was in nowise loth to go, as may be supposed. One may also guess how he was received there. Then, as soon as Ina came back with us all, the ealdorman set to work to prepare afresh the wedding that was so strangely and suddenly broken in upon, and it was likely to be little less joyous that it had been so.

On the evening before the wedding the ealdorman came to me, when the day's duties were over, and said that Elfrida wished to speak to me. So I went, of course, not at all troubling that the ealdorman could not tell me what was to be said, for there were many things concerning tomorrow's arrangements with which I was charged in one way or another.

So I found her waiting me alone, in that chamber off the hall where her father and I spoke of the poisoning.

"I have not sent for you for nothing, Oswald," she said, blushing a little as if it were a hard matter she had to speak of. "There is somewhat on my mind that I must needs disburden."

"Open confession is good," I said, laughing--"what is it?

"Well--have you forgotten your vow of last Yuletide?"

"Not in the least. Would you have me do so? For that were somewhat hard."

"No--but yes, in a way."

There she stopped for a moment, and I waited for her to go on, not having any very clear notion of what was to come. She turned away from me somewhat, letting her fingers play over one of the tall horns on the table, when she spoke again.

"It has been in my mind that you--that maybe you thought that I have been hard on you--in ways, since we spoke in the orchard."

So that was what troubled her, but I did not see why she should have spoken of it, seeing that a lady has no need at all to justify her ways in such a matter, surely.

"No," I answered, "that I never thought. If my vow displeased you, or maybe rather if I displeased you thereafter, I had no reason to blame any one but myself for the way in which it was needful that I should be shewn that so it was. It was just the best thing for me, for it cured me of divers kinds of foolishnesses."

"That is what I would have heard you say," she said with a light-hearted laugh enough, while her face cleared. "Now I can say what I will. Do you know that you have kept your vow to the full already?"

"Not at all. There are long years before you yet, as one may hope."

"Ay, Oswald, and through you those years seem bright to look forward to. See, through you has come Erpwald, and now you have kept his life for me at risk of your own. All my life long I shall thank you for those two things. Surely your vow is fulfilled, for this will be lifelong service. There is more that I would say to you, but I cannot."

She turned away again, weeping for very happiness, as I think, that could not be told, and I had no word to speak that was worth uttering, though I must say somewhat.

"It will be good to think of you two together--"

"In the place you have given us," she broke in on me. "Love and a home for all my life! What more could your vow have wrought than that? Let me go, Oswald, or I shall weep. It was a good day that sent you to be my champion."

Then she stepped swiftly to me and kissed me once, and fled, and I do not mind saying that I was glad that she had gone. Too much thanks for things that had been done more or less by chance, and as they came to hand as it were, without any special thought for any one, are apt to make one feel discomforted.

The wedding on the morrow I have no skill to tell of, but as every one has seen such a thing, that hardly matters. I will only set down that never had I seen such a bright one, or so good a company, there being all the more guests present because many who came to the levies stayed on to do honour to the ealdorman and his daughter. Elfrida looked all that a bride should, as I thought, and also as the queen said in my hearing, so that I think I cannot be wrong. I gave her Gerent's great gold armlet, having caused it to be wrought into such a circlet for her hair as any thane's wife might be well pleased to wear.

As for Erpwald, he was dazed and speechless with it all, but none heeded him, though indeed he made a gallant groom, for that is the usual way as regards the bridegroom at such times. Which is perhaps all the more comfortable for him.

Then was pleasant feasting, and after it some of us who had been Erpwald's closer friends here rode a little way with those two wedded ones on the first stage of their homeward journey. The Sussex thanes and their men were with them as guard, and they rode on ahead and left us to take our leave.

And by and by, after a mile or two, the rest turned back with gay farewells, and left me alone with the two, for they knew that I was their nearest friend, and would let me be the last to speak with them. We had not much to say, indeed, but there are thoughts, and most of all, good wishes, that can be best read without words.

"There is but one thing that I wish," Elfrida said at the very last, even when I had turned my horse and was leaving them.

"What is that?" I asked, seeing that there was some little jest coming.

"Only, that I had seen the Princess Nona."

I laughed, and so they were gone, and I went back to Glastonbury, wondering if Elfrida guessed what my thoughts of that lady might be. I had not said much of her to any one, except as one must speak of people with whom one has been for a while.

Strangely enough had come to pass that which I vowed to do for Elfrida, though not in the way which had been in my mind when I drank the Bragi bowl. Presently, when I came back to the ealdorman's house, I had to put up with some old jests concerning that vow, which seemed to others to have come to naught, but they did not hurt me.

Three days after the wedding Thorgils came to Glastonbury with his charge, and glad enough I was to hand it to Herewald, as I have already said, and to get the care of it off my mind. Yet I will say that by this time there had come to me a knowledge concerning this gold which was pleasant. Only the other day I had been but the simple captain of house-carles, though I was also the friend of a mighty king, and foster son of a prince indeed, and that had been all that I needed or cared for. Lately there had come a new hope into my life, and it was one that was far from me at that time. But now, when the time came for me to go to Dyfed for Owen, I should go with power to choose lands and a home for myself and for that one whom I dared now to ask to share it. And that was the only reason that I cared to think of the new riches at all. If that hope came to naught I should certainly care for them or need them little enough, for my home would be the court as ever.

Better to me than the gold was a letter from Owen. The honest Norseman had gone out of his way to put in at Tenby, knowing that I should be glad to have news thence, and not troubling about Mordred who was waiting release, at all. So he had seen Owen, who was well as might be, he said.

"With two holes in one thigh, and his left arm almost growing again like a crab's claw. I do not think that he was in the least surprised to hear of the war, nor indeed of its end. All he wanted to know was of you, as it seemed, at least from me. So it was also with Howel and the princess. It was good to see their faces when I told them of the fight at the camp, and how you won glory there. Nevertheless, I was half afraid that I made the fighting a bit too fierce over Erpwald, for the princess turned pale enough in hearing how you were knocked over. You ken that I am apt to make the most of things when I am telling a story. My father was just the same, and maybe my grandfather before that, for saga telling runs in the family."

I laughed at him, but in my mind I thought of the day when I saw Elfrida pale as she heard of Erpwald's danger at Cheddar, and I wondered.

Then I turned to Owen's letter, and it was long and somewhat sad, as may be supposed, for this war had a foreshadowing of long parting between him and me. But he said that he had known it must come, having full knowledge, before Morfed the priest took him, how the war party were getting beyond control. Wherefore he saw that he and I had been saved much sadness by his absence, and it remained to be seen how we should fare when he returned. At least, we should meet soon in Dyfed, for he mended apace.

I need not tell all of that letter, for it was mostly between us twain. But in it were words for Ina concerning peace, such as an ambassador from the British might well speak, and they helped greatly toward settlement by and by. And so the letter ended with greetings from Howel and Nona, and many words concerning their kindness to him.

But when I spoke to Thorgils of crossing soon to bring Owen back he shook his head.

"I suppose he has even made the best of things in the letter, but if he can bear arms again by Yule it will be a wonder," he said. "Yet he is well for so sorely wounded a man."

Then he promised that it should not be so long before I heard news from Owen again, for he had yet to make several voyages before the winter. And he kept his promise well, for I think that he made one more than he would have done, for my sake solely, though he will not own it, lest the long winter should seem lonesome to me.

For I will say at once that Owen did not come back by Yule. All that went on in the Cornish court I do not know, but it seemed that Gerent thought it well that he should not return until the last hope of victory over Wessex had passed from among his people; and it may be that he did not wish it to be thought that Owen had any hand in bringing about the peace which he must needs make. He would see to that, and take all the blame thereof himself, caring nothing for any man, if blame there should be from those who set the war on foot.

So although I waited to hear from time to time as Thorgils came and went, getting also word from him when some Danish ship crossed to Watchet, nought was said of Owen's return. And I was not sorry, for as things went I could not have gone to Dyfed to meet him.

There was the new land we had won to be tended, and for a time the planning for that was heavy enough. All men know now how it ended in the building of the mighty fortress of Taunton at the southern end of the Quantock hills, to bar the passage from West to East for all time. There is no mightier stronghold in all England than this, at least of those built by Saxon hands, and there has been none made like it since Hengist came to this land. It stands some two miles from where the Romans set Norton, for they had the same need to curb the wild British as have we, and the place they chose for their ways of warfare needed little amending for ours.

While that was building, Ina dwelt in the house of some great British lord at the place we call South Petherton, not far off from the fortress. As the place pleased him, presently he had a palace built there for himself, which, as it turned out, Ethelburga the queen never liked at all. However, that came about in after years. All day long now he was at Taunton, taking pride in overseeing all, so that there is no wonder that the place is strong.

As for me, I was with Herewald the ealdorman on the new boundary line with the levies and the king's own following, guarding against any new attack, and trying to win the Welsh to friendship. That was mostly my work, as I knew the tongue, and they knew me as Owen's foster son. We had some little trouble with them for a time, but soon, as they came to know the justice of the king, and that he did not mean to drive them from the land, they became content, and indeed there were many who welcomed a strong hand over them.

Presently there would be Saxon lords over the manors as Ina found men to hold them, but there would be no change beyond that. Freeman should be freeman, and thrall thrall, as before, each in his old holding undisturbed, with equal laws for Saxon and Briton alike.

Now, one day when I came to the house of the king at Petherton on some affairs I needed his word concerning, presently there came a message to me that Ethelburga the queen would speak with me, and, somewhat wondering, I was taken to her bower, and found her waiting for me.

"Oswald," she said, after a few words of greeting, "there is one who wronged you once, and has come to ask for your forgiveness. What answer shall I give?"

"Lady," I said, "I can remember none who need forgiveness from me now. Those who wrought ill against Owen have it already, or are gone. I have no foes, so far as I know, myself, and truly no wrongs unforgiven."

"Nay, but there is this one."

"Why then, my Queen, that one must needs be forgiven, seeing that I know not of wrong to me."

I laughed a little, thinking of some fault of a servant, or of a man of the guard, of which she had heard. But she went to a settle hard by and swept aside a kerchief which lay on it as if by chance, and under it were two war arrows. And I knew them at once for those which had been shot into our window at Norton and had vanished.

Now I will say that the sight of these brought back at once some of the old feeling against those who, like Tregoz, had sought Owen's life and mine, and my face must needs show it.

"Ay," the queen said, seeing that, "these are indeed a token that forgiveness is needed."

Then I remembered that there was but one who could come here with these arrows, though how she had them I could not do more than guess. It could be none other than Mara, the daughter of Dunwal.

Then suddenly, from among the ladies at the end of the room, one who was dressed in black rose up and came toward me, and she was none other than Mara herself, thin and pale indeed, and with the pride gone from her dark face. Her voice was very low as she spoke to me, and her bright black eyes were dim with tears.

"I do not ask you to forgive my uncle, or indeed my father--for what they planned and well-nigh wrought is past forgiveness," she said, "Forget those things if it be possible, but forgive my part in them."

"I have done that long ago, lady," I said in all truth.

I knew that she must have been made use of by the men in some ways, but I did not think at all that she had wished ill as they wished it, since I knew that Morfed had trained the Welsh girl to the deed at Glastonbury.

"Ay," she said sadly. "But forgetfulness is not forgiveness. You do not know how I carried messages between my father and uncle, when one was in bondage and the other in hiding, so that their plans were laid through me. I am guilty with them. Therefore I would hear you say at least that you will try to forgive before I pass from the world into the cloister where I may pray for them, and for you also, if I may."

Then I said, with a great pity on me for this lady whom I had known so proud and careless:

"Lady, I do forgive with all my heart. I do not think that you could have stood aloof from your father, and I do not think that you are so much to blame in all the trouble as you would seem to make me believe. In all truth I do forgive."

She looked searchingly at me while I spoke, and what she saw in my face was enough to tell her that she had all she needed, and with one word of thanks she went back to the ladies, and one of them took her from the room.

"She goes into my new nunnery at Glastonbury tomorrow, Oswald," the queen said, "and now she will rest content. It was a good chance that brought you here today, my Thane, for she had begged me to send for you, and that I could hardly do, seeing that one knows not where to find you from day to day. I could tell her truly that I knew I could win your forgiveness: but that would not have been enough for her, I think."

So Mara passed into the nunnery, and unless she has been one of the veiled sisters whom one sees in their places at the time of mass, I do not know that I have ever set eyes on her again. I do not think that it was the saddest end for her.

CHAPTER XVII
HOW OSWALD FOUND A HOME, AND OF THE LAST PERIL OF OWEN THE PRINCE.

All that winter, and through the spring, men toiled at the great fortress, but Ina went back presently to Glastonbury, or to others of his houses, after his wont, now and then riding even from far to us to see how all went. And I was fully busy in the new province, for we made a roll of those who owned land there, that all might be known to the king, and that matter was set in my hand for those reasons which had made me useful already in quieting the country. Moreover, the years at Malmesbury had made me able to write well, and now I was glad that I had learnt, though indeed it went sorely against the grain with me to do so at the time. Truly, I had to go on this errand of the king's with sword in one hand and pen in the other, but I daresay I did better, and fared less roughly, than would one who could not speak to the British freemen in their own tongue. At least, if a man was sullen when I came to him, he was, as a rule, pretty friendly when I left, for he knew that no harm was meant him, and that to be on this roll meant that on his lands he was to bide in peace.

And I may not forget that Evan helped me greatly in the matter, for he knew almost all of the best freemen.

When the walls were strong, in the midst of the new fortress they built a good house for Ina, and we thought that he meant to live here at times, for he had it fully furnished, even to the rushes on the floor, after Easter. By that time I had leisure to spend the holy season with the court at Glastonbury, for there was peace everywhere. And there I had a visit from Thorgils, who brought good news from across the sea. He had made his first voyage of the year, and had seen Owen, who was himself again, if yet weak.

He had not written to me, but sent word by the Norseman that he did but wait for me to come for him, if I might. If not he would come alone; but it seemed to him that we should have to part when we reached this side of the channel, for he must go to Gerent at once.

Next day Ina and the queen must needs pass to Taunton to see the place, for he said that when I might go for Owen depended on its readiness. So we rode with but a small train, meaning, after seeing the fortress, to go on to Petherton for the night, which was quite a usual plan with the king nowadays, since all this building was on hand.

So we went round all the walls, and saw the new bridge across the Tone River, and then went into the hall that stood, as I have said, within the walls of the fortress itself. There all was ready for the king, even to a fire on the hearth in the middle of the great hall, which was fully as large as that at Glastonbury itself. I had not seen this house of late, and now the king would have me go all over it and tell him what I thought thereof.

Indeed, there was nought to say of it but good, for it would be hard to find one better planned in all Wessex, as I think, whether in the house itself, or about the buildings that were set along its walls without for the thralls and workshops, or in the stables and other outhouses. It was indeed such a house as any thane would be proud to hold as his home.

Presently, therefore, after seeing all, the king and queen and I stood by the hearth in the hall again, and Ina asked me my thoughts of it. And I told him even as I have written, that all was well done and completely.

"Why, then," he said, "let me come and stay here now and then."

I laughed at that.

"I have heard, my King, of house-carles who led their masters, but that is not our way. Where the king goes the household follows, in Wessex."

He laughed also, for a moment.

"Long may it be so," he said. "Nevertheless, I think that I shall have to be as a guest here now and then."

Then Ethelburga smiled at my puzzled face, and spoke in her turn.

"Why, Oswald, it seems to me that you are the only man in all Wessex who does not know who is to live here."

"It is always said that the king himself will make it one of his palaces, lady," I answered.

Then Ina set his hand on my shoulder, and made no more secret of what he meant.

"I want you to bide here, my Thane, and hold this unquiet land for me. There is not one who can better rule it from this fortress for me than yourself; and the house and all that is in it is yours, if you will."

Then for a moment came over me that same feeling of loneliness that had kept me from taking Eastdean again, and with it there was the thought that I was not able to take so great a charge on me.

"How can I do this, my King?" I said, not knowing how to put into words all that I felt. "I am not strong enough for such a post."

"Nay," he said gravely. "It is said of me that I do not do things hastily, and it is a true word enough, seeing that I know that I often lose a chance by over caution, maybe. Answer me a question or two fairly, and I think you will see that I may ask you to bide here."

Then he minded me that I alone of all his athelings knew this Welsh tongue as if born thereto, and also that men knew me as the son of Owen the prince, so that the Welsh would hardly hold me as a stranger. That I had found out in these last months while I had been numbering the freemen and their holdings; and as I went about that business I had seen every one that was of any account, so that already I knew all the land I had to rule better than any other. That task, however, had been set me, as I know now, in preparation for this post.

I had no answer to make against all this concerning myself, for it was true enough, but I did not speak at once. It did not follow that I could rule as I should, even with all this to help me, and I knew it.

"What, is more needed?" Ina said. "Well, I at least have had a letter from Owen by the hand of Thorgils yesterday. See what is written in it."

He set the writing in my hand, and turned away while I read it. It was meant for my sight as well as his, for he had written to Owen concerning this post for me. And after I had read it all I could say no more, for Owen told how he would help me in all ways possible, and also that he knew how Gerent himself would be more content in knowing that no stranger was to be over the land he had lost.

So I gave the letter back to the king's hand, and said plainly: "I think that I may not hold back from what you ask me, my King, after all that Owen says. Nevertheless I--"

"But I am certain that you will do well," said Ina. "Now I shall miss my captain about the court, but I need him here. So you must even stay. There is Owen on the west to help you keep the peace in one way, and Herewald on the east to help you with the levies if need be. Fear not, therefore. It is in my mind that you will have an easier time here than any other I could have bethought me of, if I had tried."

Then, as in duty bound, I knelt and kissed the hand of the king in token of homage, and he smiled at me contented.

"You will be the first ealdorman of Devon, Oswald, when the Witan meets," he said; for it needed the word of the council of the thanes to give me the rank that was fitting.

Then when I rose up and stood somewhat mazed with the suddenness of it all, Ethelburga the queen, who had stood by smiling at me now and then, said: "This is your hall, Oswald, remember. But it needs one thing yet. You were wrong when you said it was complete."

I looked round and saw nothing wanting, from the hangings on the wall to the pile of skins on the high place seats.

"There are the pegs for the arms of the house-carles," I said, "but no arms thereon yet. That will soon be mended. And I have to set up a head or two of game, to make all homely, maybe?"

"More than that, Oswald," she said, laughing. "Strange how dense a man can be! It is a mistress who is needed. Else the women of Devon will have no friend at court."

I laughed, a little foolishly, perhaps, not having any answer at all, and Ina smiled and went out into the court by himself, saying that he would not meddle with such matters. So I was left to the queen by the hearth.

"Jesting apart, Oswald," she said, "I had hoped that vow of yours would have led to somewhat, and whose fault it was that nought came of it I do not know. However, no harm seems to have been done, and that may pass, though indeed Elfrida was a favourite of mine. But see to it that next time you are no laggard. Now, when are you going to Dyfed?"

Then I suppose my face told some tale against me, for the queen laughed softly.

"Soon, Oswald?"

I could not pretend to misunderstand her then, but when it was put to me so plainly it did not seem to me all so certain that my suit would fare better than my vow. I had no fear once that the last would not have been welcome, and was mistaken enough. Now, perhaps because I was in real earnest, I did doubt altogether.

"What, do you fear that there is no favour for you, my Thane?" Ethelburga said, with a smile lingering round the corners of her mouth.

"I do not see how there can be," I answered. "I am not worthy. It is one thing for the princess to be friendly with me, and another for her to suffer me to look so high."

I spoke plainly to the queen, as I was ever wont since I was a child in her train and she the kindly lady to whose hand I looked for all things, and from whom all my earlier happinesses had come. She was ever the same, and I know well that her name will be remembered as one of our best hereafter. It was almost therefore as mother to son that she spoke to me, rather than as mistress to servant.

"But you had no doubts at all concerning Elfrida."

"That was foolishness, my Queen, and I see it now. This is different altogether."

"I know it, and it was my fault in a way. Still, you were then but the landless house-carle captain, and yet you dared to look up to the daughter of the ealdorman. Now you are the Thane of Taunton, and to be the first ealdorman of Saxon Devon, with house and riches at your back, moreover. And she of whom you think is but the daughter of a Welsh princelet."

"Nay, my Queen, but she is Nona."

"Go your ways, Oswald," the queen said, laughing--"of a surety you are in earnest this time. Nay, but I will jest no more, and will wish you all speed to Pembroke. If there is no welcome, and more, for you there, I am mistaken, for you deserve all you wish."

So we spoke no more, but joined the king. Presently, when I came to think of what the queen had said of my changed rank and all that, I saw that she was right, and it heartened me somewhat. Not that I thought it would make any difference to Nona, but that it surely must to Howel, which was a great matter after all.

In a week Ina gathered the Witan of Somerset here to Taunton, first that the last stone of the fortress should be laid with all solemnity and due rites, even as the foundation had been laid with the blessing of Holy Church on it, and then that he might take counsel for the holding of the new land. Then in full Witan I did homage and took the oaths that were fitting, and so the king girt my sword on me afresh as I sat at the foot of his throne as the first ealdorman of Devon; and the Witan confirmed his choice, also making sure to me all dues that should come to the man who held the rank. They seemed well satisfied with the king's choice of me, and that was a good thing, for I will say that I had somewhat feared jealousy here and there. I do not think that their approval was due to any special merit of my own at all, but it was plain that I stood in a halfway place, as it were, between the two courts in a way that was in itself enough to make the choice good policy.

After that Ina bade me go to Dyfed, while he was yet in the west, and would set all things in train for me, choosing my house-carles, and setting such men as I could work well with in places of trust in the land. There was much for the king to do yet.

"Therefore take what time you will, Oswald," he said kindly. "You will be busy enough when you come back, and I can trust you not to overstay your time. If Owen can come to speak with me bring him, but that is doubtful yet."

One may suppose that I did not delay then. I sent Evan to Thorgils, and asked him to give me a passage over, and so had a fortnight to wait for him, as he was on his way from some voyage westward at the time. Then a fair summer sailing and a welcome from the Danefolk at Tenby, where we put in rather than make for the long tidal waters of Milford Haven against a southwest breeze.

There the Danes must needs set themselves in array in all holiday gear that I might ride to Pembroke as a prince's foster son, with a better following than Evan and my half-dozen house-carles, and I rode with fifty men after me, so that the guard at the palace gates might have thought that Ina himself had come to see Owen, and there was bustle of welcome enough.

And so there were wonderful greetings for me, from Owen first, and afterward from Howel and from Nona, and I will not say much of them. If one knows what it is to see a father whom one had left weak and ill, strong and well and fully himself again; if one has met a good friend after absence; if one knows what it may be to see again the one who is dearest in thought, there is no need for me to try and tell the greeting, and if not, I could not make it understood. Let it be therefore. It was all that I looked for, and I was more than content.

And yet, for all that, it was a long week before I dared to tell Nona that which I would, and how I did so is another thing that I cannot set down. Maybe all that I need say is that I need not have feared, and that the new hall at Taunton waited for its mistress from that hour forward.

And so at length I knew that I must be away, and I rode to Tenby to see Thorgils, and found him in the haven, begrimed and happy, with men and boys round him at work on the ship everywhere, painting and scraping in such wise that I hardly knew her. From stem to stern she was bright green instead of her sea-stained rusty black, and a broad gilt band ran along her side below the oar ports. A great red and gold dragon from one of the warships of the Danes reared its crest on the stem head, while its tail curved in red and gold over the stern post, and even the mast was painted in red and white bands, and had a new gilt dog vane at its head.

"Here is finery, comrade," I said. "What is the meaning thereof?"

"Well, if you know not, no man knows. I have a new coat for tomorrow's wedding, and it is only fit that the ship that takes home the bride should have one also. Wherefore the old craft will be somewhat to sing about by the time I have done with her."

Then he showed me a new red-striped sail that Eric had given him, and an awning for the after deck which the women of the town had wrought for the shelter of the princess whom they loved. It seemed like a good speeding to Nona and to me.

And so it was at the end of a fortnight thereafter. It would be long to tell of the morrow's wedding, and then of days at Pembroke before we sailed, passed all too quickly for me. But at last we stood with Owen on the deck of the good ship while all the shore buzzed with folk, Welsh and Danish alike, who watched us pass from Dyfed to the Devon coast, cheering and waving with mighty goodwill, and only Howel seemed lonely as he sat on his white horse, still and yet smiling, with his men round him, where the cliff looks over the inner harbour, to see the last for many days of the daughter he had trusted to my keeping.

We cleared the harbour, and then where she had been lying under the island flew toward us under thirty oars the best longship that Eric owned, for it was his word that as the Danes had seen me into Pembroke by land, so they would see Nona from the shore with a king's following by sea, and that was well done indeed. The old chief himself was steering in full arms, and all the rowers were in their mail and helms, flashing and sparkling wondrously in the sun as they swung in time to the rowing song as they came. And all down the gangway amidships between the rowers stood the armed men who should take their places when their turn came, full sixty warriors, well armed and mail clad as if they had need to guard us across the sea.

I suppose that there is no more wonderful sight than such a ship as this, fresh from her winter quarters, and with her full crew of three men to an oar in all array for war, and Owen and I gazed at her in all delight. As for my princess, she had more thought for the kindliness of the chief in thus troubling himself and his men, I think, for she could not know the pleasure it gave each man of the Danes to feel his arms on him and the good ship swinging under him again after long months ashore.

"There is another ship in the offing," I said to Thorgils presently, when we, with the Dane just astern of us, were some five miles from land and had ceased to look back to Tenby. Nona had gone into the cabin away from the wind, which came a little chill from the east on the open sea, and maybe also that she felt the chill of parting from her father more than she would have us know.

"Ay," he said, looking at the far vessel under his hand, "I do not make out what she is--but if she is a trader--well, our Danes are likely to get some reward for their trouble. They will not have come out for nothing."

I laughed, for any trader in the Severn sea knew that he must be ready to pay more than harbour dues if he had the ill luck to meet with the Danes.

They would make him pay for freedom, but would not harm him unless he was foolish enough to fight.

So we held on, and the strange sail, which was seemingly beating up channel against the wind, put about and headed for us somewhat sooner than Thorgils expected.

"She is making mighty short boards," he said. "She should surely have headed over to the coast yet awhile. Would have fetched a bit of a breeze off the land there, maybe."

Thorgils watched this vessel curiously, for there were things about her which seemed to puzzle him. The men, too, were beginning to talk of her and watch her. And presently I saw that our consort, the Dane, had slackened her speed, so that there was a mile of water between us astern.

"Oh ay," said Thorgils, as I spoke of this, "they mean to pick her up when we have passed her. They can overhaul her as they like."

Now we drew near to the strange ship, and it seemed to Owen and me, as we stood side by side on the after deck beside Thorgils at the helm, that we saw here and there among the men on her deck the sparkle of arms as she lifted and swayed to the waves. She was a long black ship, not like the Dane at all, and her sail was three cornered on a long tapering yard, quite unlike ours, which was square. Thorgils said that she was a trader from the far south, a foreigner, even from so far as Spain, though why she was here he could not tell. Mostly such never came round the Land's End.

"She wants to speak with us," he said presently. "I suppose she has lost herself in strange waters."

The vessel was right across our bows now, some half mile away, and her tall sail was flapping in the wind as she hove to. Thorgils put the helm down so as to pass to windward of her, and as he did so the sail of the stranger filled again, and she headed as if waiting to sail with us for a while. Now we could see that many of her crew, which did not seem large, were armed, and I thought little of that, seeing that there were Danes about. But Thorgils waxed silent, and sent a man to the masthead suddenly, for some reason which was not plain to me.

No sooner was the man there than he shouted somewhat in broad Norse sea language, which made our skipper start and knit his brows.

"How many?" he asked.

"Like to herrings in a barrel.--More than I can tell," the masthead man answered.

Then Thorgils turned to us.

"This is more than I can fully fathom," he said, leaning on the helm a little, so that the ship edged up a trifle closer to the wind steadily. "She has her weather gunwale packed with men, who are hiding under it--armed men. On my word, it is well that Eric is with us."

Owen and I looked at one another. If I had been alone, or with him only, I think I should have rejoiced in this seeming chance of a fight at sea, but with Nona and her maidens on board there was a sort of terror for me in what all this might mean.

No honest vessel hid her men thus, and waited for the coming of two strangers.

"Get your arms on, prince and comrade," said Thorgils. "It is in my mind that these are desperate folk of sorts. We are pranked up with that dragon like any longship, and here is Eric astern of us, and yet there is some look of fighting in the hiding of these men. Will they face two of us, or what is it?"

"We may not fight with the lady on board, Thorgils," Owen said under his breath. "If so be we can get away from them we must. Yet it will be the first time that Oswald and I have thought of flying."

"There is no merit in staying for a fight if there is need why one should be out of it," Thorgils said. "See, she is going to try to get to windward of us, and now will be a bit of a sailing match."

Then he called one of the men, and he came aft and took a pole with a round red board on its top from where it hung along the gunwale, and, standing on the stern rail with his arm round the high stern post, waved it slowly. He was signalling to Eric as Thorgils bade him.

The ship forged up into the wind closer and closer, and the spray flew over her bows as she met the sea. But the strange vessel was no less weatherly, and kept pace with us, and now Eric was bearing down on us more or less, sailing a little more free than we, though he also had to luff somewhat to keep near us, taking a long slant across our course as we sailed now.

I sent Evan for our arms, for the men were arming silently. They were in the chests in the fore cabin where I had once been bound, and Nona knew nought of possible trouble on hand. To keep her from it altogether I went to the low door of her rude shelter before I put on my mail, and looked in, telling her to keep the cabin closed against the spray that was flying, and had a bright smile for my thought. Then I went back to the deck and armed, and all the while the two ships reached to windward, but even in that little time I saw that the stranger had gained on us. The man was at work signalling to Eric again.

"We shall know if he means fighting in no long time," said Thorgils to me. "If he does I think that he is going to be surprised."

"How?"

"Well, unless every man on board is clean witless they must deem us both harmless. Maybe they have heard of a wedding party that is to cross and are waiting for us. Otherwise it seems impossible that they will face us and the Dane as well."

Now Eric was back on his old tack, and passing astern of us. I saw the glint of his oar blades, which had been run out from their ports ready to take the water if need was presently.

And then we knew that his help would be wanted. Suddenly the strange ship's head flew up into the wind and she was round on the other tack, paying off wonderfully quickly; and as she did so, from under her gunwale, where they could be hidden no longer, rose the armed men, seeming to crowd her deck in a moment. She was full of them from stem to stern, and our men shouted. She had won well to windward of us.

But Thorgils had known what was coming, and had kept his quick eye on the helmsman of the stranger. Even as her helm went down for the luff his went up and the men sprang to the sheets, and we were tearing across her bows even as her sail filled on the new tack, and heading away lift by lift toward Eric. And Eric hove to to meet us, and his sail fell and his oars flashed out and took the water, and he made for us like the sea dragon his ship seemed.

"Down with you men under cover!" roared Thorgils. "Arrows, comrade!-- Down with you!"

The strange ship was only a bow shot from us, if a long one yet, but she was overhauling us apace.

I saw her men forward bending their bows, and the Norsemen of our crew came aft with my men under the break of the deck on which we stood, where they were in cover. Evan ran to me with his shield up.

"Evan," I cried, "shield Thorgils." And I set myself before Owen with my own shield raised to cover him, and he laughed at me grimly.

He set his own alongside mine, and we three stood covering Thorgils. The Norseman's face was set and watchful, but his blue eyes danced under the knit brows, and I do believe that he was enjoying the sport.

Ay, and so would I but for her who was so close to me. It was the first time I had known aught but joy in battle, and what all my strange new thoughts were I cannot say. I would not pass through that time again for worlds.

Then the first arrow fled from the enemy toward us, falling short by a yard or two, and at that there came one who looked like a chief, and stood on the high bows and hailed us in Welsh.

At sight of him Evan cried out, and Owen started.

"Daffyd of Carnbre, Morfed's kinsman," Owen said to me quietly. "This is the last of the crew who followed Morgan."

"Likewise the last of Daffyd," Thorgils growled grimly. "Look!"

But I could not. Now the arrow storm swept on us, and all the air seemed dark with shafts which dimpled the sea like a hailstorm, and clanged on our shields and smote the decks with a sharp click from end to end of the vessel. Even at that time I saw that some of the arrows were British, but more of some outland make with cruelly barbed heads. One or two went near my helm, and I had several in my shield, but none of us were hurt.

I had to watch them for the sake of Thorgils, who was unmailed, and I could not look where he pointed ahead of us.

Then of a sudden the arrows ceased to rain on us, and there went a cry as of terror from the decks of our enemy. The wild war song of the Tenby Danes rose ahead of us, and I turned and looked. Eric was close on us, and his men had risen from under the gunwales, where they too had been hiding until the foe was in their grasp, and now the dragon was on her prey, and that prey knew it. And yet Evan had need to shield me as I turned, for the chief whom they called Daffyd was urging his men to shoot, and himself snatched a bow and loosed an arrow at us harmlessly.

It was wonderful. Under the sweep of the thirty long oars the dragon ship tore past us, hurling the white foam from her sharp bows, while the thunder of war song and breaking wave and rolling oars filled my ears and set our men leaping and cheering as they saw her. Eric was on the high forecastle, and he waved his broad axe at us gleefully, and all along the decks the fighting men stood above the armed rowers; one shielding the toiler, and one with bent bow ready, steady as oaks on the reeling deck, and cheering us also with lifted weapons.

The foe saw, and her oars ran out too late. The dragon met her, and thus, checking her speed as she passed her, swept her crowded deck with arrows at half range; and yet the foe held on after us, for the men of Daffyd and of Morgan were bent on ending Owen if they themselves must die. The arrows were about us again, and Eric must turn and be back to our help. It seemed that the foe would be on us before that help could come.

I did not know the handiness of the longship under oars. She was about even as I looked again from the foe to her. And her sail was hoisted, and under that and oars alike she was back on the foe; and then the men of Daffyd forgot him and us in the greater business of caring for themselves, and left him raving on the foredeck, to seek shelter while they might.

Then I suppose the helmsman was shot, for the ship luffed helplessly, and in a moment the stem of the viking was crashing on her quarter, and the grappling irons were fast to her. Thorgils laughed and luffed at once.

"Somewhat to sing of," he said cheerfully, as he hove to to watch the fight.

That it was in all truth. We were but a bow shot off, and could see it all. We heard the ships grinding together, and we heard the shout of the Danes and the outland yells of the Welsh, and we saw the vikings swarming on board while the axes flashed and the war song rose again.

"Eric has a mind to pay them for nigh spoiling a wedding voyage," quoth our Norseman.

It was no long fight, for I suppose that there are men of no race who can stand before the Northmen at sea, at least since we have forgotten the old ship craft of our forefathers. From stem to stern Eric led his men, sweeping all before him, some foemen even leaping overboard out of the way of the terrible axes, and so meeting another death. I think that the Welsh chief Daffyd was the last to fall before old Eric himself. And then was a great cheer from the two ships, and after it silence.

Then Eric hailed us, and Thorgils ran out his oars, and we went alongside the Danish ship. And at that time Nona came from the cabin, and called me, looking wonderingly at the arrows that littered the deck at her feet.

"Oswald, what is it all?--Do the good Danes leave us?"

Then she saw my mail, and paled a little.

"Fighting! and I not with you?" she cried. "Is any one hurt?"

But I went to her side and told her how things had gone, asking her to bide in the shelter yet, for we had things to see that were not for her. And so she went back again and closed the door, being assured that the danger had passed.

We went on board the Danish ship, for there was not enough sea to prevent our lying gunwale to gunwale for a moment. Both Owen and I would find out if possible how all this came about. There was a row of captives on the deck of the enemy waiting question, and I looked down on them from beside Eric.

Swarthy men and black haired they were, speaking no tongue which we knew, and one of them was black as his hair. I had never seen a black man before, and he seemed uncanny. The Danes were staring at him also, and he was grinning at them with white teeth through thick lips in all unconcern. Many of these men had chains on their legs, and this black among them.

"Chained to the oar benches they were, poor thralls," Eric said. "We could not bide that, so we cut them free. Then they fell on their lords and rent them."

Owen shuddered. He had seen the southern galleys before, and knew why no man was left alive of the foreigners who had fought. Our kin do not slay the wounded. But there were some Britons left among the captives, and one of them cried to Owen by name for mercy.

We had that man on board the Dane and questioned him, and learnt all. He had no reason to hide aught when he was promised safety.

Daffyd had heard that we were to cross from Tenby, having had all the doings of Owen spied upon since the winter. Then he learned that when I came over Owen was to return, and therefore he had my doings watched also. He hired this foreign ship in Marazion, where she put in for trade just as he was wondering how to compass our end on the journey, promising her fierce crew gold of his own and all plunder there might be, if they would help him to an easy revenge. So they came into the Severn sea, and lay for a fortnight or more under Lundy Island, watching for us as a cat watches for a mouse, and getting news now and then from Welsh fishers from Milford Haven.

It was from them that Daffyd learned of my wedding, and so it came to pass that neither he nor the strangers thought for a moment that our two ships held aught but passengers and much plunder, with a princess to hold to ransom, moreover, for the taking. They took no account of the few house-carles we might have with us, and even I knew nought of the crossing of the armed Danish ship with us, which was planned so that it came as a pleasant surprise to us all. Thorgils was right, and it had been a terrible one for them.

So the plunder fell to Eric, and it was worth having. There was the ship and arms and captives, and the gold of Daffyd, and that of the traders, moreover, with some strange and precious woven goods from southern looms, silken and woollen, which yet remained in the hold, wondrous to look on.

Now, in halting words enough I went to thank Eric and his men for that which he had done for me and mine, which indeed was more than I knew how to put into words.

"Hold on, comrade," he said, staying me. "I will tell you somewhat. Good friends enough we are with Howel nowadays, but it was not always so. It was the doing of your fair princess that things came not to blows between us at one time, for we held that he was unreasonable in some matter of scatt {ix} to be paid. She settled that matter for us with wise words, and we hold that to her we owe it that we are in Tenby today. Howel could starve us out any time he chose. And that the prince will own to you if you ask him, being an honest man, if hasty. We shall miss Nona the princess sorely-- good luck to her."

Then he must needs have all the bales of rich goods set on board our ship, as a wedding present to Nona, and so set a crew on board the prize, and she left us, heading homewards to Tenby. We went back to our own ship at once after this was done, but Eric would see us safely to Watchet before he was satisfied, and so we took up the quiet passage again, little harmed enough. Eric had a few wounded men, but we had not suffered from the arrows.

Presently the stars came out, and Nona and I sat with Owen under the awning in the quiet of the calm sea, while the men rowed under the shadow of the sail that held a little wind enough to help them homeward, and we went over all the things that the day had brought us. And Owen said:

"Now you may be at rest concerning me, Oswald, for there is not one left to lift a hand against me of whom I need think twice. Daffyd was the last of the crew to which Morgan and Tregoz and Dunwal belonged, for Gerent has the rest in ward safely; and there they will bide, if I know aught of him, until I have to beg him to set them free beyond the shores of Cornwall."

I will say now that this was true, for thence forward no man lifted hand or voice against my foster father. The war and its hopeless ending quieted the men whom Morfed had led, and there was peace, in which men turned to Owen as the one who could keep it, and had given wise counsel which was once disregarded.

So it came to pass that I took home Nona with me, and set her as princess in the hall at Taunton amid the rejoicing of all the Welsh folk who were under me; for, as Ethelburga the queen had said, they knew that they had a friend in her. And here we have bided ever since, and are happy in home and friends and work, for all seems to have gone well with us. And as to those good friends of ours, there may yet be a little to tell before I set the pen aside.

Owen passed to Exeter at the time we came home, for he would see his uncle before he went to speak with Ina. But presently he was back with us at Taunton, bearing with him a wondrous present for the bride from

Gerent, and good and friendly words for me which promised well for the peace of the border, at least while he lived. And seeing that he lives yet, with Owen at his right hand, that has been a long time.

Now Owen comes and goes, and none think it strange that he is most friendly with Ina, for men have learnt that in the peace of the two realms is happiness.

Presently Jago came back to Norton, for I needed some British adviser at hand, for Evan, faithful and well trusted as he is as our honest steward, and able to tell me of the needs of the people, knows nought of the greater laws and ways, and Herewald minded me of him. They had ever been good friends, and I could fully trust him. So he rebuilt his house at Norton, where the land lay waste round the old Roman walls which our Saxons hate, and there he is now, helping me mightily with his knowledge of the Welsh customs, which I do not wish to interfere with more than needful.

For, in the wisdom of Ina, we did not follow the old plan of driving out and enslaving all the Welsh folk in this new-won land, as had been the rule in the days of the first coming of our forefathers when Saxons were few. Those manors whose owners had fallen or would not bide under the new rule, Ina gave to thanes of his own, and the men of Somerset and Dorset took what land they would where the freeman had left them, but all others he left under new and even-handed laws in peace.

So I had to content the men of both races as well as I could, and men say that I wrought well. At least, I have had no murmuring, and I may deem that they are right.

As one may suppose, there is no more welcome guest in our hall than Thorgils, and at times he brings Eric or some other Tenby Dane with him if a ship happens to cross hither. Once a year also he brings Howel, and there is feasting in our hall, Saxon and Norseman, Briton of the west and Briton from over sea together in all good fellowship.

One evening it came to pass that Thorgils sat in our hall, which was bright with the strange stuffs that came from the ship of Daffyd, and we talked of the old ship a little, after he had sung to us. And then I said idly:

"She must be getting old, comrade. When am I to give you that new craft we once spoke of?"

Whereon he looked at Nona suddenly, and said:

"I mind that old promise. But now there is a ship of another sort that will be a better present. I will ask for that."

"What is it?"

"Build us a church at Watchet, and set there a priest who shall teach us the way of the Christian. We have seen you forego a blood feud and do well to the innocent man whom our faith would have bidden you slay, and it is good. We know you for a brave warrior, and your faith has not taken the might from your heart as we were told it must. Only let the priest be a Saxon."

Then he added, as if thinking aloud:

"Ay, Odin and Thor and the rest of the Asir are far off from us here. Our old faith falls from us, and we are ready for the new. Let it be soon."

There I think that the hand of Nona wrought, for the Norse folk fairly worshipped her. So it was not long before that good friend of mine, the Abbot of Glastonbury, found me the right man, and one day thereafter Nona and I stood sponsors for Thorgils and one or two more whom we knew well, at the font in the new church which the gold of Mordred built instead of the ship, and soon all the little town was Christian in more than name.

There is happiness at Eastdean, and we meet with Erpwald and Elfrida at the house of her father now and then, and they have been here also. But I have never had time to go to Eastdean again, though it is a promise that we will do so when we may.

It is the word of Ina my master that all things go well where I bear rule for him, and I fear little blame, if little praise may be for me, when Owen comes to us from time to time. If there is any praise, it is due to my fair British princess, who is my best adviser in all things.

So there is peace; and some day, and that no distant one, there will grow up here a new race in the west, wrought of the blood of Saxon and Briton and Norseman; and the men of that Devon and Somerset that shall be, will have the doggedness of the Saxon and the fire of the Welsh and the boldness of the Norse, to be first of all England, maybe, in peace and in war, on shore and at sea. And that will have been brought to pass by the wisdom of Ina, whose even laws are held the wisest that the race of Hengist has ever known.

It is in my mind that the lesson of the wisdom of equal rights for all men, whether conquered or conqueror, is one that will bide with us in the days to come, and be our pride.

Now it seems that I have told my story so far as any will care to hear it. But if there has been aught worth telling it has centered round that one who took me from the jaws of the wild wolf in the Andredsweald. First in my heart, and first in the hearts of his people now at last, must be set the name of my foster father, Owen--the Prince of Cornwall.

THE END.

NOTES.

i The national weapon. A heavy blade between sword and dagger, with curved back and straight edge, fitted for almost any use.

ii The fine to be paid in amends for an open "manslaying" in quarrel or feud.

iii The ancient Welsh province now represented by the county of Glarnorgan.

iv Tribute due to an overlord by the settlers.